GREAT THINKERS
ON GREAT
QUESTIONS

RELATED TITLES PUBLISHED BY ONEWORLD:

God, Chance and Necessity, Keith Ward, ISBN 1–85168–116–7
God, Faith and the New Millennium, Keith Ward, ISBN 1–85168–155–8
In Defence of the Soul, Keith Ward, ISBN 1–85168–040–3
The Phenomenon of Religion, Moojan Momen, ISBN 1–85168–161–2
The Sense of God, John Bowker, ISBN 1–85168–093–4
A Theory of Almost Everything, Robert Barry, ISBN 1–85168–123–X

GREAT THINKERS
ON GREAT
QUESTIONS

Edited by Roy Abraham Varghese

ONEWORLD

OXFORD

A Oneworld Book

First published by Oneworld Publications 1998
First published in trade paperback 2009

ISBN 978–1–85168–555–1

Cover design by www.fatfacedesign.com
Printed and bound in Great Britain by TJ International, Padstow

Oneworld Publications
185 Banbury Road
Oxford OX2 7AR
England
www.oneworld-publications.com

For my father, M. Abraham Varghese,
and mother, Leela Abraham,
and my grandparents M. M. Varghese
and Rachel Varghese,
who taught me the answers
to the Great Questions
through their lives of faith, hope and,
above all, unconditional love.

CONTENTS

* Follow-up questions and answers included.

* Follow-up questions and answers included.

* Follow-up questions and answers included.

Part IV: IS THERE A GOD?

Great Question 10: *The existence of God has been one of the most hotly debated issues in the history of human thought. What are your own conclusions on the question of God's existence and on what basis do you affirm or deny the existence of God?*

Great Question 11: *What bearing, if any, does science have on religion – particularly with respect to the questions of God's existence, the origin of the universe, and the possibility of miracles?*

* Follow-up questions and answers included.

* Follow-up questions and answers included.

* Follow-up questions and answers included.

CONTRIBUTORS

1. *Sir Alfred Ayer*, b.1910–d.1989. Wykeham Professor of Logic, Oxford University, 1959–78; President, Society for Applied Philosophy, 1982–1985. Delivered the Gifford Lectures. Works include *Language, Truth and Logic* (which introduced Logical Positivism to the English-speaking world); *The Foundations of Empirical Knowledge* and *Concept of a Person*.

2. *G. E. M. Anscombe*, b.1919–d.2001. Professor of Philosophy, Cambridge University; Honorary Fellow of St. Hugh's College and of Somerville College, Oxford University; Fellow of the British Academy. Widely recognized as one of recent history's leading moral philosophers, her works include *An Introduction to Wittgenstein's Tractatus*, *Intention*, and *Three Philosophers* (with Peter Thomas Geach). Also translator and co-editor of the posthumous writings (including *Philosophical Investigations* and *On Certainty*) of Ludwig Wittgenstein.

3. *William P. Alston.* Professor of Philosophy, Syracuse University; past President, American Philosophical Association; past President, Society for Philosophy and Psychology; founding editor of the journals *Philosophy Research Archives* (now *The Journal of Philosophical Research*) and *Faith and Philosophy*. A distinguished contributor to the philosophy of language and the philosophy of mind, he has also been described as "one of the foremost contributors to the analytical philosophy of religion." Editor of the Cornell Studies in Philosophy of Religion. Works include *Philosophy of Language*, *A Realist Conception of Truth*, and *Perceiving God: The Epistemology of Religious Experience*.

4. *C. T. K. Chari.* Former Professor of Philosophy, Madras University. Member of the Prime Minister's Council of Indian Philosophy. Published extensively on subjects ranging from Hindu philosophy to logic, linguistics, information theory, mathematics, quantum physics, and parapsychology. Contributor on reincarnation to Wolman's *Handbook of Parapsychology*.

5. *George F. R. Ellis.* Professor of Applied Mathematics, University of Cape Town and Queen Mary College, University of London; Past President of the International Society of General Relativity and Gravitation; Fellow and Past President of the Royal Society of South Africa; Founding Member and past Member of Council of Academy of Science of South Africa; Fellow of the Third World Academy of Science; Fellow of the Royal Society; author of numerous works on the evolution and density of the Universe and co-author (with Stephen Hawking, his former fellow-student) of *The Large-Scale Structure of Space-Time.*

6. *John Foster.* Fellow, Brasenose College, Oxford. Works include *The Immaterial Self.*

7. *Owen Gingerich.* Professor of Astronomy and of the History of Science, Harvard University and former Chairman of the Department of the History of Science. Past Chairman of the US National Committee of the International Astronomical Union. Delivered the George Darwin Lecture, the most prestigious lecture of the Royal Astronomical Society. Asteroid 2658=1980CK was named in his honor by the International Astronomical Union. Works include *Album of Science: The Physical Sciences in the Twentieth Century, The Great Copernicus Chase and Other Adventures in Astronomical History,* and *The Eye of Heaven: Ptolemy, Copernicus, Kepler.*

8. *Gerard J. Hughes.* Former Chairman, Department of Philosophy, Heythrop College, University of London and former Master, Campion Hall, University of Oxford. Works include *Authority in Morals, The Nature of God,* and *The Philosophical Assessment of Theology* (edited).

9. *Brian Leftow.* Nolloth Professor of the Philosophy of the Christian Religion, Oriel College, University of Oxford and former Professor of Philosophy, Fordham University. Editor of a series of volumes on philosophy and the divine attributes. Works include *Divine Ideas* and *Time and Eternity.*

10. *H. D. Lewis.* Former Head of the Department of the History and Philosophy of Religion, London University. Past President of the Mind Association and of the International Society for Metaphysics; former Chairman of the Council of the Royal Institute of Philosophy and Editor of the Muirhead Library of

Philosophy from 1947 to 1978. Delivered the Gifford Lectures. Books include *The Elusive Mind*, *The Self and Immortality*, and *Our Experience of God*.

11. *Bernard J.F. Lonergan*, b.1904 – d.1984. Former Professor of Philosophy, Gregorian University and Boston College. *Time* magazine noted that he "is considered by many intellectuals to be the finest philosophic thinker of the 20th century"(*Time*, April 20 1970). Over a hundred and fifty doctoral dissertations have been written on his work and an entire conference of fellow-philosophers was convened to study his work. "77 of the best minds in Europe and the Americas gathered to examine Lonergan's profoundly challenging work." Works include *Insight*, which was described as having "become a philosophic classic comparable in scope to Hume's *Inquiry Concerning Human Understanding*," (*Newsweek*, April 20, 1970), *Method in Theology*, and *Philosophy of God and Theology*.

12. *John Lucas*. Emeritus Fellow, Merton College, Oxford University; Past President of the British Society for the Philosophy of Science; Fellow of the British Academy. Delivered the Gifford Lectures. Works include *The Freedom of the Will*, *The Nature of Mind, and Development of Mind*.

13. *Ralph McInerny*. Michel P. Grace Professor of Medieval Studies, University of Notre Dame; Director of the Jacques Maritain Center. Past President of the American Metaphysical Society and of the American Catholic Philosophical Association. Appointed to Bush's Committee on the Arts and Humanities and elected to Catholic Academy of Sciences. Delivered the Gifford Lectures. Editor, *The New Scholasticism*. Works include *The Logic of Analogy*, *Thomism in an Age of Renewal*, and *Boethius and Aquinas*.

14. *Sandra Menssen*. Associate Professor of Philosophy, University of St.Thomas. Co-editor of *Logos: A Journal of Catholic Thought and Culture*. Has published extensively in philosophy of religion, biomedical ethics and gender studies, and is co-author (with T. D. Sullivan) of *A Ship for Simmias? Philosophical Objections to Revelatory Claims*.

15. *Hugo Meynell*. Professor of Religious Studies, University of Calgary. Fellow of the Royal Society of Canada. Works include

God and the World, *The Intelligible Universe*, and *The Theology of Bernard Lonergan.*

16. *Russell Pannier.* Professor of Law, William Mitchell College of Law, St. Paul. His previous publications have been in the areas of logic, metaphysics, jurisprudence, and constitutional law.

17. *Alvin Plantinga.* John A. O'Brien Professor of Philosophy, University of Notre Dame. Past President of the American Philosophical Association and the Society of Christian Philosophers. Fellow of the American Academy of Arts & Sciences. Delivered the Gifford Lectures. Plantinga has been described as "the most important philosopher of religion now writing." Works include *God and Other Minds*, *The Nature of Necessity*, and *Warrant.*

18. *Josef Seifert.* Rector, International Academy of Philosophy, Liechtenstein, and founding co-director, International Academy of Philosophy, Irving, Texas. Member, European Academy of Sciences & Arts. One of the most prominent contemporary proponents of phenomenological realism, he has published extensively in English and German on epistemology, metaphysics, philosophy of mind, and philosophy of religion. Works include: *Back to Things Themselves: A Phenomenological Foundation for Classical Realism*, *Gott als Gottesbeweiss: Eine phänomenologische Neubegründung des ontologischen Arguments* (*God as Proof of God's Existence: A Phenomenological Foundation for the Argument for the Existence of God from the Necessary Divine Essence*), and *Leib und Seele.*

19. *T. D. Sullivan.* Aquinas Professor of Philosophy and Theology, University of St. Thomas, St. Paul. Has published extensively in logic, ethics, metaphysics, and the philosophy of religion. Co-author (with Sandra Menssen) of *A Ship for Simmias? Philosophical Objections to Revelatory Claims.*

20. *Leo Sweeney*, b.1918–d.2001. Research Professor of Philosophy, Loyola University, Chicago. Past President of the US Section of the International Society for Neoplatonic Studies; Past President, American Catholic Philosophical Association. Works include *A Metaphysics of Authentic Existentialism*,

Authentic Metaphysics in an Age of Unreality, and *Divine Infinity in Ancient and Medieval Thought.*

21. *Richard Swinburne.* Nolloth Professor of the Philosophy of the Christian Religion, Oxford University. Fellow of the British Academy. A distinguished contributor to philosophy of science, philosophy of mind, and philosophy of religion, he is the leading living proponent of rational "argumentative" theism. Delivered the Gifford Lectures. Works include *Space and Time, The Coherence of Theism,* and *The Evolution of the Soul.*

22. *Keith Ward.* Gresham Professor of Divinity, Gresham College, London. Former Regius Professor of Divinity, Oxford University. Fellow of the British Academy and member of the Governing Council of the Royal Institute of Philosophy. He is one of the most prominent contemporary philosophers of religion in the United Kingdom. Works include *God, Faith and the New Millennium, Concepts of God, In Defence of the Soul, God, Chance and Necessity, Pascal's Fire,* and *Re-thinking Christianity.*

INTRODUCTION

A RETURN TO UNIVERSAL EXPERIENCE

To thine own self be true – Hamlet

As humanity embarks upon a new millennium, it faces a startling paradox: an ever-increasing influx of information is matched by an ever-decreasing confidence in the capacity to know. Many prominent philosophers of recent times may better be described as anti-philosophers because of their tendency to see philosophical problems merely as linguistic muddles and their conviction that the human mind is incapable of actually knowing anything; nihilists like Richard Rorty even say that "the best hope for philosophy is not to practice Philosophy"[1] and that we must "drop the idea . . . that Truth is 'out there' waiting for human beings to arrive at it."[2] Skepticism has left its mark on modern science as well: the journal *Nature* ran an article in which two scientists indicted the four most influential philosophers of science of the last century, Karl Popper, Imre Lakatos, Thomas Kuhn, and Paul Feyerabend as "enemies of science" for whom "the term 'truth' has become taboo" and whose skepticism and nihilism "may be impairing scientific progress at this moment."[3] Books and articles heralding "the end of science" are paralleled by proclamations of "the end of philosophy."

But the whims and fancies of fashionable speculation will not change the "hard facts" of the human condition – or snuff out the Great Questions that keep coming back to the major fields of human inquiry despite having been repeatedly certified as "meaningless." Almost everywhere we look in modern science, age-old questions have re-surfaced in scientific garb.

Current cosmological accounts of the origin of the universe raise the kind of questions that are answered in cosmological arguments for God's existence. The anthropic principle in astrophysics and the genetic blueprint revealed by molecular biology furnish the building blocks for new versions of the teleological argument. The new sciences of chaos and complexity have underlined the radical contingency of the universe – an insight that had driven thinkers in previous centuries to postulate a Necessary Being. The present-day fascination of scientists with the phenomena of consciousness and language – and the failure to satisfactorily explain either in physicalist terms – has brought a new awareness of the body–mind problem. And, at least according to some observers, the popular quest for a final theory in physics is simply a subliminal quest for God. "A lot of my colleagues like the idea of final theories because they're religious," says Mitchell Feigenbaum, the best-known exponent of the science of chaos, "and they use it as a replacement for God, which they don't believe in. But they just created a substitute."[4] Stephen Hawking even ends his best-selling *A Brief History of Time* with the comment that if we find out "why it is we and the universe exist . . . it would be the ultimate triumph of human reason – for then we would know the mind of God."[5] And the devout search for extra-terrestrial intelligence by many atheists sometimes seems like a subconscious quest for an intelligence beyond us that can explain our being here. If nothing else, modern science has brought the Great Questions back to the table.

But the Great Questions are philosophical questions, not scientific ones. Science can only speak to what is observable and quantifiable. Questions about purpose, the origin of being from non-being, the soul, and moral value fall outside the scientific domain of the strictly empirical. These are metascientific questions – questions that have traditionally been addressed by philosophers.

Despite the fact that nihilism afflicts much of modern philosophy, it must be said that not all recent philosophers have turned their backs on reality, rationality and truth. The question of God, the greatest of the Great Questions, has returned to the contemporary conversation. "In a quiet revolution in thought and argument that hardly anyone could have foreseen only two decades ago, God is making a comeback. Most intriguingly, this is happening . . . in the crisp, intellectual circles of academic philosophers," began a famous article in *Time*.[6]

In *Cosmos, Bios, Theos* twenty-four Nobel Prize winners and thirty other scientists pondered the Great Question of the origin of the universe and the existence of God. *Great Thinkers on Great Questions* is a comprehensive sequel to *Cosmos*. In this volume the concern is with fifteen Great Questions – and the answers to them from great thinkers, philosophers, and scientists, who have helped shape the direction of modern thought. The Great Questions listed here were presented and answered in a variety of forums and modes. In some cases, the contributors responded to the questions in writing. In other instances, there were personal interviews with the contributors. In the latter instances, the interview format inevitably led to follow-up questions that are also included here. Clearly then, there is a stylistic variation in the way in which the contributors responded to the questions.

The contributors to this book agree, for the most part, that the Great Questions are meaningful questions which can, in principle, be answered accurately. Moreover, their answers generally coincide with the answers of common experience. The common, unifying theme of the contributions here is indeed the defense of the obvious, the attention to the universal experience of humanity. In essence, this volume reconnects the intellectual enterprise to the fundamental insights of universal experience. The objective of this collection is not to present diversity for its own sake but to build a bridge between modern thought and the body of truth that has seemed obvious to the majority of the human race. In the current intellectual environment of unprecedented confusion, the great thinkers interviewed here have developed a modern version of the perennial philosophy, the wisdom of the ages. It is to be hoped that the next revolution in modern thought will be a return to these truths revealed in universal experience. At this juncture, a brief overview of the essential elements of universal experience, as I understand them, will be helpful as an introduction to the rest of the volume.

FROM COMMON SENSE TO SAPIENTIAL SENSE

It is my contention here that it is a fact of universal and immediate experience that human beings are not only capable of knowing but that they are indeed endowed with a knowledge-base encompassing essential and ultimate principles of reality. It is this knowledge-base that underlies all thought and rationality and every exercise of the human mind. For clarity's sake, I will call the distinctively human capacity to know fundamental truths about reality our "sapiential sense" (from homo sapiens) and the truths to which this "sense" is privy, the database of sapiential sense or, better still, "sapiential sense-data." Our sapiential sense is a dynamic interface between thoughts and things that discerns the actual in the perceived and that is presupposed by all acts of knowledge. Sapiential sense-data comprises the set of fundamental pre-philosophical and pre-scientific truths that can neither be demonstrated nor denied.

What I call here sapiential sense and sapiential sense-data have been loosely called many other things: common sense, illative sense, noetic structure, intuition, right reason, first principles, perennial philosophy, self-evident facts, properly basic beliefs, the given. Unfortunately, these terms have acquired too wide a range of variously applicable definitions and ambiguous connotations to be meaningful in the present discussion. Consequently a fresh set of terms – drawing attention to the fact that we are indeed sapient beings – may be helpful at least in identifying and dissecting this fundamental framework of human experience that is as obvious as it is obscure. (A discussion of the varieties of knowledge, the distinctions of empirical/metaphysical, a priori/a posteriori and analytic/synthetic, is not required for our present purpose.)

These introductory remarks may well be greeted with skepticism: How do we know that we have the kind of sapiential sense outlined here? If it exists, how do we access or utilize it and how do we distinguish sapiential sense-data from its counterfeits?

Such questions make the relatively simple and basic reality we are considering seem esoteric and remote. But in discussing sapiential sense we are merely pointing to the obvious and the immediate, drawing attention to something we have had and worked with all our lives. For some, the discovery of sapiential sense may be as exciting as the discovery of the man in Molière's play who realized he had been talking prose all his life.

But how do we know that we do indeed know? Pause for a moment and consider some of the things of which we are certain. We know that at this very moment we are reading this essay, that this essay had at least one author, that the print marks on these pages contain a message, that this message may well describe our own experience accurately.

On a higher plane, we know without a doubt that rational inquiry requires a rational order of things, that two contradictory assertions cannot both be true (for example, the same object cannot exist and not exist at one and the same time), that a valid inference from a valid premise leads to a valid conclusion, that the mind is capable of knowing truth (we cannot deny this statement without assuming that the mind is capable of knowing the truth of the denial), that every phenomenon has an explanation, that something cannot come from nothing (here we are talking of absolute nothing, not a something disguised as nothing), that the world exists, that we exist (to the student who asked how she knew she existed, her wise professor replied, "And who's asking?"), that intention presupposes intelligence (here the reference is to obvious instances of intentional activity).

How do we know that these affirmations are true and how can we demonstrate their truth? Well, we know them to be true because that is what our minds tell us – instinctively, immediately – but we cannot demonstrate them to be true because all demonstrations would presuppose their truth. Empirical evidence is of no relevance because no amount of empirical evidence can show a statement such as "every phenomenon has an explanation" to be definitively true or false – a phenomenon that appears not to have an explanation may have an explanation that cannot be detected with the available apparatus (the claim that quantum physics shows the causeless creation of something from nothing is just wrong: Paul Davies points out "The processes represented here do not represent the creation of matter out of nothing, but the conversion of pre-existing energy into material. We still have to account for where the energy came from in the first place."[7]) Similarly the claim that the world exists cannot be empirically demonstrated because all such demonstrations already presuppose the existence of the world. A logical argument would not be applicable either because the conclusions of such an argument are already presupposed before the argument gets under way.

Nevertheless, we know that these affirmations are true affirmations and if any interlocutor wishes to deny them the burden of proof lies with the interlocutor (though it is hard to see how a proof for the denial is even conceivable). In making such affirmations, we are remaining true to self-evident facts while those who deny them are flying in the face of these facts.

It is our ability to know these indemonstrable but indisputable truths that, for want of a "cleaner" phrase, we call sapiential sense. Sapiential sense is the mind's ability to "see" the truths that constitute reality, grasp things as they are in themselves. The "seeing" of these truths transcends the scope of the scientific method (which is limited to the data of the senses) and of logic (which is limited to "unpacking" the conclusions already contained in premises). "Knowledge," writes Illtyd Trethowan, "is basically a matter of seeing things . . .

arguments, reasoning processes, are of secondary importance and this not only because without direct awareness or apprehension no processes of thought could get under way at all, but also because the point of these processes is to promote further apprehensions."[8]

Sapiential sense-data, the truths grasped by sapiential sense, are incorrigible – they cannot be false and cannot be shown to be false – and indubitable – they cannot be rationally doubted. These truths are confirmed both by our everyday experience and by the collective experience of humanity. They are part of the universal heritage of the human race. Perhaps the most powerful testimony to the truth of sapiential sense-data is the field of study that is considered most inimical to sapiential sense – science. Scientific activity, discoveries, inventions, theories, laws, experiments, the spirit of science, the scientific method, would be impossible without total reliance on the insights of sapiential sense. On the one hand, science is entirely an empirical activity centering on the observable and the measurable. On the other hand, science cannot proceed at all without making fundamental assumptions that cannot themselves be proved scientifically: that the world exists, that the human mind can know truth, that reality is intelligible and also rationally ordered, that all phenomena can be explained. These assumptions are not empirically demonstrable but they must be presupposed by all empirical inquiry. These are truths that we recognize because of sapiential sense. We are, of course, free to deny these truths. But, if we do so, we cannot consistently do science or even live. To "work," science is dependent on sapiential sense.

Sapiential sense, however, cannot do what science can do. It cannot explore the quantum or intergalactic realms. It is not a method of observation or a means of measurement. It is not even a source of scientific theories and cannot evaluate the soundness of such theories. It deals strictly with those truths that we know to be true independent of any observation or measurement and that cannot be proved to be true by any amount of observation or measurement. Nonetheless, there can be fruitful interactions between science and the fundamental framework underlying it. Sapiential sense, when applied to the "hard facts" of science, may read between the lines and discover new dimensions to these "facts." It is sapiential sense that marvels at the fine tuning of fundamental constants revealed by modern astrophysics and the intricacy and depth of the genetic text carried in our cells.

IDENTIFYING SAPIENTIAL SENSE

In distinguishing the operations of science from the operations of sapiential sense we recognize that the latter is applicable only within definite parameters. Sapiential sense-data manifest certain characteristics. They are not the end-products of logical argument or empirical demonstration. They have an a priori character – their truth is known independent of sensory experience and inferential cogitation. But how can sapiential sense-data be distinguished from mere opinion and sheer speculation, judgments in economics and politics and the social sciences, and superstitions like belief in astrology and UFOs?

The difference between sapiential sense and other ways of knowing can be recognized by reference to certain conditions and criteria:

• No claim or theory that requires empirical evidence to establish it is a datum of sapiential sense. Data in the natural sciences can only be obtained by the application of the scientific method. Data in the social sciences pertains to the behavior of human persons and communities and is dependent on speculation deriving from empirical investigation. Both the natural and the social sciences sometimes make assumptions about the nature of the human person that cannot be supported by any amount of empirical study.

• Arguments and theories in mathematics and logic also fall outside the purview of sapiential sense. Nevertheless, they cannot start from ground zero and are dependent on certain axioms and premises that cannot themselves be proved by the arguments or theories. The axioms and premises are the starting-points from which a deductive argument is built and implicitly "contain" the conclusion. (Philosophers like Bertrand Russell have even pointed out that the whole of mathematics can only give us tautologies.) Of course, it is possible to increase one's knowledge through an argument because we find out what is indeed "contained" in the premises. Moreover, inductive arguments are probabilistic in nature and therefore their conclusions give us new, albeit revisable, information. At least in certain cases, the validity of the premises of a logical argument can only be discerned by sapiential sense and cannot be demonstrated in any other way.

These distinctions open the door to a fuller understanding of sapiential sense and its database. Sapiential sense-data are:

1. affirmations
2. affirmations of such a fundamental nature that they are presupposed by (and therefore lie beyond) our abilities and activities of empirical and logical investigation – they are both meta-scientific and meta-philosophical
3. obvious and immediately known to all human beings
4. entirely congruent with ordinary experience without contradicting it at any point
5. marked by a fundamental coherence, clarity and simplicity
6. presupposed by all of our intellectual activity
7. impossible to deny without implausible rationalizations and absurd consequences
8. only "seen" to be true and, therefore, self-guaranteeing and self-authenticating (the truth of what is "seen" cannot be demonstrated with external criteria)

The recognition of sapiential sense is by no means a green light for superstitions and fanciful beliefs, as can be seen by analyzing belief in astrology and UFOs.

Astrology is the claim that there is some correlation between planetary movements and our daily lives, a rather nebulous pseudo-scientific hypothesis. This is obviously an empirical claim and therefore needs to be empirically tested. There is currently no scientifically reliable evidence to support it. Belief in UFOs is based on data that is purportedly empirical, i.e. claims made by certain individuals that they have witnessed certain phenomena that they interpret as evidence for the existence of UFOs. Such a belief is not, in any sense, a datum that is independent of experience and available to all human beings.

It should be clear by now that sapiential sense does not give us any privileged position when it comes to the empirical. Sapiential sense is not a substitute for the sciences, natural and social. Neither is it a substitute for scholarship. Many thorny issues in economic theory, historical analysis and philosophical and mathematical investigation can only be resolved by painstaking analysis and study. Some of these issues cannot be resolved at all. And certainly sapiential sense, as outlined here, bears no likeness to the concept of "innate ideas." Moreover, there are certain questions that lie beyond human reason (including sapiential sense) and answers here, if any, can only come from divine revelation.

Nevertheless, when a field of study deals with foundational questions like the origin of everything or the nature of the human person, sapiential sense can act as litmus test. It is by no means unreasonable to expect some connection between the sophisticated statements of a philosophical system and our ordinary experience, especially when such a system claims to be an adequate interpretation of ordinary experience.

Litmus-test judgments of interpretations of ordinary experience do not require philosophical sophistication. As Dr. Johnson noted, we do not have to be carpenters to decide if a table is good. Virtually any philosophical position, however ludicrous, can be argued for extensively and plausibly.

OBSTACLES TO THE OPERATIONS OF SAPIENTIAL SENSE

Deploying sapiential sense sometimes means playing the part of the boy who observed that the emperor wore no clothes. It is a task that must be undertaken with complete confidence in the essential integrity of our most fundamental perceptions of the Real and a refusal to be intimidated by the pretensions of sophists. In describing Behaviorism, the British thinker C. D. Broad accurately described the characteristics of any philosophical system that denies the data of sapiential sense: it is one of "the numerous class of theories which are so preposterously silly that only very learned men could have thought of them. But such theories are frequently countenanced by the naive since they are put forward in highly technical terms by learned persons who are themselves too confused to know exactly what they mean."[9] Cicero said long ago, "There is no opinion so absurd but that a philosopher hasn't expressed it."

The wide range of differences in the views held by various thinkers on even the most fundamental issues can be attributed to two factors: the first is the tendency to adhere to views and schools of thought that are fashionable in one's own intellectual environments (about which we should remember: what is contemporary is temporary) and the second is a refusal to remain faithful to the voice of sapiential sense.

Most modern thinkers are simply confused by the sheer quantity of data pouring in from every direction. Since it is not humanly possible to keep up with all this data – let alone make sense of it – they have retreated into reductionism, relativism and outright nihilism. What should be realized is that no amount of empirical information can nullify the insights of sapiential sense. It is sapiential sense which helps us make sense of the ever-increasing influx of information. But sapiential sense-data are not formed from or affected by such information. These sapiential insights, however, provide the modern thinker with a frame of reference within which new information can be assimilated and categorized without the loss of nerve that is now a familiar feature of the intellectual scene.

The two greatest enemies today of sapiential sense – and, therefore, of rationality and truth and of human knowledge itself – are relativism and reductionism. It is widely assumed that (a) we cannot know anything with certitude because we cannot trust our minds and (b) everything in our experience can be understood and explained purely in terms of physics, chemistry, genetics, psychology, economics, and sociology. At the extreme end of the spectrum of relativism are nihilism and deconstructionism. In the case of reductionism, the extremes are empiricism, positivism, and materialism.

These assumptions and thought-forms cannot but paralyze the progress of knowledge: in the absence of any notion of truth there can be no knowing. The relativist and reductionist onslaught on truth and knowledge is fundamentally a consequence of denying or ignoring the essential datum of sapiential sense presupposed by all inquiry: that our minds can and do tell the truth. From the standpoint of sapiential sense, relativism and reductionism are simply denials of obvious and integral elements of our everyday experience. In a sense these denials are useful in illustrating the inevitable logical end-result of denying sapiential sense. Ultimately the only enduring response to relativism and reductionism is a fundamental recognition and acceptance of the facts that we *do* know and of the fact that we *can* know. Arguments refuting relativism (for instance, the self-contradiction implied in affirming that we know we cannot know) may help trigger an awareness of sapiential sense and, in the first part of this volume, the contributors show why neither relativism nor reductionism are philosophically tenable.

While counter-arguments in this vein are both forceful and necessary, they are not a substitute for what is more foundational: an awareness and confident application of sapiential sense, the guarantor of the mind's ability to tell the truth. For reasons of space, we cannot study further the historical expressions of sapiential sense other than to say that it has been ably defended and expounded by a variety of thinkers ranging from Cicero, Aristotle, Thomas Reid and G. K. Chesterton to various Thomists, Phenomenologists and analytic philosophers. Two of the most influential philosophers of recent times (who are both contributors to this volume), Bernard Lonergan and Alvin Plantinga, have developed their own distinctive and sophisticated formulations of this fundamental framework of human knowledge.[10]

To be sure, arguments rooted in so-called "common sense" have been criticized even by some realist thinkers, including two as diverse as Etienne Gilson and Lonergan. Gilson, for instance, thought the weakness of such arguments lay in their being based on an "unjustified and unjustifiable instinct." Lonergan noted that "common nonsense" is sometimes mixed in with "the cherished convictions and slogans" of common sense. Others have criticized "common sense" for being so loose and variable in its expressions and conclusions.

It must be remembered that "common sense" as it pertains to opinion, speculation and "instincts" or "intuitions" is not what we are talking about here, although its critics often caricature common sense itself carelessly. Sapiential sense-data concerns insights that are pre-philosophical and meta-philosophical, insights presupposed by and subsequently refined in philosophical arguments or in the kind of dialectical process developed by Lonergan. Sapiential sense is rationality itself, and at its most fundamental level rationality can be experienced and exercised but not demonstrated. Admittedly, while sapiential sense serves as a reliable starting point for further intellectual activity, there is no reason to remain at the starting point.

A realist of Gilson's generation, D. J. B. Hawkins, has given a fair description of the relation between philosophy and a common sense that incorporates elements of sapiential sense:

> Reflection assures me that there are a number of points, relevant to philosophical inquiry, about which I am already genuinely certain, and their evidence is such that nothing could upset them. . . I am in possession of many truths about what things exist or have existed, whose evidence is quite unshakable, and these are often relevant to philosophy. There are what would normally be described as facts of experience, such as the existence of the self as a unitary being persisting through time and the existence of an external world and other men. . . That we are genuinely certain implies that the belief is more than instinctive, that its object is presented to us as a fact and that on the plane of common sense

its evidence is in itself. These facts have to be submitted to philo-sophical analysis, but they cannot be explained away by it, because their certainty is prior and independent. Consequently common sense often provides a negative test of the validity of philosophical conclusions. If these contradict commonsense truths, or make it impossible that we should know things which we do in fact know, they are certainly false.[11]

Gilson himself shows the necessity and even the nature of sapiential sense in the same book in which he criticizes "common sense":

> If we turn to the testimony of experience, which we should do at the beginning of any undertaking, it would seem difficult to desig-nate by any other word than "evident" the type of certitude we have concerning the existence of the external world. The actual existence of the page I am writing or the one you are reading is not an intellectual evidence of the axiomatic type, for it is possible for this page to be elsewhere, nor would it be self-contradictory for this page to have never been written. On the other hand, I need not ask that it be accepted as a postulate, for sensible perception is nor-mally accompanied by an immediate certitude so clear that we hardly care to question it. No one really doubts that sight, touch, hearing, taste and even smell are normally competent to attest to existence, and whenever it is necessary to verify the existence of anything, it is to the testimony of one or more of the senses that we turn. This conviction of the reliability of our senses is simply the self-evidence of our experience. Since we are here concerned with self-evidence, it is futile to demand a demonstration."[12]

GOD, THE SOUL AND OTHER CENTRAL INSIGHTS OF SAPIENTIAL SENSE

The application of sapiential sense can be usefully illustrated in addressing two of the Great Questions, the existence of God and the existence of the soul.

Our awareness of the existence of God springs from a variety of sources: the insight that something cannot come from nothing is almost instinctive and forms the basis of the cosmological and tele-ological arguments for God's existence; the awareness of a transcen-dent reality at work in their lives has been another starting point for many people; again, the conviction that there is an absoluteness about our experience of right and wrong leads to an awareness of the divine reality underlying the moral order.

In *Cosmos, Bios, Theos*, I tried to show that the metascientific principles of the intelligibility and rationality of reality presupposed by the scientific method called out for an ultimate explanation for the existence of the universe.

In the constant quest for explanations that ground the perception of intelligibility and rationality, the human mind confronts the challenge of explaining the existence of the universe. "Why is there something rather than nothing?" asked Leibniz – a "why" question that is just as much about ultimate origin as it is about ultimate purpose. The question is equally forceful whether the universe has trillions of galaxies or whether all that exists is a grain of sand. How did it get here? It is now in being. How and why was it brought into being? Did it create itself? Or was it always here with no beginning and, presumably, no end? But to say that it always existed is still not an explanation of its existence. It is, rather, a putative, highly speculative description that is, by the nature of the case, incapable of scientific verification (how is it possible to prove that matter and energy have no beginning and no end?). And a description is not an explanation. The assertion that the universe always existed is not, to my mind, an explanation for this reason: even if we admit the assumption of an eternally existing universe we are still left with the problem of explaining and accounting for the phenomenon of an eternally existing universe. The mathematics and the mechanisms behind the processes that culminated in the universe we inhabit have been the objects of plausible and often fruitful speculation. But the question of ultimate origin – an ultimate explanation for the mathematics and the mechanisms – continues to elude and baffle the most ingenious theorists.

Science takes as its starting-point the metascientific principle of explanation, the principle that reality is intelligible and rational and that there is an explanation for everything. Most cosmological and teleological arguments are based on the principle of explanation and their validity is bound up with the validity of this principle as an essential and ultimate principle of reality. In its most common forms, cosmological arguments begin with the premise that any thing which exists must have an explanation adequate to fully account for its existence either in itself or in something else.

The only viable explanation for the existence of any one of the entities or all of the entities that make up the universe would be the existence of an ultimate uncaused being – a being that did not receive existence from anyone or anything else and can completely explain its own existence. This self-explanatory being is commonly called "God" and is the explanatory ultimate demanded by all non-self-explanatory entities from sub-atomic particles to galaxies. Cosmological arguments do not reason from the fact that everything in the universe has a cause in space and time to the conclusion that the universe has a cause in space and time: these arguments point out, rather, that everything in the universe is non-self-explanatory, which means that the explanation of the universe does not lie in itself but must lie in a self-explanatory being.

The train of thought that leads from the universe to a transcendent self-explanatory being is, above all, the response of rationality to the facts of experience. "The direction of thought towards the unconditioned (God)," writes Copleston, "is simply the movement of reason itself in its process of understanding in a given context . . . The completely isolated finite thing is unintelligible, in the sense that reason cannot rest in this idea but strives to overcome the isolation . . . Some of those who speak of things as being 'gratuitous', *de trop* or 'just there', betray by the very phrases which they use the fact that their reason is not satisfied with the idea of a finite thing as 'just there'". By refusing to apply the principle of explanation to the universe, the atheist "simply puts a bar to the movement of understanding in a certain context because, for reasons which it can be left to others to determine, he does not wish to travel along a path which, as he sees clearly enough, leads in a certain direction".[13] Because it rises in the "movement of reason," rational theism (as opposed to fideism) has been described as the "ultimate rationalism," "the fulfillment of human rationality." The existence of God, then, is an inescapable insight, the greatest insight, of sapiential sense.

A number of the thinkers who have led the return to theism in modern philosophy – notably Richard Swinburne, Alvin Plantinga and William Alston, who have developed their distinctive lines of argument and reflection – are contributors to this volume.

Another Great Question that is addressed by sapiential sense is the existence of the soul. In this area, as is the case with the existence of God, the burden of proof is on the materialist who denies a reality of which we are conscious at every waking moment. The existence of non-physical properties in human experience has not only been recognized by most of humankind but even by most philosophers until Descartes. The philosopher of science Karl Popper noted that "All thinkers of whom we knew enough to say anything definite on their position, up to and including Descartes, were dualist interactionists."[14]

Even the foremost proponent of logical positivism in the English-speaking world, the late Sir Alfred Ayer, whom I interviewed for this volume, acknowledges here that the mental is clearly distinct from the material and that he sees no grounds for identifying the two.

In addressing the question of the existence of a mental reality that is not reducible to the physical, the layperson is on the safe and secure ground of everyday experience. Our experiences of subjectivity, identity, intentionality, insight and thought are not only undeniable but they are undeniably different from all experience of the physical. As Richard Swinburne has written, "Much philosophical ink has been spent in trying to construct arguments to deny what seems to stare us in the face – that conscious events are distinct from brain events."[15]

In an unintentionally hilarious comment on the body–mind problem, *Time* magazine opined, "After more than a century of looking for it, brain researchers have long since concluded that there is no conceivable place for such a self to be located in the physical brain, and that it simply doesn't exist."[16] This "conclusion" is reminiscent of the remarks made by the first Soviet cosmonaut to orbit the earth: he was quoted as saying that he had failed to find God in outer space and therefore God does not exist. In both instances, the investigators had not only looked for the realities in question in all the wrong places but had entirely misunderstood the very nature of these realities. Neither God nor the soul have ever been thought of as occupying space – and, as a matter of fact, great brain scientists of recent times, ranging from C.S. Sherrington to Wilder Penfield to John Eccles accepted the existence of a non-physical reality separate from the brain. The very idea that the self (if it exists) must be located in the brain betrays a state of conceptual confusion on a par with the notion that we can find "time" by dismantling a clock.

Materialism is demonstrably helpless in addressing the issues of perception, self-consciousness, intention, identity and language, and a number of recent philosophers have developed incisive critiques of materialism from these uncontroversial starting-points: David Lund (*Perception, Mind and Personal Identity*), David Braine (*The Human Person: Animal and Spirit*), John Foster (*The Immaterial Self*), Richard Swinburne (*The Evolution of the Soul*), H. Robinson (*Matter and Sense*) and Geoffrey Madell (*Mind and Materialism*). A few excerpts from Lund's *Perception, Mind and Personal Identity* show how the most sophisticated theories of materialism and physicalism fail to account for the data of universal experience:

> What it is like to be conscious or to have experience is a reality
> which the materialist seems unable to acknowledge, but the full
> extent of his difficulty is obscured until we see the implications of
> the fact that this is a reality for a subject. I argue that I have direct
> awareness of myself – that "I" is a referring expression and that
> when I use it to refer to myself I refer to a subject known to me by
> acquaintance. This is the ground of the unity of my experiences at
> a time as well as across time . . . Their unity consists simply in the
> fact that all of them are mine . . . The subject of experience,
> though ontologically fundamental, is unknown to materialism. It
> cannot be known by description: it has a uniqueness other than
> the uniqueness of a particular which uniquely satisfies an individ-
> uating description. Awareness of it does not consist in the aware-
> ness that a certain set of properties is instantiated. It is accessible
> only by taking the perspective of the first person – a perspective
> which itself has no place in the centerless objective order of mate-
> rial reality. But the existence of a subject of experience also indi-
> cates that there can be no satisfactory materialist treatment of con-
> sciousness or the qualitative character of the mental. For if the
> subject is a non-physical particular, the claim that its acts or states
> of awareness are irreducible to anything physical seems undeni-
> able. And the same must be said of properties instantiated in those
> states in individuals dependent upon them.[17]

It appears that there can be no satisfactory materialist treat-
ment of either the qualitative phenomenality of experience or the
intentionality of consciousness, that is, prior to bringing the fact
that we have self-consciousness into consideration. But if, as I
have argued, we are led to acknowledge the existence of a subject
of consciousness, the case for materialism is lost.[18]

We have an epistemic awareness of a mental reality as it is uninterpreted, more specifically, that we are directly aware of (or
acquainted with) the qualitative character of our experience, of
our acts or states of consciousness, and of ourselves in having
experience. And it seems clear that if any of these arguments are
successful, then materialism cannot be true. For each of them
would have us acknowledge the essential involvement of consciousness in experience, whether it is the experience of being a
subject or an experience having a qualitative character. But, as we
have seen, the materialist apparently has no place for an occurrent
or categorical consciousness. . . The claim that consciousness
poses a formidable challenge to the materialist is uncontroversial.
What seems clear now is not only that that challenge has not been

met but that it cannot be met without some plausible grounds for
taking consciousness to be, if not simply an illusion, then certainly a good deal less than what it introspectively appears to be . . .
But now we have reached the conclusion that all of these
approaches fail; and there are no others. Thus again the conclusion that materialism fails seems inescapable.[19]

Braine takes language as his starting-point and argues that the
process of linguistic understanding neither operates through a bodily organ nor has a neural correlate. And the logician Peter Geach, by
reference to the atheist philosopher W. V. O. Quine, shows how
materialism is at odds with logic: "Quine's logical theory is at odds
with his naturalism. For Quine's naturalism commits him to holding
that no rigorous sense can be made of the verb 'to say' (which is
incorrigibly intentional); not even if we were to take the impersonal
sense of 'to say' as fundamental, the sense in which not men but sentences say things. The sad result is that Quine's weapon against
ontological obfuscation loses its sharp edge; he *cannot* in disputa-
tion make clear what he means by ontological commitment, because
so to do would mean bringing prominently forward a notion that
the severer muse would ban."[20]

In a debate with the behaviorist B. F. Skinner, Brand Blanshard
showed how even perception poses a major challenge to the materialist:

Images have always offered special difficulty for the behaviorists,
and I do not want to exploit that difficulty unduly. So perhaps I
should add that precisely the same difficulty is occasioned by ordinary perception. Professor Skinner uses the example of seeing a
rainbow in the sky. What is it that we are here responding to? He
does not, as Watson did, develop the fact of light impinging on
nerve ends. He holds, and rightly, that these are not what we see;
what we are seeing is the reds, greens, and yellows of the bow in
the sky. But then these reds, greens and yellows are not really
there at all. Would any responsible physicist admit for a moment
that they are? He would admit, of course, that the vibrations are
there, but that is a quite different matter. The whole tradition of
physics from Newton down has relegated the reds, greens and yellows to sensations, sense-data in our minds, caused indeed by
outer vibrations, but utterly different from them. . . In his last
important book in philosophy [Bertrand Russell] holds that everything we directly perceive exists in consciousness, and that the
entire world of physical science is a speculative construction built

on that foundation. And about the secondary qualities such as colors, sounds and smells, physics would surely agree with him. Regarding these qualities, Professor Skinner seems to me caught in a dilemma. If he puts them in physical nature, he is at odds with science. If he puts them in consciousness, he abandons behaviorism. And I doubt if he can find an ontological purgatory between these two.[21]

We must note here that the differences between Aristotelians/Thomists and Platonists/Cartesians on the exact constitution of the human person (the soul as form of the body vs. mind–body dualism) do not affect the central issue of the intellect. Both traditions agree – against materialists and physicalists – that the intellect is intrinsically immaterial (as Aquinas said, the soul's intellective cognition is an activity performed "on its own, in which the body does not share").

It should be obvious that as long as we are true to ourselves, we can find the ultimate answers to most of the Great Questions in sapiential sense-data (for instance, the reality of our freedom, of our experience of moral obligation, and so on). Sapiential sense is useful also in detecting error.

An instance of error-detection concerns reincarnation. We note that the theory is implausible not just for the philosophical and empirical reasons adduced later in this anthology but because it denies our immediate and ultimate awareness of personal identity. If we take our irreducible experience of self-hood seriously, we cannot conceive of this self unconsciously going through various animal and human bodies before finally dissolving in a spiritual ocean. Everything that the reincarnationist tells us about the self is contrary to all that is known about the self in human experience. Similarly, the idea of pantheism, the idea that we are all part of God, is entirely foreign to our experience of the irreducible distinctness and identity of the self. Still less plausible is the idea that we will somehow merge into God: the immaterial nature of the soul precludes us from thinking of it as something that can be cut up, or merged with, some other entity. Moreover, our awareness of the radical difference between our finite selves and the Infinite makes it unthinkable that there could be any "dissolution" of human souls in God.

Now, it is obvious that the instances above are not proofs or disproofs. They simply show that the burden of proof is with those who reject what is obvious in human experience. And claims which contradict the obvious simply cannot be accepted or even be taken seriously, as Peter Geach points out: "When we hear of some new attempt to explain reasoning or choice naturalistically, we ought to react as if we were told someone had squared the circle or proved √2 to be rational: only the mildest curiosity is in order – how well has the fallacy been concealed? Least of all should we be impressed by the alleged human production of artificial intelligence in machines: there is little more ridiculous than the spectacle of a man inferring from the existence of a machine that produces language and calculations because of people's designing it and giving it a program, that human beings are themselves such machines fundamentally, only their coming to be can be explained without bringing in any notions of plan and intention."[22] In the same vein, Lonergan writes: "I do not think it difficult to establish God's existence. I do think it a lifelong labor to analyze and refute all the objections that philosophers have thought up against the existence of God. But I see no pressing need for every student of religion to penetrate into that labyrinth and then work his way out."[23]

In approaching the Great Questions, then, we are concerned not so much with giving arguments as with drawing attention to what is obvious in our immediate experience, for it is here that we find the Ultimate Answers.

Roy Abraham Varghese

NOTES

1. Richard Rorty, "Pragmatism and Philosophy," in *After Philosophy* ed. Kenneth Baynes, James Bohman and Thomas McCarthy (Cambridge: The MIT Press, 1987), p. 28.
2. Richard Rorty, "Science as Solidarity," in *Dismantling Truth* ed. Hilary Lawson and Lisa Appignanesi (New York: St. Martin's Press, 1989), p. 13.
3. T. Theocharis and M. Psimopoulos, "Where Science Has Gone Wrong", *Nature*, October 15, 1987, pp. 595–8.
4. John Horgan, *The End of Science* (New York: Helix Books, 1996), p. 222.
5. Stephen Hawking, *A Brief History of Time* (New York: Bantam, 1988), p. 175.
6. Richard Ostling, "Modernizing the Case for God," *Time*, April 7, 1980, p. 65.
7. Paul Davies, *God and the New Physics* (New York: Simon and Schuster, 1983), p. 31.

8. Illtyd Trethowan, *Absolute Value* (London: George Allen & Unwin Ltd, 1970), p. 5.

9. C. D. Broad, *The Mind and Its Place in Nature* (London: Kegan Paul, 1925), p. 623.

10. See the discussion on "Lonergan's Negative Dialectic" in *International Philosophical Quarterly*, September 1990, for the relevance of Lonergan's approach to the Deconstructionists and other "post-modernists."

11. D. J. B. Hawkins, *Approach to Philosophy* (London: The Paladin Press, 1938), pp. 19-21.

12. Etienne Gilson, *Thomist Realism and the Critique of Knowledge* (San Francisco: Ignatius Press, 1986), pp. 180–1.

13. Frederick Copleston, *Religion and Philosophy* (Dublin: Gill and Macmillan, 1974), p. 174.

14. Karl Popper and J. Eccles, *The Self and Its Brain* (1977), p. 152.

15. Richard Swinburne, "The Origin of Consciousness," in *Cosmic Beginnings and Human Ends* ed. Clifford N. Matthews and Roy Abraham Varghese (Chicago: Open Court, 1995), p. 358.

16. *Time*, July 17, 1995, p. 52.

17. David H. Lund, *Perception, Mind and Personal Identity* (Lanham: University Press of America, 1994,) pp. xvii, xviii.

18. Ibid., p. 230.

19. Ibid., pp. 231–2.

20. Peter Geach, *The Virtues*, (Cambridge: Cambridge University Press, 1977), p. 50. In "The Given" (*Philosophy and Phenomenological Research*, June 1986, pp. 597ff.) Bredo Johnson develops a limited defense of "immediate experience" in the face of the standard criticisms of the given of Quine, Wilfrid Sellars and Nelson Goodman. The writings of Illtyd Trethowan, in my view at least, seem to be more successful in taking experience on its own terms in this area.

21. "The Problem of Consciousness – A Debate" B. F. Skinner and Brand Blanshard, *Philosophy and Phenomenological Research*, pp. 321-1.

22. Peter Geach, *The Virtues*, (Cambridge: Cambridge University Press, 1977), pp. 52–3.

23. Bernard Lonergan, *Philosophy of God, and Theology*, 1973, pp. 55–6.

Part I:

CAN WE KNOW AND KNOW THAT WE KNOW?

RELATIVISM

Great Question 1: *It is commonly believed that "truth" is simply a product of perspective or genetics or cultural environment. We are told by relativists that the human mind cannot really know anything. What is your assessment of relativism?*

RICHARD SWINBURNE

"It is commonly believed that 'truth' is simply a product of perspective or genetics or cultural environment." Well, this doctrine cannot be, in general, true because it is clearly self-defeating. If there isn't such a thing as truth, then this view, that truth is a product of perspective or genetics, cannot itself be true. So the general doctrine cannot possibly be true. What is more plausible is that on some matters human beings cannot know anything; there isn't a truth in some areas or, at any rate, a truth that human beings can discover. For example, it might be (though I don't think it is the case) that there are no truths of morals. The doctrine that there are no truths of morals would not be self-defeating in a way that the general doctrine "there are no truths" is self-defeating because there might be truth in some other discipline, say metaphysics, but not in morality.

However, I think the way to approach this question is simply to say that in this matter, as in all matters, one ought to believe what seems obviously to be true and to start from there. And what seems obviously to be true is that there are some simple truths about what we observe around us. That this table is brown, that the clock is now pointing to nine o'clock and so on; and equally much, jumping the gun a bit to your Question 10, it seems pretty obvious that certain things are wrong and certain things are good. It is wrong to torture children and it is good to feed the starving, and so on. If we are ever to have knowledge about anything, we must start from what seems most obviously true – and there are plenty of simple, obvious truths, both about the immediate data of experience and about moral matters. What seems obviously true may not be true. But it is rational to believe that it is true because that is the way it seems to be until some-body's got a stronger argument against it. And once one does that then it does seem there are quite a lot of things that one can know.

And also I am not very happy about any attempt to draw a rigid line, saying that humans can have knowledge in this area but not in that area. I think any attempt to draw the line saying "this is what we can know" and "that is what we can't know" is in danger of being self-defeating, because in saying that there is an area of knowledge, area of truth, to which we cannot have access already commits us to the view that there is something we know about it and that it is too big for us to know very much more about it. So any attempt to draw the line between truths we can know and truths we can't know already presupposes we know a tiny bit about the latter sort of truths. The only thing to do in any field is to proceed and see how far we can get. Some things are obvious and some things aren't so obvi-ous. Let's see how strong the arguments are, starting from the things which are obvious for different kinds of knowledge, and maybe some things can be known fairly well and other claims to knowledge are weak. I don't feel happy with any general doctrine that we can't have knowledge in this area, or certainly not, for reasons I have already given, that we can't know anything at all.

HUGO MEYNELL

What you rightly say "is commonly believed" is in fact self-destruc-tive. Is the proposed truth, of perspective or genetics or cultural envi-ronment? If so, there is no good reason to believe it. If not, it falsi-fies itself. All forms of relativism may be disposed of by similar argu-ments. Now I maintain that Kant was right in holding that there are certain a priori principles of reasoning that have to be established by something other than deductive logic, and which are presupposed in all of our commonsense and scientific reasoning. I should say that these assumptions, and the reasons why we tend to know what is absolutely true and to know and do what is absolutely good to the extent that we thoroughly apply them, have been set out more bril-liantly and persuasively by [Bernard] Lonergan than by anyone else. He summarizes them in what he calls the "four transcendental pre-cepts:" be attentive, be intelligent, be reasonable, be responsible. Being attentive is a matter of attending to experience in a very wide sense, including our feelings and the operations of our minds as well as the contents of our senses. Being intelligent consists of hypothesizing, of envisaging possibilities that may explain this experience, of asking "What?" and "Why?" One is reasonable so far as one selects as probably true the hypothesis or possibility that best fits the relevant experience in each case, rather than one that gratifies our desires, or calms our fears, or panders to our self-esteem, and so on. Finally, to be responsible is to act in accordance with the value-judgment at which one has reasonably arrived. Deductive logic facilitates the operation of intelligence and reasonableness; one makes deductions from hypotheses, and rejects those hypotheses, deductions from which are falsified by experience, retaining (usually only provisionally) those which are corroborated by it. It is true that, by itself, or even in combination merely with experience, deductive logic can discover nothing new. On the other hand, there are no other ways of reliably discovering what is true and good than being thoroughly attentive, intelligent, and reasonable; "scientific experimentation and philosophical argumentation" are simply ways of applying these precepts to get to know different aspects of reality.

Suppose someone – say a positivist or behaviorist – denies that the mental operations enjoyed by the transcendental precepts actually occur, or that they are essential to the discovery of what is true and good. Lonergan shows that these denials are self-destructive. There are few people who are going to admit that they have never had the experience of seeing or hearing or feeling anything. Secondly, it is not very common (though I have seen it done) for people to assert that they have never hypothesized, never envisaged a possibility, and never understood or even misunderstood anything. But if you are going to be a consistent materialist or reductionist in psychology, this is exactly what you must say, for example, claiming that people are in the last analysis simply machines who react to schedules of positive reinforcement acting on biological predispositions. Rare, too, as Lonergan says, is the researcher who will say that she has never actually made a reasonable judgment, and certainly not in forming the opinions expressed in the paper which she is now delivering before her learned colleagues. Finally, it is not very frequently that an author confesses that he has never made a responsible decision in his life, least of all in presenting this particular book to the public. (Though I could cite one case, of a deconstructionist literary critic.) If obedience to the precepts is presupposed in all of our knowledge-claims and value-judgments, then they can be established on the ground that their contradictories are self-destructive. Descartes, in rather similar vein, pointed out that

I cannot coherently think that I am not a thinker, or argue that I am not an arguer. Likewise, I cannot reasonably and responsibly state that I am not at all a reasonable and responsible person. So much for the a priori characteristics of our way to knowledge that cannot be reduced to logic in the strict sense. (When Spock exhorted Kirk to "be logical, Captain", he in fact was reminding him to be thoroughly attentive, intelligent, and reasonable.)

And, of course, if the real world is nothing other than what our true judgments are about, and our reasonable judgments tend to be about, then it follows that on the whole we should trust the deliberations of scientists as yielding the best available account of what actually is so, rather than what grandfather thinks when he looks at his tea-leaves. The reason is that we think they are specially qualified to propound hypotheses and make judgments in accordance with the available evidence on matters within their competence. It could, of course, turn out that grandfather happens to be right, on the nature of gluons or the constitution of quasars; but this could only be established by even more intelligence and reasonableness applied to the relevant data by those who are in a proper position to do so. Now relativism is wholly inconsistent with all this. The virtue of relativism, such as it is, is as a reaction against people in Western society who use their own cherished beliefs and assumptions as a kind of juggernaut to knock down traditional and non-Western points of view, when in fact there is probably a great deal that we can learn from these. If we Westerners have been especially attentive, intelligent and reasonable with respect to some matters, with regard to others we seem to have been mighty insensitive, stupid, and silly.

People tend to be relativistic on moral matters, even when they are not so about matters of ordinary fact. Here again there may seem good reason for this, if one does not think the matter through. I understand that there is a district in the Sudan where, if you are an unmarried woman, it is thought extremely indecent for you to go around with clothes on; whereas, I am credibly informed, in North America it is considered just as indecent for you to go about unclothed. Relativists infer, from examples like this, that morality, value, and responsible conduct are completely relative to social milieu. But in my view this is a boneheaded conclusion. What the example really shows is that the universal moral principle, that you should not give offense to those among whom you live without very good reason, dictates that a young woman in the one place should on the whole go around without clothes, and in the other with clothes. (There might, of course, be special countervailing circumstances; think of Lady Godiva.) The ultimate moral criteria can be outlined roughly as follows. We have a conception of what a happy, fulfilled, and self-realized life might be like; we ought to promote it as far as possible and ensure that some people shouldn't have it at the expense of others. To this end, local customs and traditions have to be taken into account. I conclude that the principles of truth and value which I have tried to sketch and justify are quite incompatible with relativism; though there is a kind of dogmatic and shortsighted absolutism, which would impose on everyone the customs and conventions which happen to suit one's own society or group, against which moral relativism is an understandable though confused protest. Some customs, however deeply entrenched in a culture, are absolutely bad; female circumcision is an obvious if distasteful example.

ALVIN PLATINGA

Why should I believe that truth is simply a product of perspective or genetics or cultural environment? Is this being proposed to me as something that is really true, is it being proposed to me as a product of genetics? If all the relativist is really telling me is just that from his perspective that is what truth is, then of course I agree with him. From his perspective that is what truth is. But from my perspective it's dead wrong. The fundamental problem here, a fundamental problem for relativism – apart from just the fantastic nature of it (it's extremely difficult to believe that it isn't really just true that $7 + 5 = 12$, but only true from somebody's perspective or point of view), apart from the sort of incredibleness of it, the main problem is that it completely does away with the possibility of disagreement. It looks like people actually disagree. One person says: it is wrong to discriminate against people just because of their color; someone else says no, it's right to do that; and each person thinks that what they say is true. The relativist comes along and tells us that the whole presupposition of their debate is false: there isn't any such thing as truth. All there is really is truth-from-a-perspective. So (according to the relativist) the one person is saying "from my perspective, it is wrong to treat someone badly just because of their color;" and the other person is saying "from my perspective that is not bad." But then we no longer have a disagreement. Each person is just explaining how things stand from his or her perspective and each person can perfectly well agree with the other person that from that other person's perspective, that is indeed how things look. There is no longer any opportunity for disagreement. Relativism ordinarily begins from an acute awareness of human disagreement: this disagreement, the relativist thinks, suggests that we can't really know much of anything. But then relativism ends by denying that there is any such thing as disagreement.

So it seems to me there are two problems with relativism. First it denies that there is any such thing as disagreement. Second, it is at most dubiously coherent, because it looks like the relativist is trying to tell us a truth: that truth is just a product of perspective or is always relative to a perspective. It looks like the relativist wants to assert that; but from their own perspective they are not really asserting that. From their own perspective, they are only asserting that from their perspective that is the way things stand. But of course that isn't news, and it isn't startling, and isn't really what they want to claim.

GERARD J. HUGHES

Uncontroversially, different individuals, and the members of different cultures, interpret the world in different ways: illness might be attributed to the activity of a virus, or the malice of an ancestor, or the wrath of a god; color-words are notoriously culture-dependent; moral codes differ one from another, and so on. Our various languages and cultures show that we interpret the world we live in in a multitude of ways. Equally uncontroversially, such facts do not of themselves entail that everyone's view is equally correct, or that it is never possible to say that a particular way of interpreting the world is simply mistaken. Popular expressions of relativism, such as "It is true for them that she fell ill because her dead mother-in-law had it in for her", or "It is true for them that cannibalism is morally permissible" are often no more than confused ways of saying "They believed that her dead mother-in-law caused her illness", or "They cannot be blamed for cannibalism, given their sincere beliefs". Nothing follows about the truth of those beliefs, one way or the other.

More sophisticated forms of relativism are more difficult both to state and to assess. For instance, it might be argued that since all our thought and language already presuppose an interpretation of the world, it makes no sense to ask what the world is like "in itself", uninterpreted. There is no neutral Archimedean point from which the truth of various interpretations might be assessed.

Of course, it makes no sense to ask whether something has color independently of any possible perceiver; color essentially involves a relationship between objects and perceivers; equally, it makes no sense to ask whether a whale is a mammal independently of any language users who employ the words "whale" and "mammal". It still remains the case, though, that the world is the way it is, and the way it is might justify classifying parts of it as whales, or mammals, or both. If such classification is justified, then it will be true to say that whales are mammals. What sort of justification might be involved here? I take the answer to this question to involve some version of pragmatism. That is to say, the test will be some form of success. If we adopt some particular understanding of (a part of) the world, we might then discover that we can interact with it more predictably, control it more tightly, understand it more coherently and in progressively simpler terms. This encourages us to believe that we have got it right. Of course this type of criterion will not yield equally definite results in every case. Truth is therefore not equally easy to determine in every instance.

If all our human interpretations are in this way checked against the world, one might expect them gradually to converge. I believe that they do, and that the differences between cultures are less radical than is often supposed. Many of the differences that there are can be explained by differences in technological expertise (say, between Aristotle and ourselves, or between someone from the developed West and a member of a remote Papuan tribe), or by differences in ease of access to information, and so on. Anthropological studies, far from lending support to relativist theories of truth, seem to me on the contrary to demonstrate the possibility of mutual comprehension, and to show that the fundamental modes of human thinking are universally shared. In evolutionary terms, it might be argued that we have succeeded as a race precisely because we are reasonably successful in understanding the world as it is; in theistic terms, it might be argued that God has so created us as to be able to grasp the truth about our world.

Relativism has more often been advanced as an account of morality than as an account of knowledge generally. This is easy to account for, since the test of successful interaction with the world is here less easy to apply than it is in, say, medicine, or chemistry. While I shall offer some further thoughts on truth in ethics in the next section, it is worth remarking here that many allegedly relativist views of ethics are not relativist at all. For example, it is an absolutist, not a relativist,

view, that differences in circumstances will often mean that people
should act differently; and it is surely obvious that people living in different social, environmental, and economic settings will for that very
reason have different moral obligations towards one another. It is no
part of the absolutist's view that everyone ought to behave in precisely the same way, no matter who or where they are. Secondly, it is no
part of the absolutist's view that there must be only one correct answer
to the question "What is it permissible to do in these circumstances?"
And finally, an absolutist can, and indeed should, maintain that each
person has a moral duty to act as they honestly and sincerely think
best, even if those beliefs are in fact mistaken.

I therefore think that the absolutist is in a much better position
to explain both the progress of science and the ways in which we
succeed in understanding and learning from societies other than
our own.

I also think, contrary to what is often supposed, that it is the absolutist rather than the relativist who can give a proper account of the
value of tolerance. On the relativist view, truth is self-contained,
immune from criticism by any "external" views which might be held
by other cultures. There may be practical or political reasons why relativists will decide not to be intolerant of other cultures, and indeed
they may believe (and therefore hold that it is true for them) that they
should be tolerant. But this belief itself will have no more than a relative truth. In contrast, absolutists will hold that the sincerity of their
own beliefs is no guarantee whatever of their truth; there may be
much to be learnt from other ways of seeing the world, other ways of
structuring society, other ways of leading the moral life. The views of
others deserve respect not for merely practical reasons, but because
they may be a source of enlightenment and knowledge.

JOSEF SEIFERT

It is perhaps too much to assert that it is commonly believed today
that what we call truth is simply a product of perspective or genetics or cultural environment. But it is true that skepticism and relativism in countless forms are very much prevalent today. The
relativist who says that truth is relative contradicts himself, however, because, in so saying, he claims truth for this very judgment.
Thus he claims that it is actually so that truth is relative. Hence,
he claims that his own position is true because it is adequate to
reality. For he believes that as a matter of fact truth is relative,

and thus that relativism is true. Consequently, any relativism pre-supposes the absolute truth of its own position, of its content and of its reasonability, and in particular of the proposition of the rel-ativity of all truth. But relativism also presupposes the truth of all the reasons which lead the relativist to adopt his relativism. We can see from the internal contradictions of relativism that it cannot possibly be correct.

But in addition we can refer to countless evident truths which we can gain in mathematics, even in the sphere of chess theory[1], in the recognition of our own existence and in the infinite variety of our own experiences and acts which are accessible to us through undeniable evidence, in the insights into mathematical objects and the laws that govern them, into laws governing colors, motions, the moral order, the nature of love, the nature of promises, etc. For example, truths such as that colors are necessarily extended, that motion necessarily pre-supposes time, that to respect the rights of other persons is necessari-ly good, while to disrespect them, to murder or to rape others, is not only an evil such as pain, but a moral evil – all these and innumerable other universal truths about the essences of things are supremely intel-ligible to the human mind. The same applies also to the laws of logic.

This immediate access to evident truths (however difficult and arduous the path that leads to evident truth might be) is another and more profound refutation of relativism than the understanding of its internal contradiction.

One could refute relativism and skepticism also by understanding the logical connections between the truth and falsity of propositions in formal logic and syllogisms. The way in which the premises of log-ical arguments contain their conclusion is not such that one presup-poses these conclusions but rather that the truth of the different premises guarantees the truth of the conclusion. Hence, from that point of view a conclusion of a logical argument can very well reveal something new that is not known directly but known only indirectly by means of a demonstration.

GEORGE F. R. ELLIS

In my view, this relativist stream of thought can only be pursued in relation to science by those who have had no practical experience of science. One of the most striking features of science throughout its his-tory has been how human presuppositions have again and again been proved false by the nature of reality, as exposed by the experimental method. Nature has often surprised scientists and forced them to revise their theories in the face of indisputable experimental evidence (for example in the cases of quantum theory and of relativity theory); and this is equally true in the case of mathematics, where for example the phenomenon of chaos has been hidden in simple equations until the past decade. It is untenable that the surprising theories that result are simply the result of social construction.

As regards that hard-core of relativists for whom this argument is unconvincing, my response is a challenge: if you really maintain that scientific laws are simply a social construct or the result of a choice of a language game, then let's see you change your social construct or alter your language game, and rise up and float in the air. Then you will have shown that what is identified by science as the universal law of gravitation does not have a real foundation in nature, and is just a social convention. I do not expect any successful takers.

Thus, as regards science, I suggest the situation is as believed by working scientists: while the scientific process is subject to sociological forces just as is any other human activity, and the questions scientists ask are to some extent socially determined, the answers obtained to these questions are not. Scientific discoveries explore and clarify the nature of reality and the universal fundamental structures underlying the physical universe.

Many will accept this in relation to the "hard" sciences – physics, chemistry, and mathematics in particular – but will deny its validity in relation to the social sciences, where one is indeed brought up against the bewildering variety of human behaviour and cultural systems. This leads to a denial of any universally valid patterns in human behaviour. My view is that there are indeed such threads if one looks beyond the surface layers to a deep enough level of analysis: there are universal themes at play that are worked out in a vast variety of ways in different times and places. A response I have been given is that while this may be true, the universal themes are not the exciting ones; the interesting questions relate to the variations in society (e.g. the different ways people exert social control) rather than the common behaviour (the fact that there are specific mechanisms for social control in all societies). This is a statement of interest and taste; it confirms rather than denies the point I am putting.

The analysis of Barkow, Cosmides, and Tooby proposes – with detailed examples – that there are sound evolutionary reasons for believing in a universal aspect to human behaviour. The fundamental point they make is that one should take an integrated approach to knowledge; the social sciences cannot afford to ignore scientific themes such as evolution if they wish to attain a fundamental understanding of their subject matter. However, suggest Barkow *et al*, in their analyses of human behavior, the human sciences largely ignore evolutionary aspects; and the purely cultural conclusions they derive are shaped by this method of enquiry. This position, which I believe has merit, is of course very controversial; the opposition claim is that the effect of such inherited features is minimal, culture being the major determinant of behavior. Whatever the outcome of that debate, I can give additional support to my own position by noting the universal appeal of the great plays and literature of all nations (the Greek tragedies, Shakespeare, Dostoyevsky, and so on); they could not have this universal appeal were there not a common thread of human understanding across cultures.

RALPH MCINERNY

Relativism has got to be one of the hardest things to adopt. It seems to me that you have nothing but trouble trying to hold it consistently and I think the example of Nietzsche and Rorty and other nihilists is worthwhile taking into account. Finally they don't try to justify it at all. They don't think relativism is true. If they did they couldn't be relativists. So, finally it is sort of an aesthetic stance that they take and, well, they are welcome to it, but I don't know why I should pay any attention to it. Try being a relativist and it is impossible. In order to state the position you have to negate it. And so I think it is a reductio kind of argument against relativism.

Also, we know that we know.

Yes. That's a good point. If you have doubt about knowledge, you don't have doubt about the fact that you know that, so you get caught up in the kind of usual difficulties brought against Descartes: he has great confidence in the reason in which he has no confidence. But all those arguments are dissatisfying. Reductio ad absurdum is dissatisfying because we don't need an argument for what we are getting to. So most of the time we have the sense we are playing a game, like that being played by the people who raised the difficulty. It's almost a shame to have to formulate these things on behalf of the obvious.

WILLIAM P. ALSTON

The first thing I want to say about this is that we shouldn't assimilate the question of truth to the question of knowledge. As I understand truth, that is propositional truth, the proposition that "SMU is in Dallas" is true if and only if SMU is in Dallas. That is, the content of the proposition provides the necessary and sufficient conditions for its truth. If that content is, shall we say, realized, if it obtains in the world, then the proposition is true. That is all it takes to make it true, and nothing else will suffice. So we shouldn't conflate the question of whether truth is relative to culture or society or something of that sort with the question of whether knowledge is relative in those ways. I think it is obvious there are many truths that no one has knowledge of. For a simple example, just consider the set of propositions of the form, "at such and such a time it was raining on this spot". Think of the indefinitely large set of such propositions where time stretches as far back into the past as you like. Now with respect to this particular spot where I am sitting right now, nobody knows whether it was raining at this spot exactly ninety thousand years ago. No one will and no one can ever know. God knows, no doubt, but leaving God out of the picture, as far as human beings are concerned there is an infinite number of true propositions such that no one knows them to be true, ever will know them to be true. So it is very important not to assimilate truth and knowledge, and there is a pervasive failure to grasp this point in the intellectual world today. People have just forgotten what truth is.

I can understand something of what is behind this. People may be skeptical about our ability to know certain things and they get impatient with the idea that what we say about these things has an objective truth value, even if we can't know what it is. What good is that to anybody, they ask. Well, whether it is any good to anybody or not we should face the facts, and use words coherently and intelligibly and not get everything confused. So the thing of first importance is to not get your concepts all messed up and to recognize that truth is what it is, whether it is doing us any good or not. I have published a book on this subject called *A Realist Conception of Truth*. There is a view that is fairly popular nowadays, which can be termed something like conceptual relativism or theoretical relativism. It maintains that there is a plurality of ways of conceptualizing reality, which are incompatible with each other, at least on the surface, and which are such that in principle we have no rational way of choosing between them; hence there isn't any one way, any one consistent way, the world is. I don't think the arguments for this are convincing, but even if this view is correct, it complicates the matter with respect to truth without changing the basic picture. Take a particular example of the sort of thing that is being claimed here. You might think of an Aristotelian way of construing the world as made up of a lot of individual substances, each of which endures through time, maintains its self-identity through time, interacts with others. Then contrast that with some sort of process ontology like you have in Whitehead, and you might throw in Spinoza here too, while you are at it, which is still a different story. Suppose I believe that tree out there has leaves on it. Well, I'm formulating that in an Aristotelian mode, but the reality that I am in touch with would be categorized from a Whiteheadian or Spinozistic point of view in a different way. So there isn't any one fact about that hunk of reality. There is what it is from an Aristotelian perspective or point of view, there is what it is from a Spinozistic point of view and a Whiteheadian point of view. These may be all empirically equivalent but they are different ways of categorizing the matter. This means that we have to regard what we are talking about as relative to, in this case, metaphysical schemes. But we don't have to relativize truth. We can say that to give an adequate formulation of any proposition, you have to put in a reference to the conceptual scheme or perspective from which the proposition is being asserted. There is no such complete proposition as, *that tree has leaves. That tree has leaves relative to Aristotelian metaphysics.* Truth can still be the same. It's still the case that the proposition that the tree has leaves relative to Aristotelian metaphysics is true if and only if that tree does have leaves relative to Aristotelian metaphysics. So truth is still a matter of things being as you are saying them to be. It is just that there is a plurality of different ways the world can be said to be. I think that some of these ways can be rejected as being incoherent or selfcontradictory or something like that. And in any event I don't hold any brief for this relativism, but it is a prominent view nowadays, and people are often confused about what is involved in this. It leads them to say that truth is relative, whereas truth isn't relative at all. It is what your propositions are true of that is relative according to this view.

But then knowledge is another matter altogether. The question of when you have knowledge and how strict the requirements for this are is a very complicated one. I don't think it's crucial for religion for people to have knowledge in any strict sense. There a lot of things in the Christian tradition that suggests severe limits on what we can know about God. There is, for example, the famous Pauline image in the first epistle to the Corinthians, "Now we only see through a glass darkly." I think whether we have knowledge of God depends on what is the right way to think about knowledge and what is required for knowledge. There are several strict conceptions of knowledge such that it is plausible to say that we don't, strictly speaking, have knowledge of what is proposed to us in the Christian faith. Aquinas, who was not a wishywashy, liberal, modern-day theologian, contrasted faith with knowledge, strictly so-called, and he thought we could, quite properly, have complete confidence in the articles of faith without knowing them strictly speaking. Consider the idea of faith, that is, the cognitive side of faith. (That is not the whole story about faith; faith involves trust, commitment, all sorts of other things too. But I am speaking of propositional faith, faith that such and such is the case.) Propositional faith doesn't involve knowledge. That doesn't mean that there are no grounds or bases for it, that there is no rational support for it. But that support may not be of such a kind as to amount to knowledge strictly so-called.

How does this relate to the question of certainty, quite apart from issues of faith, certainty of empirical issues, for instance, that you are seeing me. Now it could be an illusion, but at least you have an illusion of seeing me. Can you be absolutely certain about something like that?

Well, yes, I don't think we have the same kinds of problems there. Of course there are abstract, logical possibilities that can be raised here, but I don't think we should regard those as preventing one from having certainty.

How does what you said about truth relate to the correspondence theory of truth, the idea (loosely speaking) that truth relates to a correspondence between propositions and facts?

Well, the correspondence theory is a way of attempting to spell out further the sort of thing I was saying. It is an attempt to explain what is involved in propositions being true. I think the basic concept of a proposition's being true can be given just by this familiar schema "the proposition that T is true if and only if T." *Grass is green* is true if and only if grass is green. That gives you the basic concept, but then the correspondence theory is a way of trying to go further here. When you say the proposition that grass is green is true if and only if grass is green, then it looks as if you are saying that there is a certain fact, or possible fact, which is such that if and only if that fact obtains then the proposition is true. So that must mean there is some way in which this proposition is related to that fact differently from the way it is related to other facts, because it is this fact rather than any other that has to obtain in order for the proposition to be true. So what is that relationship? Various difficulties have arisen in trying to specify that relationship. But that shouldn't inhibit us from thinking that we have the basic concept straight.

> *How would such a statement as "it is true that the world exists" be understood to be true?*

Well, now, are you bringing up some special feature of this particular proposition "the world exists"?

> *Just the fact that the world exists. I am asserting, as a matter of fact, that the world exists. Is that a truth? Is that true?*

I would say so, yes!

> *How does that tie in to what you have said about propositions and facts?*

Well, it is just more grist for the mill. That is a very special kind of proposition.

> *But it is one which can be subsumed under the correspondence theory?*

Well, I don't see why not. Of course, it may be that that is an a priori truth rather than an a posteriori truth. We can't coherently deny that the world exists. But it could still fit into the same schema.

> *And would this be an analytic proposition?*

No. The a priori–aposteriori distinction is an epistemological distinction. It has to do with what the grounds or bases for accepting the proposition are, not what it is for it to be true. The analytic–synthetic distinction: that is not an epistemological distinction but I don't think it is a distinction in modes of truth either. It is a distinction in the character of the proposition. There are a lot of problems about formulating this distinction, but certainly an analytical proposition is one the truth value of which hangs on how the constituent concepts are related to each other in a way that the truth value of a synthetic proposition doesn't. But still what it is for it to be true is the same. It is just that the kind of thing that determines that, the kind of thing that determines whether the conditions for truth are satisfied, is different in the two cases.

NOTES

1. There is an immense realm of evident truths, some of which are derived from mathematics and logic, others are grounded in the specific new structures of chess rules combined with mathematical laws, that are explored in the theory of openings and endgames of chess. See Josef Seifert, *Schachphilosophie* (Darmstadt: Wissenschaftliche Buchgesellschaft, 1989).

UNIVERSAL INSIGHTS PRESUPPOSED BY SCIENCE AND PHILOSOPHY

Great Question 2: *It is often said that the premises in an argument already "contain" their conclusions and therefore logical arguments cannot reveal anything new. Are there any fundamental insights that lie beyond scientific experimentation and philosophical argumentation to which the human mind has access?*

ALVIN PLANTINGA

I think there are all kinds of things we know pre-philosophically and pre-scientifically. We know that there are other people pre-scientifically and pre-philosophically. That is not a product either of scientific investigation or experimentation nor is it a product of philosophical insight or argument. The same goes for our belief that there has been a past, that seven plus five equals twelve, and that I had an orange for breakfast this morning. These are all not results of scientific experimentation nor a result of philosophical discussion. They are rather things that science takes for granted. Science starts from these things. In the same way, science doesn't establish that there are telescopes or other scientific instruments.

Philosophy is a bit different. It typically takes logic for granted. It is hard to say what philosophy just as such takes for granted. What you've got are lots of philosophers, and each of them takes certain things for granted. Different philosophers take different things for granted, but there isn't any such thing, it seems to me, as what philosophy, just as such, takes for granted. Descartes didn't take much for granted, and he also didn't get very far. Hume didn't take very much for granted. But Aquinas took a good bit more for granted. Different philosophers take different things for granted, but nearly all philosophers start off by taking something for granted. If you don't take anything for granted you can't really take a single step. Suppose you refuse to take anything whatever for granted: you out-Descartes Descartes. Then you can't even take logic for granted. You can't give any arguments for anything; and anyway you don't have any premises to argue from. So both philosophy and science are enterprises that start, after one already knows a whole lot of things and after one already takes a whole lot of things for granted. The human mind has access to all kinds of things that it doesn't get by scientific experiment or philosophical argumentation. Certainly the existence of God would be among these things, as would be the existence of other minds.

JOSEF SEIFERT

Not all truths can be known by logical inferences; the fundamental premises and the first principles of logic itself lie beyond demonstrable knowledge, not because they could not be known rationally or because they would just have to be assumed in blind faith, but rather because the supreme and more perfect form of evident and rational knowledge is the intuitive understanding of existence or of necessary essential truths.

RALPH MCINERNY

Absolutely. I think to be a human being is to know certain truths about the world and about oneself and it is not a matter of education, it is not a matter of gift, it is not a matter of IQ. There are drop-off points, obviously, where we are talking about someone who is impaired from using their human powers. The Aristotelian holds that we all already know things. Philosophy isn't the beginning of knowledge but presupposes that we know things, and that is a very attractive, so to speak, democratic way of doing philosophy, it seems to me, whereas most modern philosophy is very elitist.

Does the notion of fundamental insights apply also to moral truths, to our understanding of right and wrong?

Try to find somebody who doesn't have that knowledge. It is very hard, to the point of being impossible, to expunge that from the human consciousness. A lot of people accept dreadful principles of action but would still be appalled if you mistreated them. Our mothers told us, "How would you like it if someone did that to you?" That is a golden rule.

Part II:

IS MATTER THE
WHOLE STORY?

THE EXISTENCE OF THE SOUL

Great Question 3: *Do you accept the existence of a soul or mind separate from the body and, if so, on what basis?*

RICHARD SWINBURNE

Yes indeed. This is something of which I am very, very confident. I think all human beings consist of both the body and the soul. I am my body, plus my soul. These are the two parts of me and the soul is the essential part. Why do I think this?

Well, consider a thought experiment which, up to now, is just a thought experiment but in the future it certainly may be more than that, it may be really done. I have two parts to my brain, a left part and a right part, and there is reasonable evidence that people can survive with only their left brain, or at any rate their left brain plus their brain stem and maybe a few other bits. So, imagine my brain taken out of my skull in the future and imagine the left half of the brain put into an empty skull, from which the brain has been removed, and my right brain, the right half of my brain, put into a different empty skull from which the brain has been removed. And suppose these two half brains to be connected up to the nervous system of the body into which they have been put. So you have, as it were at stage one, me; and then two unfortunate people from whom brains are removed and the left half of my brain is put into one of these bodies and the right half of my brain into another. And suppose that any other bits which are necessary in order to get a functioning person, say extra bits of brain stem, to be added to each of these half brains, maybe even taken from the brain of my identical twin, so that now we have two people, each one of which differs from the previous two people, in that they have different brains from those and the central part of one of these people is the left half of my original brain and the central part of the other person is the right half of my original brain.

Now which of these people is me? There seem to be four possibilities or perhaps only three. One is that neither of them are me, that messing about with brains in this way has simply destroyed me. Or it may be that it is the person with my left-brain who is me or, thirdly, it may be the person with my right-brain who is me or, fourthly, I suppose, it might be that both are me. They couldn't literally both be me because they are different people from each other but it may be that in some sense both are partly me or something like that. Now the point is, we don't know what the answer is, and we wouldn't know what the answer is even though we knew what has happened to every bit of my brain and even though we knew exactly what were my thoughts and feelings before this operation and the thoughts and feelings of the one or two successive persons after the operation. We still wouldn't know which is me. But it is an all-important, crucial fact, whether it is the left-hand person who is me or the right-hand person who is me or whether I haven't survived the operation or whether, in some sense or other, I am both of these people. This is all-important, all-important for me whether I have survived this operation. It is a crucial fact about the world which we would remain ignorant of even if we knew what had happened to every bit of my brain and even if we knew what were the thoughts and feelings of all the people involved. We still wouldn't know which later person was the same as the earlier me and this, therefore, has the consequence that there is going to be a crucial fact about the world which we will be ignorant of if all we know about is what has happened to the material objects of the world.

So there must be an immaterial object of which these crucial facts are facts about. Only if I consist of soul and body and if what happens in the operation is that my soul goes with one part of my brain or, alternatively, with the other, can we make sense of what has happened. Our ignorance about what has happened is our ignorance of where my soul has gone and we explain why we don't know the answer, that is because we can't keep souls under observation even though we can keep bits of brain under observation. So only if we suppose there are souls can we make sense of the fact that we don't know some crucial truth about the world, with whether I survived the operation, even though we do know what has happened to every material object in the world.

So here is just one argument for the existence of a soul but basically all arguments are going to have this kind of structure to them. They point out that there is an awful number of truths you won't know about the world if you merely know what has happened to the bits of matter and what properties they have had and, therefore, there must be something extra. For example, if you merely know what is going on in a brain you won't know whether the brain is connected with one person or two persons. It is an obvious fact, say, that I might be having a visual experience and an auditory experience at the same time – I am conscious of hearing this and seeing that – but all an observation of the brain will show you is that certain visual stimuli produce effects in certain parts of the brain and certain auditory stimuli produce effects in other parts of the brain. And it may be that the brain is so disconnected that, really, there are two separate people in whom these stimuli set up mental impressions or, alternatively, that that isn't so. But mere knowledge of what happens in the brain wouldn't tell you how many subjects of experience are connected with the brain and that is often a real question when the brain has been tampered with in various ways so that the left half behaves autonomously from the right half. So I don't think you can describe, let alone explain, some basic facts about the world, "I am the same person that has had this previous experience" or "I continue to exist" or "I had this experience and that experience at the same time," unless you suppose that experiences happen to souls rather than just to brains.

ALVIN PLANTINGA

I do accept the existence of a soul or mind separate from the body. I don't think that a person is the same thing as his or her body. I don't think a person is a material object; my main reason for thinking that is a philosophical one. If I were a material object then I would have to be identical with, say, my body, or my brain, or some part of my brain, or some other part of my body. (Presumably I wouldn't be identical with some other physical object or with somebody else's body, or some collection of other people's bodies.) But (so it seems to me) I am not my body; I am distinct from my body, because it is possible that I should exist when it didn't exist. It seems to me possible, for example, that all the parts of my body should be rapidly replaced by other body parts while I remain conscious, the original parts being destroyed. This is beyond present medical science, of course, but it's logically possible that this could happen. If that were to happen, then I would continue to exist, but the thing that is in fact my body wouldn't exist. It is therefore possible that I exist at a time at which my body does not exist. So I can't be identical with my body. So I must be something distinct from it. But for any other material object, it's also possible that I should exist when it didn't. So it seems to me I am not any material object at all.

HUGO MEYNELL

Well, my views about this, I'm afraid, are rather unfashionable, but I'll grit my teeth and present them all the same. I think that there are two forms of explanation which we have of things and events, neither of which can be reduced to the other. One is what one might call agent explanation, where you explain something by reference to the intentions and purposes of persons. Why did she walk out of her office? Because she knew Roy Varghese was down the passage and wanted to talk to him about something. Other sorts of explanation don't make any such reference, as when we say that a pond has frozen because of the low temperature, or that plants have died due to lack of moisture; this is the kind of explanation which isn't agent explanation. One of the reasons, it seems to me, for the belief that we are not totally reducible to our bodies is that agent explanation cannot be reduced to explanation of the other kinds, authorities like Skinner and Freud in some moods notwithstanding. That we can in principle so reduce it is often claimed in the name of science; but the fact is that we cannot subject our mental processes to merely physico-chemical explanation without making nonsense of science. As Lonergan expresses it, if it is really true that the scientist says what she says only due to physico-chemical causation, then the scientist does not say what she says because there is a good reason for her to do so. So there is no point in listening to her. So much for a defense of the notion that we are really autonomous agents and subjects; the question is whether there is anything to autonomous subjects over and above their bodies.

I am inclined to agree with Duns Scotus, against Aquinas, that the fact that we transcend physical reality enough to get to know about it, however suggestive it is, does not of itself show that our souls are sufficiently independent of our bodies to survive their dissolution. However, I think that there are additional and rather strong reasons for believing that we survive the death of our bodies. In the early 1960s, Robert Crookall published a very important but lamentably neglected book called *The Supreme Adventure*. There he summarizes a vast quantity of data from the utterances of mediums in trance, automatic writing and reports both of the dying and of those who watch over them; and fits these together into an account of what the immediate afterlife is like for ordinary people. What I think is brilliant about Crookall is his method. He takes as his database evidence apparently bearing on the afterlife from a wide range of sources, and treats it, as he says, like travelers' tales. He asks what is the most plausible way of accounting for all this material, and carefully considers hypotheses alternative to his own. Of course, a single account of this kind bears little weight. Suppose someone says, "I think I saw my grandmother a week after her death. I got a very vivid impression of her and she told me something that I didn't know before, which she seemed to be the only person in a position to know, but which turned out to be true." One such story taken by itself will not impress, and ought not to impress, the Society for Psychical Research. But Crookall puts a huge number of such anecdotes together and comes out with coincidences which cannot at all readily be accounted for unless postmortem souls actually undergo the kinds of experience that his sources suggest. His argument is a cumulative one which establishes, as he puts it, that the survival of bodily death by the human subject, is of the same order of probability as the truth of the theory of evolution. (Crookall was a distinguished professional geologist, so he knew what he was talking about.) It is also of interest that, when Crookall's book came out, little was known about "near-death experiences". Now if you take near-death experiences on their own, one quite convincing explanation of why they are so similar is that one might expect the structure of the human brain to produce more or less identical hallucinations in a state of near-collapse. But it seems to me that this is no longer plausible, if you take the evidence from near-death experiences in conjunction with the material from other sources which Crookall has assembled and collated.

JOSEF SEIFERT

I accept the existence of a soul or mind separate from the body not only on the basis of religious faith: because of the Christian revelation, as well as because of the teaching of the Catholic Church, to which I adhere. Rather, I think that the existence of a soul, and of a separate mind which is distinct from the body, is also evident on philosophical, rational grounds. In three books which I wrote on this topic, I sought to develop many different arguments for the existence of the soul. One of them is based on the insight that any conscious activity, any act of knowing, or of free decision, can evidently never be performed by a material thing that is extended in space and has parts of its being outside of others. It is evident that the I, the Self, who performs conscious activities, is simple in the sense of being strictly speaking and absolutely indivisible; it can never consist of parts outside other parts in space. Moreover, the material world evidently is dominated by causal laws which, if matter were identical with the mind, or even only the exclusive cause of the mind, would exclude genuine knowledge and above all, freedom. But we know with evidence that we are free and therefore that our being cannot be reduced to matter. Moreover, we can be absolutely certain of our own existence because we experience and grasp it from within in an indubitable manner, but we can never be certain in the same way of any material thing for the knowledge of which we rely on our senses, on our brain and on many other forms of mediation in which in principle delusion, illusion, and deception are not totally and absolutely excluded.

In addition, we experience our own selves from within, by being ourselves, by living consciously our own life from within, in a distanceless manner. In this way, we could never know any material thing, for matter is always the object of conscious acts and never identical with this intimate inner experience we have of ourselves. Moreover, there are many further reasons which demonstrate philosophically the existence of the human soul, above all that being and substantiality are possessed by the human mind in a much more perfect way than any material things could ever possess them.

SIR ALFRED AYER

I don't think that there are independent mental properties in the sense that I don't believe there are mental properties standing out of any causal relation to physical properties. But what I don't see is a step by which you proceed from a causal relation to an identity. I do think that just as a matter of empirical fact mental properties are caused by physical properties.

Language, Truth and Logic was extremely mentalistic in the sense that it reduces physical objects to what I call sense-contents. Now sense-contents I represent as neutral. But in fact in the history of philosophy they are much nearer the mind than they are to the body. Sense-contents were the successors of Locke's "simple ideas,"

Berkeley's "sense qualities," Hume's "impressions," and so it was much more nearly mentalistic than physicalistic. It wasn't spiritualistic. But that's quite different.

Logical Positivism died a long time ago. I don't think much of *Language, Truth and Logic* is true. I think it is full of mistakes. I think it was an important book in its time because it had a kind of cathartic effect. It swept away a lot of rubbish and excited people and to a certain extent it gave a new direction to philosophy. But when you get down to detail, I think it's full of mistakes which I spent the last fifty years correcting or trying to correct.

Yes, the mental is distinct from the material in the sense that I don't see a sufficient case for identifying them. The mental is very simple. My seeing such and such, hearing such and such, or feeling such emotions, or having such and such a sensation, or whatever, with neural processes. I think there is a causal dependency but I don't see any grounds for there being an identity. My position is fairly close to [Sir John] Eccles' [a widely published dualistic scientist].

I criticize Ryle [Gilbert Ryle was the author of *The Concept of Mind*, a critique of dualism]. I did in fact argue that he hadn't made out his case. I think it is a marvelous book because I think it is stylistically brilliant. But I don't think he exorcises the ghost and I tried to show exactly why I didn't think that.

RALPH MCINERNY

[Thomas Aquinas held that the] body and soul are two different things but they make up one substance. But he also held that the shape of a thing and the thing shaped are one thing. You don't ask where the shape is independently of what it shapes. But in the case of the form that makes a human being a human being, you seem to have reason to think that it could exist independently of matter and the reason is reason. You know, our thinking does not seem to be a physical or chemical process however much it might presuppose sensation, perception, and the like. Thinking itself seems to be an activity that is quite distinguishable from any physical change or psychological change of the lower kind. Now that raises the question, does that mean that the soul is one substance and the body another? No, the body doesn't exist independently of the soul and, if the soul exists independently of the body, it is still a form that requires, for its complete existence, the body, which is the argument for the fittingness of the resurrection. So the soul separated from the body is in an anomalous position. Thomas [Aquinas] speaks of it as a quasi-substance rather than a substance, not made to exist by itself and, if it does for a time, this is not its natural state.

Consciousness is something which even animals have.

Of a sort, sure.

Would you say that consciousness is an activity of the soul just like thinking?

Sure, but I would take that to be imagining. It seems obvious that dogs have dreams and so on. They have imagination, they obviously have external senses and so forth. They have a lot of cognition and no doubt there is a great hierarchy within brute animals in terms of greater and lesser forms of cognition. But what they don't have is anything like intellection. How do we know that? The great sign of intellection is language. There is no sense, there is no univocal sense, in which anything other than a human being, in the animal kingdom, has a language. Language is the sign of abstract thinking. We know singulars but we know them as instances of a kind. In seeing you I see the thing that you see and it's only in thinking about it as red that we think of it as an instance of a color and so on. But eyesight itself does not pick up abstract concepts as universal. I take that to be a very good argument. It's a complicated one and I'm simplifying it. But it seems to me that's the best way to show that cognition, in the sense that the animals have it and that we share with them, is not what you're talking about when you talk about the basis for the separate existence of the human soul – which is intellection, which is always language [i.e. intellection as expressed in language is distictive of the human soul]. We talk metaphorically about the language of the bees and the language of porpoises and so forth, but it's because it's like language.

Would you think that the soul, say, of an animal, would have actual mental life separate from the body too?

Oh, no. There is no sign of that, there is no indication of it. The cognition that it has, which is often quite amazing, is a feature of its sensory organs only.

Let me restate that. The action is not independent of those organs. But that actual activity is in some sense distinct from the physical organ. Would you say it is a kind of mental activity which is immaterial?

In animals? No. If I called it immaterial it would be only to distinguish it from other aspects or features of animals that they share with inorganic things. But you might say that they are relatively immaterial but that wouldn't be a basis for saying that the animal soul exists independently or would survive the death of the animal.

Obviously, cognition, sense cognition, is an amazing thing and there are all kinds of degrees of it and one doesn't want to put it down. But, on the other hand, one doesn't want to blur the difference between that and intellection, and we see the difference in ourselves as well as between ourselves and, say, other animals.

Intellection is an activity of the soul which can take place without the body. Would you say that?

Yes, but exactly how don't ask me. That is why I'm very happy about the resurrection.

And that is obviously unique to human beings.

Yes. Philosophers who held the immortality of the soul didn't know what to do next and told stories and got into a kind of dualism so that the soul existed prior to the body and consequently existed after it. Aristotle is very uninformative about what the soul is going to be doing when it is separated from the body; one place where he talks about it at some length is the first book of the *Nicomachean Ethics* and it's kind of hard for us to think he is telling us very much. Thomas commenting on that congratulates him because he says, "How could he know?"

Is it ontologically possible to clone a human being? A materialist might point to the recent reports of success in cloning a mammal in claiming that it is only a matter of time before human beings can be cloned – thus eliminating the need for appealing to any non-physical component. How would you evaluate such a claim?

The question about cloning human beings is twofold: would it be possible to produce a human being in the way Dolly [the cloned sheep] was produced? That is a factual question. Say the answer is yes. If it is a human being, it must have a soul. A soul is not produced from matter but breathed into the conceptum by God. Would God grant a soul to a cloned human being? Well, does God grant a soul to a human being begotten by rape or incest? The immorality of the human means does not preclude divine causality.

There are of course many other aspects to this. *The New York Post* raised the metaphysical question as to whether you can have numerical identity as well as plurality. As far as I can see, it took a male and a female contribution to produce Dolly, so sameness here would pose no more difficult metaphysical problems than procreation.

G. E. M. ANSCOMBE

I don't know about the soul being distinct from the body. It is the principle of unity of an organism, the soul, and a living organism is a unity and the principle of unity is called the soul. This applies not just to human beings.

Do human beings have a spiritual substantial soul?

Well, that is rather obscure because since the soul is the principle of unity of an organism, the question is how can that exist when the organism is destroyed? It ought to be a rather serious question for any good philosopher, as it is a very serious question, for example, for Thomas Aquinas. I should think that it would be answered by consideration of what it is that the human soul is the principle of – a certain kind of animal called human being – and of what it does. A human being has thoughts of a sort which are to be expressed in language and I think that if somebody says that he can look into the brain and see what thoughts somebody is thinking, and there are people who do this, then he is an ass.

In a sense, from our own experience, we know that thoughts are, by their very nature, qualitatively distinct from physiological processes. Would you say that?

Yes, certainly. They may be expressed in ink, by a pen or a typewriter. I don't know that the word would be "expressed" because in order to understand what is expressed by a pen or a typewriter, you have to know the language. The producer, of course, does know the language. But we just don't know, we who can talk don't, therefore, know just what processes in the brain are involved in our thinking of various thoughts. But, of course, they are not there in the brain.

Thoughts, in some way which, no doubt, a good physiologist would try to discover, depend on our having a brain. That is not to say that the thinking is an activity of the brain.

On the other hand, Thomas Aquinas himself speculated on the idea of the separated soul.

Well, he investigated it. It was for him a serious problem precisely because he believed the Aristotelian principle – the soul is the form of the body. Here he was speaking, Aristotle was speaking, of the human soul. Aristotle also, of course, speaks of the souls of plants and other animals and, therefore, I am not, in any way, disagreeing with him, rather following him, by saying the soul is the principle of unity of any complex organism. When the complex organism is human it goes in for thinking and that is not a material activity – although if it is done with a pen or typewriter, you suppose these to be communication of thought, a physical activity. But if you don't know the language, you would not understand the activity.

When you approach the question of intention – on which you have written so much – what bearing does this have on the nature of the soul or that specific activity of the human person which is distinct from either physical objects or plants and animals? Does intention have any bearing on the issue?

Well, I disagree with those who suppose that the other animals never had anything you could call an intention. You can see that the cat is stalking a bird, for example. But I would say that an animal, at least such as we can understand their actions in that kind of way, no more calls for the possibility of acts of intention than other acts of the soul. But then I don't believe an animal, other than the human animal, has a spiritual soul. Animals other than the human animal do not, so far as we can tell at all, have what we call thinking. Of course, we sometimes would say, the bird thinks it can get out because it flies against the glass. There "thinks" refers to the "deeds." And we sometimes say that a dog dreams when it goes "woof, woof." We certainly make comparisons and see certain similarities. Human intention is a bigger thing than the cat stalking the bird and you have to distinguish between what makes an action intentional and what the intention is and also between the intentionalness of the activity and the intention or the objective or the end. Part of this, at least, is applicable to the cat stalking the bird or

the animal who dreams something. I have heard about, but have
never seen, an animal, some kind of monkey or ape, moving something to stand on it to reach a bunch of bananas. And here you could
say, well, it is the case that, if you watch it, you can see what its aim
is. This is, of course, more than you actually can see what the aim is
in the cat stalking the bird, but also you can see what its means are.
Therefore, this would be another reason where I would object to
people that think that the nonhuman animals, all of them, are incapable of intention. But the thought and calculation which must go
into a great deal of human intending cannot be supposed to be there.
It seems to me that it would be simply folly to imagine that you
could find a way of asking the chimpanzee, even if you knew its language, what it was moving that thing for.

*But don't we see some kind of primitive intention in a cat
stalking a bird, to take that example? Doesn't it leave the possibility that there is something primitively mental taking place?*

Of course, I believe that animals have, as you put it, something mental, but I don't mean something spiritual. By that it would be absurd
to deny that animals have sensation and reactions to sensation. On
the other hand, I would be inclined to say especially that that
appears to involve a mental sort of intention as in the case of the
plant. A plant, well, the plant may be such, like the sunflower, so
called, because it turns its face toward the sun, and I don't think that
we would be inclined to say that the plant is intending to be facing
the sun. The cat is more like us. You don't automatically expect the
cat to stalk a bird. It's just that you sometimes see a cat and see, oh,
I can see it is stalking a bird.

*What's the nature of the distinction between the mental which
is irreducible to the physical and the spiritual nature of the
human soul? Is it the fact that the kind of thought which
humans have is, in some sense, qualitatively distinct from the
kind of intentional activity which a cat has in stalking the bird?*

The most striking and obvious distinction is language. If somebody
with brain damage can spell out words, as may very well be the case.
I know such a case. He had too severe brain damage to be able to
speak or write. Writing is a very refined activity of the hand. It is
possible that the part of the brain which involves a fine control of a
pen enables you to learn to write. But such a person may very well

be able to spell out words by being given a clock face which has letters, instead of numbers on it, and also some words maybe by turning the hands of this clock face so that they spell out sentences. Quite obscure, I don't mean very obscure, I mean, sentences which with the mere construction of something of a sentence, that is obviously meant as a sentence, proves the presence of the intellectual soul. I know such a case.

Ergo, question, why isn't 1 a prime number? That is the question, that is something the formulation of which obviously involves what we, what *I* would call an intellectual soul. I would say that any sentence, with proper sentence construction, the grammar of language, proves the same.

I think even the materialist probably won't dispute the idea of the soul being the principle of unity. The more sophisticated materialist probably would hold to some kind of identity theory in explaining how we have thoughts which seem to be qualitatively distinct from brain processes.

Well, I think you are rather naive about sophisticated materialists. But of course, you may be defining extreme sophistication in your materialism in such a way that the materialist may say, "Yes, there is a unity. This is a unified organism." But, on the other hand, I think that I observe a realization of unity, but not if there is any intellect in the person.

Thomas Aquinas also held that the spiritual nature of the soul seemed to him to be rational grounds for affirming the possibility of the soul surviving death.

Probably he did. I would say that to him it was a problem and it is not clear that he solved the problem. I don't think I know his writing on the subject well enough to say, but I would expect that he thought that he had solved the problem. What I do note is that for him it was a problem and that is the right approach to this matter, which should be a problem.

In your view that is a problem. Would you say we cannot, without faith, affirm a life after death?

Well, now, faith can affirm that and I don't think it was faith on his part. I don't think you have to have faith to believe that the principle of unity of the human organism is a spiritual principle. But I do observe that the way in which many spiritualists talk, upon the whole, is a way which sees no more in the unity of the human organism than we would see in the unity of a bicycle.

On the further question of the survival of the soul, do you think that by recognizing the spiritual nature of the human soul, it is at least a valid inference to affirm survival?

I don't know. I think that this is really one of the many difficult questions in philosophy but all I have said so far is that I think that for the good philosopher, who is not a foolish materialist, it is still a problem, and the reason why it is a problem is that it is a pretty clear conception of the human soul, that it is the principle of unity of the human organism.

JOHN LUCAS

That depends on what you mean by "the existence of the mind" because it can be questioned in a whole lot of different ways. I would start from the principle that I am very much aware of my own self, of thinking and deciding; and I've always taken it for granted that other people are similarly thinking and deciding. Then I come across various criticisms and these are some of the quite traditional ones such as from David Hume, and of other kinds such as from Descartes, and then more modern ones from neurophysiology – and I look at those objections and find them on the whole very unpersuasive, and flawed in different ways.

So your basis, fundamentally, is commonsense experience?

That's where I start from. It depends on where I'm starting from. I might at some stage be trying to construct a deep philosophical system and might be starting from some other place, and then I might need to produce some argument to show that from that point of view you should also allow the existence of mind. But [most of the time], I'm starting from a very commonsensical point of view.

Now is your understanding of mind similar to the Cartesian dualist?

Well, I'm not sure. I'm said to be a dualist and don't regard that as any accusation but I am not in Descartes' position, and I simply draw some distinction between minds and bodies. Whether they should be described as substances, as Descartes says, I'm not sure. If

I go along that path I would need to produce a detailed account showing how they interact. The interactionist account involves considerable difficulties and I'm sometimes quite taken with the possibility of some other attempt to explain the mind and the body in terms of different sorts of predicates or different sorts of explanation. It might be that the real distinction lies not in what we say that it is but in how we understand it. I don't know about that. Whatever attempted explanation I put forward I would certainly not be denying the existence of mind.

JOHN FOSTER

What is your assessment of Daniel Dennett's defense of materialism in his book Consciousness Explained?

Although a committed materialist, Dennett recognizes that there are certain factors which seem, initially, to constitute serious obstacles to any materialist account. Two in particular – both concerned with consciousness – Dennett sees as especially crucial, and they become recurring themes in his discussion. The first is that materialism seems unable to accommodate the introspectible qualities of conscious experience. Thus when someone is in pain, or hears the rumble of thunder, or visualizes a scene in his or her mind's eye, it doesn't seem that any purely physical description of what's going on inside them (or indeed any purely physical description of any aspects of the physical world) would cover, explicitly or implicitly, the character of the experience as introspection reveals it. The second factor is that materialism seems unable to accommodate the fact that experience belongs to a conscious subject. When there is an episode of pain or hearing or visualizing, there is always someone in whom the experience occurs (someone who suffers the pain, or has the auditory awareness, or frames and witnesses the visual image), and there doesn't seem to be anything physical which could play this subject-role: ". . . the trouble with brains, it seems, is that when you look in them, you discover that there's nobody home" (p. 29). Dennett's aim is to show how, despite initial appearances to the contrary, a coherent and plausible materialist account of the mind – and in particular of consciousness and its subject – can be provided.

Dennett's basic approach, in pursuit of this aim, is to develop and defend a form of functionalism. Put briefly, what functionalism asserts is that, given any type T of mental state or activity, if F is the

functional role, or cluster of roles, which we ordinarily associate
with T (in effect, that role or role-cluster which we can see to be
rationally appropriate to the psychological character of T), then the
instantiation of T (the occurrence of a T-particular) in a given subject at a particular time consists in the occurrence of a physical state
or process which, relative to the whole physical make-up of the subject and the properties of the wider physical environment, is
equipped to play this role. Thus, on Dennett's view, for a physical
system to have a capacity for a certain kind of functional organization – a kind which enables it to execute the characteristic functions
of consciousness in that form; and for the system to embody a single subject to which the various episodes of consciousness occurring
in it belong, nothing more is needed than the fact that this organization as a whole achieves a certain kind of internal unity and coor-
dination. On this last point, Dennett thinks that the internal unity is
achieved, not at the level of the physiological hardware, but because
the different component physiological systems which make up the
brain, and which typically function in parallel, collectively realize a
serial von-Neumann-type machine: "Conscious minds are more-or-
less serial virtual machines implemented – inefficiently – on the parallel hardware that evolution has provided for us" (p. 218).

Dennett is aware that there are a number of seemingly powerful
objections to this functionalist approach. One familiar objection is
that, given that all the functional aspects of consciousness are capable of being mechanistically implemented (and this is something
which the functionalist must assume), we can envisage things or
systems which satisfy all the functional requirements of a human-
like conscious mentality without having a capacity for genuine consciousness or mentality at all. The cases most often cited here are
those of the seemingly intelligent robot, Block's Chinese Nation,[1]
and Searle's Chinese Room.[2] Another familiar objection is that we
can envisage cases in which exactly the same functional condition
obtains in different human subjects, or in the same subject at different times, but is accompanied by different kinds of experience.
Here the most famous case is that of the inverted color-spectrum, in
which we envisage two subjects who (or two single-subject phases
which) are relevantly alike in functional organization, but experience complementary color-qualia in response to the same photic
input. Yet a third objection, known as the "knowledge argument",
focuses on cases in which, owing to a deficiency in their psycho-

logical repertoire, someone does not, for a certain category of mental states, have any introspective data from which they can derive a knowledge of their experiential character. The objector then claims that, contrary to the implications of functionalism, the subject cannot acquire the relevant experiential knowledge from information about the functional roles of these states in the lives of those who have them. Probably the best known version of the knowledge argument – and the one which Dennett himself considers – is that of Frank Jackson, who focuses on the case of the scientist Mary, who, though placed in circumstances which restrict her to black-and-white vision, becomes all-knowledgeable about the neurophysiology and functioning of color-vision in others. Jackson's plausible claim is then that, despite this knowledge, Mary does not know what color-vision is like experientially, and will not learn this until she comes to have color-experience herself.[3]

Dennett tries to undermine these objections by discrediting the intuitions on which they are based. He takes the chief culprit here to be the prevalent assumption that consciousness takes the form of an inner theater – the "Cartesian Theater" he dubs it – in which items are directly presented to the conscious self in a way that is quite different from the mere reception of information or acquisition of belief.[4] Once this idea of the inner theater has been accepted, it becomes impossible to avoid the sort of objections considered: there is no way of making sense of a direct presentational awareness in purely functional terms, and it is this point which, in their different ways, the various objections exploit. Dennett's response is simply to deny the existence of the inner theater and the presentational awareness associated with it. His position is that consciousness, whether sensory or introspective, is purely cognitive – a matter of acquiring beliefs or making judgments – and that these cognitive activities (unlike the bogus presentational ones) *can* be construed in functional terms. This allows him to dismiss the objections. Thus his response to the alleged possibility of the inverted spectrum is to say that, since there is no Cartesian Theater, there are no color-qualia whose functional roles could be systemically changed in that way. Likewise, his response to Jackson's argument is to insist that, since there are no color-qualia in the relevant sense, a full physical and functional knowledge *would*, if she really possessed it, enable Mary to know everything about the visual experience of other people. As for such cases as the seemingly intelligent robot, the Chinese Nation, and the Chinese Room, Dennett now feels able to insist that, so long as they genuinely exemplified the appropriate functional organization, these physical systems would indeed have the capacity for a cognitive consciousness – which is the only sort of consciousness there is.

But why does Dennett deny the existence of the inner theater, with its distinctively presentational, noncognitive awareness? The basic reason is that he has already committed himself to giving a materialist, nondualist account of consciousness, and, as he sees, the idea of the inner theater makes no sense within that framework. This is a recurring theme. To take just one example (and a particularly clear one): in the context of his discussion of the "phi-phenomenon" (where two spots, flashed in quick succession in closely neighboring positions, appear to the subject to be a single spot which moves from the position of the first to that of the second), Dennett envisages the subject making the following "sophisticated" comment: "I know there wasn't *actually* a moving spot in the world . . . but I also know that the spot *seemed* to move, so in addition to my judgement that the spot seemed to move, there is the event which my judgement is *about*: the seeming-to-move of the spot . . ." (pp. 133–34). Confident of his materialist framework, Dennett will have none of this:

> Perhaps the Cartesian Theatre is popular because it is the place where the seemings can happen in addition to the judgings. But the sophisticated argument just presented is fallacious. Postulating a real seeming in addition to the judging or "taking" expressed in the subject's report is multiplying entities beyond necessity. Worse, it is multiplying entities beyond possibility; the sort of inner presentation in which real seemings happen is a hopeless metaphysical dodge, a way of trying to have your cake and eat it too, especially since those who are inclined to talk this way are eager to insist that this inner presentation does not occur in some mysterious, dualist sort of space perfused with Cartesian ghost-ether. When you discard Cartesian dualism, you really must discard the show that would have gone on in the Cartesian Theatre, and the audience as well, for neither the show nor the audience is to be found in the brain, and the brain is the only real place there is to look for them (p. 134).

Apart from the caricature of the dualist position whose falsity he takes for granted (a dualist worth his salt – and Descartes would be the paradigm case – does *not* envisage a kind of space perfused with ghost-ether), Dennett's reasoning is here impeccable. There is no way of preserving forms of non-cognitive presentation within the materialist framework. The crucial question, of course, is: *Why* is he so sure that dualism is false?

In his rejection of dualism is the basis of his denial of the existence of the inner theater, it also lies behind his functionalist account of cognition – and the other non-presentational psychological states and activities that the elimination of the theater leaves intact. It may be easier to entertain a functionalist account of these nonpresentational aspects of the mind than a presentation, but it still seems highly problematic. Thus whatever its functional organization, it is not easy to think of a robot as capable of real thought and belief – and even harder if we envisage it to be "crudely" mechanical, so that, apart from its "sensory" monitors, it works entirely by such devices as cogs, levers, pulleys, and springs.[5] What enables Dennett to represent his functionalist approach as correct is that, given the falsity of Cartesian dualism, there is no possibility of finding a "central conceptualizer and meaner" to be the subject of the irreducible cognitive states and activities which our initial (anti-functionalist) intuitions envisage;[6] and without such a subject, there is no serious rival to an account of cognition along functionalist lines.

It is clear from all this that Dennett's positive account of consciousness hinges very crucially on his prior rejection of dualism. This account, with its implication that there is nothing more to consciousness than the mechanistically functional organization of a physical system, is, from an intuitive standpoint, highly implausible – as the various objections reveal. But Dennett is happy to commend it to his readers because he sees that the only way to avoid these implausibilities would be to adopt a dualist position, and he takes it as already settled that dualism is not an option. Thus when he said that "in this book, I adopt the apparently dogmatic rule that dualism is to be avoided *at all costs*" (p. 37) – and the italics are *his* – he meant just that. In effect, he is saying that, however implausible the results of his subsequent investigation when considered in isolation, they should be embraced without embarrassment if they provide the best theory available within the materialist framework. The siren call of dualism is to be resisted whatever the circumstances and whatever the consequences.

> *What do you think of Dennett's arguments against the existence of a mind separate from the body, specifically with respect to the question of interaction between the two?*

Dennett begins at a familiar point, the traditional issue of dualistic interaction between body and mind:

> The standard objection to dualism was all too familiar to Descartes himself in the seventeenth century, and it is fair to say that neither he nor any subsequent dualist has ever overcome it convincingly. If mind and body are distinct things or substances, they nevertheless must interact; the bodily sense organs, via the brain, must *inform* the mind, must send to it or present it with perceptions or ideas or data of some sort, and then the mind, having thought things over, must *direct* the body in appropriate action (including speech). Hence the view is often called Cartesian interactionism or interactionist dualism (pp. 33–34).

Dennett finds such a view deeply problematic. He is particularly puzzled by the supposed directives from mind to brain:

> These, *ex hypothesi*, are not physical; they are not light waves or sound waves or cosmic rays or streams of subatomic particles. No physical energy or mass is associated with them. How, then, do they get to make a difference to what happens in the brain cells they must affect, if the mind is to have any influence over the body? A fundamental principle of physics is that any change in the trajectory of any physical entity is an acceleration requiring the expenditure of energy, and where is this energy to come from? It is this principle of the conservation of energy that accounts for the physical impossibility of 'perpetual motion machines', and the same principle is apparently violated by dualism. This confrontation between quite standard physics and dualism has been endlessly discussed since Descartes's own day, and is widely regarded as the inescapable and fatal flaw of dualism (pp. 34–35).

Dennett adds, somewhat cryptically, that "ingenious technical exemptions based on sophisticated readings of the relevant physics have been explored and expounded, but without attracting many conversions." Whatever the beliefs of these infrequent converts, Dennett is clearly not among them.

Ostensibly, the objection that Dennett is here bringing against the dualist's version of mind-to-brain causation is that it violates the principle of the conservation of energy – a principle which he takes to be scientifically well-established. However, I assume that the real objection is a more general one. For suppose the dualist were to envisage a situation in which any local gain in energy associated with the mind's influence on a particular region of the brain at a certain time was compensated for by an equivalent loss of energy in some other region at the same time. Instead of this satisfying Dennett, he would undoubtedly see it as involving a double problem: the problem of a physically inexplicable energy-increase at one point and a physically inexplicable energy-decrease at another. Dennett's real objection, I take it, is that, whatever its precise form, any set-up in which the nonphysical mind exerts a causal influence on events in the body will result in physical changes which are contrary to the requirements of physical law. The physical laws, established by physics and chemistry, require the brain to behave in certain ways in certain physical conditions, and the nonphysical mind can only exert an influence by interfering with this nomological control and producing physical results which are impossible in physical terms.

In fact, I assume that Dennett's underlying objection is even more general than this. For I take it that what, fundamentally, Dennett objects to in the dualist's view of mind-to-brain causation is that it postulates a causal influence on the physical world of a physically inexplicable kind: it violates the supposed principle that the physical world is a closed system, in which the only causal influences on what takes place within it are themselves physical – the influence exerted by prior physical conditions in the framework of physical laws. This is a still more general objection, since there are two ways in which we can envisage the mind exerting a non-physical influence on physical events without this involving any conflict with physical law. Thus, on the one hand, we could suppose that the fundamental physical laws are only probabilistic (statistical), and that, because of this, the conditions obtaining in the brain at any time leave open a range of physically possible continuations. We could then think of the interventionist causal role of the non-physical mind as that of selecting between, or at least affecting the probabilities of, these physically possible options. On the other hand, we could envisage a situation of systematic over-determination, in which the influence of the nonphysical mind, though genuinely independent, always exactly duplicates that of the current physical conditions in the brain, and is in this sense redundant. In both these cases, the influence of the non-physical mind would not come into conflict with the laws of physics and chemistry – it would leave physical science able to endorse the same nomological theories of the brain as of the rest of the physical world. But the influence would not be physically explicable and its occurrence would not be compatible with the claim that the physical world is a closed system. I take it that this, on its own, would be enough to make it anathema to Dennett.

One way in which the dualist could avoid Dennett's objection would be by embracing epiphenomenalism, which concedes that the mind does not exert any causal influence on the physical world. Thus the epiphenomenalist accepts that there is psychophysical causation from body to mind, as when physical sensory input produces a sensory experience, but denies that there is psychophysical causation in the other direction: not even volitional acts, like decisions and tryings, have any physical effects. In my view – and here at least I find myself in agreement with Dennett[7] – epiphenomenalism is not a serious option. It is not just that it is in radical conflict with our ordinary conception of ourselves as agents (in not allowing us to retain the view that what we ordinarily think of as human action is intentional in any decent sense). It is also, and more crucially, that the advocacy of the epiphenomenalist position is self-defeating. For if the mind has no causal influence on the physical world, and therefore no influence on either the formation or overt employment of the public language (not even with respect to those aspects of the public language which we ordinarily suppose to concern psychological matters), then mentality cannot even become a topic for overt discussion.[8] In particular, then, the epiphenomenalist cannot try to provide an overt expression of his view without thereby implicitly committing himself to its falsity. Whatever the merits of dualism as such, epiphenomenalism really is a position "to be avoided at all costs".[9]

However, the dualist does not need to embrace epiphenomenalism to defend himself against Dennett's objection; for there are no good grounds for assuming that the only causal influences on the functioning of the human brain are physical. What are the grounds supposed to be? It can hardly be claimed that direct research on the brain has revealed anything decisive; indeed, we have yet to devise a method of monitoring a subject's brain activity which is sufficiently wide-ranging and penetrating to provide the sort of information we need, but not so invasive as to make it illegitimate to draw any conclusions about what happens in normal circumstances. So I take it that Dennett's main point must be that the assumption is plausible in the light of the progress of physical science in general. His thought must be something along the lines of:

1. Whenever physical science has managed to conduct a thorough investigation of the working of a physical system, it has always found that it can fully explain the relevant phenomena in purely physical terms.
2. In default of any empirical evidence to the contrary, it is reasonable to extrapolate from this to the particular case of the brain, concluding that in this area too the relevant physical phenomena are, or are likely to be, physically explicable.
3. Since a situation of systematic overdetermination would be inherently puzzling (for how could it be accounted for?), it is reasonable to conclude that the only causal influences on the brain are physical.

But this line of reasoning fails at step (2). For the envisaged extrapolation would only be warranted if there were no other considerations which point strongly to a different conclusion; and obviously the dualist will point out that we already know that we have minds, and (granted the falsity of epiphenomenalism) ones which exert a causal influence on behaviour; and he will insist that the familiar objections to any form of materialist account provide a strong prima facie case for taking the mind to be nonphysical. From this standpoint, we should not expect the explanatory success which physical science has enjoyed with respect to the rest of the physical world to carry over, without qualification, to the special case of the human brain. We should be prepared for – and indeed, if we discount the possibility of over-determination, should positively expect – cases in which the non-physical mind makes its causal presence felt through the occurrence of neural events which are not amendable to a purely physical explanation.

The upshot of this is that, if he is to have any rationale for his exclusion of dualism on the grounds of its clash with physical science, Dennett will *either* need to wait for such time as direct research on the brain provides strong evidence for the claim that physical science can fully explain all that takes place within it (and the dualist will deny that there is any reason to expect such evidence to be forthcoming) or find some way of independently discrediting the familiar pro-dualist arguments. All he has done so far is to beg the question against the dualist by assuming that the latter will be embarrassed by having to envisage the nonphysical mind having physical effects which physical science cannot explain. It should also be noted that, even if future research did provide strong evidence for the claim that all brain events can be fully explained in physical terms, this would not constitute a *conclusive* argument against dualism, since the dualist could still fall back on the hypothesis if, as I believe, the prima facie case against materialism can be turned into one which is irresistible.[10]

Maybe Dennett senses that his scientific argument against dualism is inadequate. For he now goes on to put the emphasis on a different point:

> Dualism's embarrassment here is really much simpler than the citation of presumed laws of physics suggests. It is the same incoherence that children notice – but tolerate happily in fantasy – in such fare as Casper the Friendly Ghost. How can Casper *both* glide through walls *and* grab a falling towel? How can mind stuff *both* elude all physical measurement *and* control the body? A ghost in the machine is of no help in our theories unless it is a ghost that can move things around – like a noisy poltergeist who can tip over a lamp or slam a door – but anything that can move a physical thing is itself a physical thing (although perhaps a strange and heretofore unstudied kind of physical thing) (p. 35).

I take this to be a quite different objection to dualistic interaction from the one we have been considering. The earlier objection, however exactly it is to be interpreted, was fundamentally an *empirical* one: it turned on the claim that to postulate lines of causation from the non-physical mind to the body would be scientifically implausible. The new objection, if I have understood it, is of an a priori kind. It is claiming that very notion of dualistic mind-to-body causation is incoherent: whatever the status of the physicist's conservation laws, or any other putative laws of physical science, we simply cannot make sense of the suggestion that something non-physical could impart motion to something physical, or have any other kind of causal influence on events in the physical world.

But why does Dennett think that we cannot make sense of this? Curiously, he does not seem to see the need to spell out the incoherence he claims to have detected. The comparison with Casper (who is not obstructed by walls and yet can get a grip on towels) is not, I assume, intended to be taken seriously: Dennett is aware that the dualist (at least the orthodox dualist) does not think of the mind as an occupant of physical space, let alone as one with Casper's paradoxical properties. But, apart from the reference to Casper, all we are offered is the dogmatic assertion that "anything that can move a physical thing is itself a physical thing" – as if this is just obvious and something which no sensible person would think of disputing. I have to confess that it is not at all obvious to me. If there is a conceptual problem in supposing that events in the non-physical mind causally affect events in the body, it is one that I need to have explicated.

One thing which may make it seem that there is a problem here is that our conception of the nature of causation tends to be conditioned by the ways in which causality typically operates in the physical realm. Typically, when one physical event causes another, the two events are either spatially contiguous (or coincident) or connected by a spatiotemporally continuous series of events through which the causal process passes. This feature of physical causation may make it seem that causation has to operate by means of spatial contact – that spatial contact is the essential mechanism for causal contact – and once this is accepted, causation between physical and non-physical events is automatically excluded. The exclusion, of course, would apply with equal force to dualistic causation in both directions – from body to mind as much as from mind to body.

If this is how Dennett sees the problem, the dualist has a simple and effective answer. For even if physical causation typically, and perhaps always, operates through spatial contact, it is conceivable that it should not. There is no conceptual difficulty in envisaging a case in which a physical event in one place causes a physical event a mile away, without there being any chain of events between them. Moreover, it is easy to envisage the sort of evidence which would persuade us that such cases occur – for example, a constant correlation between the occurrence of the one type of event and the immediately subsequent occurrence of the other, an inability to detect any intervening mechanism, and an inability to provide a causal explanation of the second event in any other way. Indeed, it was once assumed that gravitational causal influence operated over spatial distances in just this way. But if there is no conceptual difficulty in envisaging causation-at-a-distance in the physical realm, then dualistic causation should not be excluded, or regarded as conceptually problematic, purely on the grounds that there is no spatial contact between the non-physical mind and the body.

Another way the putative problem is sometimes posed is by saying that, on the dualist view, we cannot understand how psychophysical causation operates: we simply have to accept it as a brute fact, with no further explanation, that certain types of neural event directly cause certain types of mental event, and vice versa.[11] But again I am not impressed. For why should any explanation be demanded? Trivially, if causation is direct, there cannot be any question of an intervening mechanism; and presumably the notion of direct causation is not as such problematic. Maybe Dennett would say that we cannot understand why the neural events have these psychological effects or why the mental events have these physical effects: the most we can hope to do is bring the causal pairings under covering laws. But what I cannot see is why these why-questions arise. In the physical realm too our explanation of causation has to terminate in the postulation of certain causal laws, without any further explanation of why these laws obtain. So why should the dualist be required to do more? Why should the dualist be called on to offer a deeper mode of explanation than that which is available to physical science?[12]

Admittedly, some materialists would argue that it is precisely the relationship between psychophysical causation and the covering laws which turns out to be problematic on the dualist view. In fact, there are two quite different lines of argument here, one trying to show that the dualist cannot envisage psychophysical laws which cover the causal pairings in a sufficiently determinate way, the other trying to show that the dualist cannot envisage psychophysical laws at all.[13] Both these arguments turn on issues of considerable technical complexity, which I do not have space to discuss here. I have, however, examined them in detail elsewhere and, in each case, tried to vindicate the dualist position.[14] In any case, there is not the slightest suggestion that, in his rejection of dualism, Dennett has either of these arguments in mind.

NOTES

1. See Ned Block, "Troubles with Functionalism," in *Perception and Cognition: Issues in the Foundations of Psychology, Minnesota Studies in the Philosophy of Science ix*, ed. C. W. Savage (Minneapolis: University of Minnesota Press, 1978.)
2. See John Searle, "Minds, Brains, and Programs," in *Behavioural and Brain Sciences* 3 (1980), no. 3.
3. For my own version of the knowledge argument, and for my evaluation

of Jackson's, see Foster, *The Immaterial Self* (London: Routledge, 1991), ch. 3, sect. 4.

4. The most important difference is that presentation is an unmediated relation between the relevant item and the subject; it does not break down into the occurrence of a more fundamental psychological state, which is not essentially perceptive of that item, together with further facts (e.g. about how that state/state-instance and the item are qualitatively and casually related).

5. This is how I set up the case in Foster, *op. cit.*, ch. 3, sect. 5. Incidentally, I am inclined to think that the functional role of thought and belief in our lives is not of a purely mechanistic kind, and so is not capable of being exactly reproduced in a robot.

6. See *Consciousness Explained*, (Boston, MA: Little, Brown & Co., 1991), ch. 8.

7. Thus see *Consciousness Explained*, ch. 12, sect. 5.

8. For more detail, see Foster, *op. cit.*, pp. 190–3.

9. This is a slight oversimplification. As I have shown elsewhere (*op. cit.*, pp. 192–3), there is an exotic way in which the epiphenomenalist could avoid the charge that his position is self-defeating. For, by postulating a form of divinely pre-established psychophysical harmony, he could represent our situation as one in which human mentality is relevant to the ultimate explanation of human behaviour, without having any causal influence on it. In such a case, it is arguable that its explanatory relevance would be enough to allow mentality to become a topic for overt discussion.

10. Again, there is the same oversimplification as I mentioned above in note 9. For, in addition to the overdetermination hypothesis, the "exotic" form of epiphenomenalism (with a divinely pre-established psychophysical harmony) would also be an option. I have tried to construct an irresistible case against materialism in *The Immaterial Self, op. cit.*

11. Thus see Thomas Nagel, *Mortal Questions* (Cambridge: Cambridge University Press, 1979), p. 187.

12. Admittedly, there are certain factors which can make it seem that a deeper mode of explanation is available in the physical realm. Thus see Foster, *op. cit.*, pp. 161–2.

13. We owe this second argument to Donald Davidson. See, in particular, his "Mental Events", in *Experience and Theory*, L. Foster and J. W. Swanson, eds. (Minneapolis: University of Minnesota Press, 1970).

14. Foster, *The Immaterial Self*, ch. 6, sects. 3–4.

THE FREEDOM OF THE WILL

Great Question 4: *Are human decisions entirely shaped by heredity and environment or are human beings capable of free choices? On what basis is it possible to accept the reality of free will?*

GERARD J. HUGHES

It has often been argued that were all our choices determined by our heredity, upbringing, and the impact of our environment, then moral responsibility would be a chimera. This argument has been questioned, but, I think, unsuccessfully. The ability to choose one way or another, given all the beliefs and desires that we have at that moment, is surely integral to our concept of what it is to be morally responsible. Of course, the mere fact that determinism would undermine our picture of ourselves as morally responsible, free beings is not of itself a conclusive argument for the falsity of the deterministic account. Perhaps our picture of ourselves is simply a mistaken one. Still, it is a picture which is deeply embedded in our whole way of life and our whole system of values; and that fact alone does, I think, constitute important evidence in its favor. It should not be abandoned without the very best of reasons.

One type of argument which is advanced in support of the conclusion that we are not free is a kind of "slippery slope" argument. It is alleged that it is becoming more and more obvious that the workings of our minds are intimately bound up with processes in our brains; and, on the assumption that the workings of our brains obey the deterministic laws of the physical universe generally, it is surely becoming more and more difficult to maintain that our minds can function in the indeterminist manner required by free will. Moreover, as our knowledge of human psychology increases, we have gradually come to see that many of our emotions, desires, and psychological traits can be explained in physical terms: sometimes by appeal to genetics, sometimes by appeal to changes in the chemistry of the brain, or to some form of brain-malfunction.

There are several problems with this argument. One, but perhaps the least important, is that it is not at all evident, and indeed is probably false, that the physical world is a wholly deterministic world. Secondly, it assumes without evidence that the events in our brains must have a causal explanation of a physical kind, by which I mean an explanation in terms of the laws of physics and bio-chemistry, and which is part of a chain extending beyond the agent into parents, sensory inputs, and other features of the external environment. In short it assumes that the agent cannot cause such brain-events in a way which is not explicable in physical terms. Of course the physical world is the world as described in terms of physics; but it is quite another matter to assert, as the argument we are considering does, that the facts of physics are the only possible, or the only ultimate, facts.

The most serious flaw in the argument is that it ultimately discounts the importance of the kinds of explanations of free choices which are relevant, and does so in a way which is self-defeating. Let me explain. Assume a non-determinist account of the decay of a radioactive atom. That this decay has no causal explanation, is in fact random, does not in the least tempt us to suppose that the atom freely chose to alter. Free will is not randomness, but purposiveness. We take ourselves to be free because we take ourselves to form beliefs by processes of reasoning. We can decide to allow one picture of what can be done, in terms of values which can be achieved or desires which can be satisfied, to predominate over alternative pictures. I can choose to stay at home and have an early night because I feel tired, or I can choose instead to visit a friend because I feel lonely. Choices are not random, but purposeful.

It does not matter whether each of these choices could be "tracked" in terms of the brain-states which accompany them. The important point is whether or not there is any causal explanation of this choice rather than that one, granted that there is a purposeful explanation of the choice I actually make. If it is true that we are wholly determined, we seem to be forced to accept a completely mechanistic understanding of ourselves. This mechanist view damages more than our notion of free will; it damages equally our notions of belief and the rational appraisal of evidence and argument. Our very belief that determinism is true (or false) is itself the product of a mechanistic process, not of a rational process of argumentation. To be sure, that the truth of mechanistic determinism wholly undermines our notion of the rational thinking, choosing self is not a completely knockdown argument against it. But it is very odd to accept a conclusion which undermines the very notions of "acceptance" and "conclusion".

I conclude then that we do have free will. But I do not want to be dogmatic on how far our freedom extends, or precisely how free will is related to habit, routine, and settled character traits. To make a free choice one has to be able to present more than one alternative to oneself as in some way good; and it may well be that a given individual might, for a variety of reasons, simply be unable to present some things in this light. I think we understand too little of the interconnections between intellectual appraisal, emotions, and desires to be more precise.

RICHARD SWINBURNE

Yes, I believe human beings are capable of free choices. Not, of course, totally free choices. We are all subject to various influences from environment and heredity but I think we have the power to resist those to some extent. We have a limited free choice.

Why do I think this? Well, I think any argument I give will be a fairly complicated one and, therefore, I can't give it in full in this context. But the first thing I would draw attention to is that modern science teaches that the most fundamental laws of nature are the laws of quantum theory and the laws of quantum theory say that the very small bits of matter, the electrons, the protons, etc., of which our universe is made, only behave in statistical ways, that is to say there is a 50% probability that an atom will decay after a certain time, a 70% probability that if the photon goes through this slot it will end up in this place on a photographic plate, and so on. Now, in general, the indeterminacy of nature on the small scale averages out on the large scale. That is to say, to take an analogy, suppose that whether a coin falls heads or tails is an indeterministic matter, a 50% chance of heads and a 50% chance of tails. It will nevertheless follow that if you toss a coin a thousand times, approximately 500 of them will be heads and 500 tails. That is to say, small scale indeterminacies average out on the large scale. Now the photons and protons are the real vehicles of indeterminacy rather than the tossings of coins. But the same will follow: in general, small-scale indeterminacy produces large-scale virtual determinism.

But not always – because it is perfectly possible for us to construct a machine whereby small-scale indeterminacy produces large-scale indeterminacy, for example to set up a device so that whether a hydrogen bomb exploded was determined by some very small-scale goings-on. That is, in general, any device which is constructed of the fundamental particles is an averaging device: it averages out the indeterminacies of the small-scale. But there can be devices which multiply the indeterminacies of the small-scale. And it is a serious question whether the brain is one of these latter sorts of device. I think the evidence suggests that it is, that is, the brain has the feature that a very small variation in the position of some particle in the brain is going to make a very large-scale difference to what the body does. So, although nature is very largely deterministic, I think there is reason to suppose that the brain is exempted from that, in the sense that the small-scale indeterminacies of matter show up in the case of the brain on the large scale. And, therefore, since the brain is not fully deterministic there is room, as it were, for the soul to influence how we behave without upsetting the laws of nature.

Now what I have done so far is to point out that it is compatible with quantum theory that the soul shall act with undetermined actions, that is have free will. But I think there is a more positive argument in favor of this which I cannot give you in full detail but I just refer to the outlines of it. The argument is this: human beings, or, at any rate, many of us, are counter-suggestible, in the sense that we have it in our power to make false any prediction which some scientists might make about our behavior. Now, if there is a true deterministic theory of human behavior, which scientists could learn, then if they know this theory and if they observe my brain, on the basis of this, they will be able to predict what I will do. But, since I am so counter-suggestible, if they tell me this prediction I will do the opposite. So, it would seem that there could not be such a truly deterministic theory because it could always be shown false.

But, of course, it is not quite as simple as that because it may still be that there is a true deterministic theory, because it may be that the very fact of these scientists telling me that I will do X does alter my brain in such a way as to make it the case that I will do Y instead, that is to say deterministically. So somebody who notices the fact of human counter-suggestibility, and yet nevertheless claims that there is a true deterministic theory of human behavior, will have to say that what is peculiar about humans is that, although you can predict their behavior from observing their brain states and the true deterministic theory, telling them what they are going to do will always alter their brain states in such a way that it is the new brain state which will determine their behavior. You can't ever succeed in conveying to people true information about what they are going to do. But I do have an argument which says that, although that is a possible scenario, it is most unlikely that the true deterministic theory will have this characteristic. I am not going to give this in detail but it is in print. The argument goes that for almost all possible deterministic theories of human behavior it should be possible to tell a subject what they will do in such a way that it will not affect their behavior, and therefore it follows that, if telling them what they will do does affect their behavior, it is most unlikely that there is a true deterministic theory of their behavior. And, therefore, I argue that although it is possible we don't have free will, probably, very probably, we do.

ALVIN PLANTINGA

Of course human beings are capable of free choices. On what basis is it possible to accept the reality of free will?

We all believe (unless corrupted by philosophy) that on many occasions we could have done something different from what we did do. That seems to me to be part of what one naturally believes. We naturally believe that there are other people, that there is an external world and so on. We also believe, in the same way, naturally and initially, that on many occasions we could have done something different from what we did do. Not only do we naturally believe that, but we naturally believe other things that imply it; for example, that some actions are wrong and deserve blame, or even punishment. If it weren't possible for a given person not to have done what that person did on a given occasion, then the whole idea of blame, the whole idea of holding the person responsible for what he or she did, would make no sense.

So the only question here is this: are there any reasons for thinking people don't have free will? Well, there are two kinds of reason people have suggested. One is that the very idea of free action is incoherent. That argument typically goes like this: "If your decision or behavior is not determined, then it must be just by chance that you do what you do. But something that is done just by chance is not something for which one is responsible. So you can be responsible for something only if it is somehow determined that you do that thing." This seems to me to be a crazy argument. Human beings are created in the image of God; our idea of what God is like is that He is both free and not determined to do what He has done by circumstances beyond His control. He freely chose to enable human beings to achieve salvation through the life and death and resurrection of Jesus Christ. He wasn't obliged to do that; He wasn't determined by outside circumstances to do it. He could have done otherwise. But it certainly isn't just a matter of chance that He did that. The same goes for us. If I freely decide to contribute $200 to Habitat for Humanity, or to get married, if I do this freely, then it is not the case that (given what has already happened) I couldn't possibly have done something else. Nor is it the case that my doing it is just a matter of chance, just a matter of pure accident. The claim that what I do is either determined or else just chance is wholly ridiculous. So, I'm not impressed at all by this argument.

The other kind of argument is that science somehow shows us that determinism reigns and that human beings are entirely determined by heredity and environment. But this too is just baloney. Science doesn't show any such thing at all. I don't know of any theorem in physics or psychology according to which human beings don't have any freedom. Perhaps some scientists assume this, but it is just an assumption, not an established scientific result; and it's certainly hard to see how such a thing could be established.

HUGO MEYNELL

It seems clear to me that heredity and environment limit us in all kinds of ways; that's something on which people who feel morally superior to criminals may care to reflect. In Dickens' novel *Barnaby Rudge*, there is a wild man who seeks to destroy everything, but with a brother who is a very good man and does all the right things. If I remember rightly, someone remarks to the good brother that it is wonderful he's such an estimable character, when the other, who has just come to a bad end, has been so prodigiously evil and destructive. He replies that, on the contrary, it would have been a miracle if his brother had been anything other than he was, given the sufferings and indignities to which he had been subjected during his upbringing.

But all the same, it seems to me that the case for at least a limited freedom of will is compelling. There is a rather subtle philosophical argument for its impossibility, which goes like this. Any human action is either explicable or it is arbitrary. If it is explicable, it is predetermined, and so not free. But if it is arbitrary, this is inconsistent with anyone reasonably or willingly performing it. So if every action has got to be either determined or arbitrary, then free will just disappears out of the picture. Now it seems to me that this dilemma is a false one, though the point about arbitrariness is fair enough. As I sometimes tell my classes, if I stood on my head in class and sang the *Marseillaise* in Hungarian, they would not infer that I was exercising my free will. Rather they would whisper to one another, "We've always feared that he had some dreadful mental affliction, and now we know for certain." The medical authorities would probably attribute my action to an abnormality in the chemistry of my brain, or something like that.

However, one sees what is wrong with the dilemma, determined or arbitrary, if one takes a typical example of a moral decision. Suppose a tray of cream puffs is close to you and unattended; and you have a strong impulse to steal one and eat it. Evidently one of two things can happen. Either you can clench your teeth and stick to your moral principles; or you can yield to your baser impulses, pounce incontinently on the cream puffs and stuff one or two of them into your mouth. Now, the point is that neither of these outcomes is arbitrary or inexplicable; whether you yield to your inclinations or refrain from doing so, in either case your action can be explained. The determinist will say, but if your desires were stronger, that was what caused you to steal the cream puff; while if your moral principles were the stronger, that was what caused you not to. This, however, is to presuppose determinism rather than to argue for it; because which impulse will win out, on indeterminist principles, will probably be up to you.

A lot of the underlying grounds of determinism, of course, are scientific; philosophers from Descartes to Kant were always finding rather implausible ways of accounting for how human actions could be at once free and determined by mechanical causation in common with all other physical events. But science itself depends on the autonomy of human subjects in saying things because there is good reason to say them, rather than because they are predetermined to do so due to their physical and chemical makeup. Agent causation – you might call it "soul causation" – evidently goes along with the kind of view that I have outlined, where there are some events at least, reasonable and reponsible human actions, which are neither arbitrary, nor totally predetermined. And, of course, it is a cliché by now, but I think it is important in this connection, that we now have good reason to believe that physical science, at the level of nuclear physics, is itself irreducibly statistical. So many of the older arguments against free will, which presuppose that science is essentially deterministic, are now out of date. I think there is more and more reason to believe that Aristotle and common sense are right, that human agents are in a special sense causes of their own actions, genuinely responsible for whether they perform them or not.

JOSEF SEIFERT

Human decisions are certainly not entirely shaped by heredity and environment. That human beings are capable of free choices, we know with an immediate knowledge which is not less certain than the knowledge of our own existence. For the fact that we can perform acts the source of which is in ourselves and which (as St. Augustine says in *The City of God*) would not have been at all if we had not wanted to perform them, and of which we can know, as Aristotle puts it in the *Eudemian Ethics*, that humans are lord over the existence or non-existence of their own actions, is absolutely evident. To deny our free will is always a metaphysical construction or a belief which flatly contradicts the evidence of our experience. Whenever we feel guilty for something, we have the knowledge and evidence of our freedom. When we make a promise to another person, we know that they are free to accept or to reject our promise, and that we are free to keep it or to break it. The meaning of the promise involves necessarily the awareness of the freedom of the one who makes it. Whenever we make a resolution, regret or repent an action we have committed, or praise someone for what they have done, we presuppose freedom. The pagan Roman philosopher Cicero insisted that the whole legal system and countless human actions are accompanied by this evidence of freedom. Therefore, it is quite in accordance with human reason to accept freedom. The evidence of freedom is indeed so great that I would reject any religion as evidently false which denies this truth which each one of us knows indubitably: that we are free.

Of course, one can also accept the fact of human freedom on the basis of religious faith. The whole Old and New Testament make absolutely no sense without freedom. The original sin of Adam and Eve and its consequences would be an illusory comedy if God determined Adam and Eve to sin. The same is true of Satan's fall and punishment, if God had forced Satan from eternity to sin. As a matter of fact, any such deterministic metaphysics, as it is unfortunately also contained in many Christian Confessions, such as in a strict Calvinism, would turn God himself into the devil. For if He were the cause of sin, He alone would be responsible for the moral evil of his creatures.

As sin is absolutely connected with the reality of human or angelic freedom, so is also redemption and justification. For it is clear that the call to holiness, to conversion, which John the Baptist addressed to humankind, would all be comical farces if we were just marionettes and puppets in the hands of God, and were only led to whatever we do by the divine will, and lacked any freedom of our own. The drama of redemption, the call to conversion and holiness, the justification through an act of faith, which, while being rendered possible through divine grace, is nevertheless fully free and our own responsibility – all of these religious truths depend on the reality of freedom. For this reason, I hold the truth that humans are free also because it is revealed by Divine Revelation and is a central tenet of the Catholic and of any authentic Christian faith. But this religious faith in freedom is wholly compatible with human reason; even more: its content (human freedom) coincides with the object of the rational knowledge that humans are free.

This is not to deny the assertion of Protestants that we are saved only through God's grace, but it is to deny that we are saved through God's grace alone without any free action and cooperation of humankind, as Augustine put it marvellously: "*Qui creavit te sine te, non te iustificat sine te*" (He who created you without your cooperation does not justify you without your cooperation).

RALPH MCINERNY

You can reduce to absurdity the questioning of it [free will]. Most people who have thought about that in the past, about the denial of free will, would say it would render human life, as we talk about it and know it, nonsensical, because we hold ourselves accountable for what we do, we hold other people accountable for what they do, we raise our children urging them to act this way as opposed to that way, and what the denial entails is that all that is nonsense. Well, it's the denial that's nonsense, I would say. There is no reason to accept the denial.

Is it one of those things which we know from experience?

Yes, and it is one of those things, not just personal experience, but it's the experience of the race, and it is comic for someone to pop up and say I think free will is an illusion. This is a lonely voice in a crowd of people who know better, and why we should attend to that voice as if it alone is significant I've never understood, particularly because we seem to have the freedom to listen or not listen to that sort of nonsense.

JOHN LUCAS

[Since 1959, in a series of books and papers, the Oxford philosopher-mathematician J. R. Lucas has applied Gödel's Theorems to the mind–body and free will–determinism discussions. Gödel's Incompleteness Theorems showed the inherent limitations of formal systems. For instance, the consistency in terms of number theory of a formal system cannot be proved within the system. Lucas points out that computers, being formal systems, are necessarily limited by the kind of limitations of formal systems delineated by Gödel. Since the human mind is not similarly limited, the mechanist is mistaken in modeling it on a machine. No representation of a mind by a computer or Turing machine, writes Lucas, "could be correct, since for any such representation there would be a Gödelian formula which the Turing machine could not prove, and so could not produce as true, but which the mathematician could both see, and show, to be true." These kinds of applications of Gödel's Theorem received popular prominence through the works of Roger Penrose.]

How would you characterize your approach to the existence of mind and to determinism in your book Freedom of the Will? *Is it based on Gödel's theorem?*

I'm never quite certain when it comes to Gödel's theorem. I'm dealing with a whole lot of objections that people put forward; and again I'm starting from the position that we have normal experience making up our minds, and that we think it is up to us what we decide, and we believe that we are free; and then this runs into a number of very different difficulties, and I try and go into those and show that there has been some misconception about the nature of the argument. So at the end I go back to a rather commonsensical position and that's where the buck stops. That is the view I started with and the one that I've ended with; and I've refuted, I think, some of the more popular objections to freedom, but I haven't proved that it exists starting from any other position.

You appeal to experience and the buck stops here?

Yes. I appeal to experience. Each of us has experience of being an agent, of making up our mind for ourselves. That is what we all know, but sometimes can't believe in. So I then try and go to instances where it is, indeed, the case that we make up our minds for ourselves, and there aren't conditions forcing us to – there are no laws of nature which make it inevitable that we should decide in one particular way – and I discuss various different sorts of determinism: logical determinism, theological determinism, psychological determinism and physical determinism; and I examine how each of those is argued for in a rather different way. And in each case I show that argument won't work, so at the end of it, the sensible thing is to believe what we have always learnt from our experience: that we make up our minds for ourselves, and decide what we shall do, and that we are responsible for what we decide to do.

But you do think Gödel's theorem is relevant in discussing the issue?

Yes. I think that this is relevant as a very particular tool against a very particular, although quite widespread, form of determinism. The mechanists have what looks like a strong case and many people are worried by it. The point of the Gödelian argument is that it is one that gets under the cover of the mechanistic contention, and they are faced with something which is expressed in their own terms, and is something they can't just brush off.

What kind of reception has your application of Gödel's theorem had from the mechanists?

Highly hostile. This makes me think that I've touched on a raw nerve. I notice that a great many mechanists froth at the mouth at the mere mention of my name. They often say how wrong I am but they don't actually read the argument. Often they say that the mind isn't better than all possible machines. But I didn't say that it was: what I said was that the mind wasn't the same as any particular machine. This is the argument which I tried to make clear; but they have really not listened, and are really barking up the wrong tree. Other critics will attend one point but, in the course of this, concede that various other points, which other mechanists had attacked, are quite all right. Now that doesn't add up to the critics' having no case. But I do think that if I had got my argument seriously wrong, it would have become very clear what this wrong point was: and the mere fact that there is such a wide disparity between the points that mechanists make against me leads me to think they aren't very good ones.

What is Professor Peter Strawson's general response to your approach?

I don't think I've ever heard him address this question. He is not of a mathematical turn of mind. He has put forward many arguments of very great subtlety, but has kept away from the mathematical end of philosophy. And this is generally true in Oxford. There is a sharp division between the mathematicians and the rest.

I think the mathematical mappings in your book have not been addressed by a lot of philosopher-critics.

Yes, well, this is the difficulty. Gödel's Theorem is difficult. It takes a lot of time to fathom it, and people haven't got a long time to spend on it, particularly if, as many people feel, I am only proving what is obvious anyhow. Many people reckon that it is obvious that minds aren't machines: why spend so much time proving the obvious? My answer is, "I'm very glad that it is obvious to you, and maybe you are quite right not to waste time on it, but my arguments were addressed against another target, the mechanist position which did not allow that it was obvious that minds were not machines, and which would not acknowledge the cogency of any arguments except mathematical and logical ones."

How did Sir Alfred Ayer respond to your application of Gödel's Theorem?

He was not a mathematician. I criticized him in *Freedom of the Will.* In some public meeting I voiced that particular criticism, which is a mathematical one, and he flanneled out of the question with a vague answer. And I think he would have still been quite likely, in an unguarded moment, to use the same argument against free will as he did then, although he did mellow and did become more cautious.

Antony Flew mentioned that your book had substantially changed his views.

Yes, he and I used to be very much opposed and now [he's] not so very much opposed but, of course, one thing is that as time goes on, one realizes how very grateful one needs be to one's opponents, for stimulating one to articulate and argue for one's own views.

How about Professor Gilbert Ryle?

He wouldn't have seen that there was a problem or that my argument was at all relevant. He had a different set of mind and I wasn't really arguing with him. He had a certain doctrine that humans weren't machines and simply weren't minds either. I think he missed a good many points. Although he did open up quite a lot of interesting questions, his account was defective in some ways, for example, about introspection. From his position, I wasn't saying anything of interest. He wouldn't have thought I was addressing a real question; and to convince him that it was would have been a long labor, which neither he nor I had time to entertain.

How would you distinguish animals from human beings?

I think animals suffer pain and in a few cases are able to exercise a certain amount of foresight, to know fear from other animals, and can just occasionally exert a bit of originality, but very, very little, very elementary, and in practical terms have no real sense of deliberation and foresight and of deliberation and responsibility.

LIFE AFTER DEATH

Great Question 5: *Do you believe in a life after death and, if
so, why?*

JOSEF SEIFERT

I do believe in an everlasting life after death and the resurrection of
the body. In addition, I am also convinced about the immortality of
the human soul for philosophical reasons. While the Christian faith
in the resurrection of the body is based on the overwhelming event
of the resurrection of Christ and the witnesses who perceived his res-
urrected body and who handed down to us the knowledge of this
event, there are also purely philosophical arguments for the immortality of the human soul. The most convincing of these arguments I
find are those which are based on the following two premises: the
first ground of these arguments is that all the most significant acts
and activities of the human person remain unfulfilled, and would be
contradicted in a tragic manner, without immortality. In all knowledge of the truth we aim at a lasting contemplation of the truth, and
we reach something that is timelessly true. Even the knowledge of
the historical past reaches a truth about what has happened, which
can never pass away. Most of all, the knowledge of the eternal
truths, of the essences of mathematical objects, of the nature of
moral actions, of sin, etc., aims at something lasting and at something which will never pass away. This is most of all true of our
knowledge of God as the eternal and absolute ground of all things.
Therefore, in all acts of knowledge man aims at eternity, and at a lasting cognitive union with truth and above all with the truth about
those things which are eternal. Therefore it would contradict the
deepest principle of life of the person, it would contradict the vocation of the soul to contemplate and be related to an eternally valid
truth, to be destroyed in death forever. The same is true about morality which requires the perfect justice of reward and of punishment.
Our conscience tells us that we deserve punishment for morally evil

acts and that reward is due to morally good acts. Therefore, perfect
justice is never realized in this world in which the innocent victims
of Nazi-terror die just as much as the greatest criminals who torture
them. Thus, in the light of the objective metaphysical exigency that
justice be realized, this world of ours cannot be the only world. For
the meaning and value of the world itself would be undermined in a
most horrible way, if there were no life of man after death in which
justice will triumph.

Also the desire for happiness cries out for immortality. Let us
summarize the argument of St. Augustine to this effect: If a state of
our feeling is such that we are indifferent towards its continuation,
we cannot be said to be happy. For if we are truly happy, we want
this happiness to last forever and can exclaim with Goethe's Faust:
"*Verweile doch, du bist so schön.*" Even the atheist Nietzsche said:
"Woe speaks: pass away, but pleasure desires eternity, it desires
deep, deep eternity."

Most of all, the transcending acts of striving for moral perfection
and of interpersonal love desire eternity. If we love a person, as
Gabriel Marcel puts it, we say to the other, "Thou will not die." For
we desire happiness and thereby necessarily also immortality. We
desire a union with the other person which is much more perfect
than the one we reach in our present life; and we want this union to
last forever, etc. Thus the meaning of human existence and of the
world order as such would be shaken entirely if humans were to die
like a mouse or a rat.

The second pillar on which this argument rests is that such a metaphysical contradiction to the very meaning and vocation of the human
person cannot actually exist. This requires us at least to understand
the inner truth of the described goods: it cannot be that that which is
the most noble, such as faithful human love or moral goodness, can
lie and announce an immortality which does not exist! It is impossible
that the holiest parts of human experience are just lies! The inner truth
of these experiences gives us hope, and in a certain way prophetically
proves that they are not in vain and meaningless.

But the ultimate foundation of the second premise is no doubt the
existence of God. If we can know that an infinitely good God exists,
then we can be quite certain of the immortality of the soul. For then
it is impossible that that which – in virtue of the deepest nature and
dignity of the person – is required for the fulfillment of the meaning
of personal existence, namely immortality, be not given in reality.

RICHARD SWINBURNE

Yes. Well, if we are both souls and bodies, then if our body is destroyed there is a soul left. That doesn't mean to say that the soul will necessarily survive. All that the arguments I gave earlier show is that I currently consist of both a soul and body. It is possible that when my body is destroyed, my soul also in some way ceases to exist. That may or may not be the case. So we need a further argument to show that when my body is destroyed my soul does continue to exist. I think that argument will be a very indirect one, that is to say, it would be an argument for the existence of God and it would then be an argument showing that God has revealed certain things, including that there is life after death and, therefore, that is reason for believing it. I happen to think, as a Christian, that He has revealed various things in the Bible and through the Church and it is a central item of Church doctrine that there is life after death and that is my reason for believing it. I believe it because I believe argument shows that there is a soul which can survive; argument shows that there is a God; argument shows He has revealed Himself in a certain way; argument shows that among the items of that revelation are that there is life after death and that is my reason for believing it. I don't think that pure philosophical arguments can show there is life after death – in the sense that I think that any argument for life after death has to go via argument for the existence of God. I think there are such arguments and there are arguments for the truth of the Christian revelation and, therefore, good arguments for life after death.

GERARD J. HUGHES

Surely no traditional theist could deny outright the possibility of a mind existing independently of a body. God, after all, is traditionally believed to be a person with a mind and a will, even if we are far from clear what God's mind or will are like; and God is not traditionally thought to have a body.

That being said, however, it just might still be worth asking whether even God's disembodied mind must be thought of as a wholly immaterial mind. Physicists in recent years have taught us that apparently quite different things, such as matter, energy, space, time, and gravity, are by no means independent of one another. Indeed, in some extreme circumstances these apparently diverse items seem almost interchangeable. I am in no position even to comment on these cosmological speculations, but they might serve to make us somewhat more hesitant to say that we understand what matter is, or how matter relates to such things as minds, and even "disembodied" minds.

Be all that as it may, it seems to me that the more we learn of neuroscience, the less likely it appears that a human mind or soul could exist independently of matter. More generally, I think that being somehow embodied is so central to our notions of being a human person, and to our concept of personal identity, that a Platonist or Cartesian identification of ourselves with our minds or souls is a less likely view than a more Aristotelian one, in which we are bodies with a whole range of capabilities, including the capability of thought and decision-making. I do, however, have a fairly open mind on the details of what would be required for us to retain our individual identity. I would assume that to retain my identity after death, I need to be able to recognize my habits of mind, my patterns of desire and interest, my reactions to people and situations, as mine, the ones I am familiar with. I assume, too, for the reasons given above, that in order to do this, I must in some sense be embodied. But, just as the notion of "matter" is only imperfectly understood by us, so, too, in my view are the notions of "space", "time" and "body"; so questions about what a body capable of sustaining my mind would have to be like, or where or when such a body would be, seem to me almost totally mysterious.

I believe in life after death on Christian grounds. That is to say, I take it to be an integral part of Christian revelation, and I think there are general rational grounds for accepting that revelation as true. For the reasons given in the previous two paragraphs, I have no clear view on what form such life after death might take, or by what mechanism it is achieved. I believe that it must be a life in which my deepest aspirations are fulfilled; in which the limitations of the ways in which we can here and now understand one another, or understand the being of God, are transcended. Beyond that, we can do no better than express our hopes and beliefs in whatever language we can devise to capture what is essentially a mystery beyond our present experience.

REINCARNATION

Great Question 6: *What is your assessment of the theory of reincarnation?*

C. T. K. CHARI

First of all, Hinduism is not committed absolutely to belief in reincarnation. It is not as if Hindu metaphysics condemns every soul to be reborn. In all the systems it is recognized that there are souls that are not reborn at all. Indeed the goal of Hindu metaphysics is not to be reborn. The cycle of rebirth is a fallen state. What the Western reincarnationist does not realize is that the cycle of births and rebirths is a fallen, sinful state. Redemption lies in going beyond the cycle. Even when there is belief in reincarnation in Hinduism it has a secondary place. The goal in all systems is to go beyond reincarnation.

Further, the redeemed state cannot be the end-product of a series of rebirths of the self. What kind of self? Not the last self. Memories cannot be extinguished for such a self. Forgetting is only temporary and this is part of the condition here. In the redeemed state, it's not the last self in a temporal series. All the memories have to be integrated. Once more we see that it is not reincarnation at all. It's some concept of survival, personal survival. In Hindu theistic systems it's a person. All the conscious states are synthesized, integrated. That in itself seems to me an objection to reincarnation in the usual popular sense.

So from a metaphysical standpoint that's an objection to the theory of reincarnation.

Yes. There are supporting grounds also. In the theistic systems, for instance, two kinds of consciousness are found and distinguished. An empirical, objective consciousness, flickering and coming and going, and a more substantive consciousness that is grounded only in God, a personal God. It's the substantive consciousness which finally survives death and is immortal. The accidental, flickering consciousness which comes and goes is not immortal. It seems to me this in itself opens the door to an explanation of the so-called memories of previous lives. Maybe they pertain only to flickering consciousness. Flickering consciousness is not an island. Flickering consciousness is one with many other centers of flickering consciousness so there could be contagion, reaction, interaction at an empirical level.

Such a distinction is not explicit in Western science: this distinction between flickering object-consciousness and a more substantive subject-consciousness which alone is grounded in a personal God and that survives. It's not the flickering consciousness which survives or is immortal because it is easily open to other influences, other centers, at an empirical level when we act, interact. Much of the so-called parapsychological evidence is in the empirical category only. The very term "flickering" implies it is not steady. Consciousness studied by science, brain–mind studies, does flicker, all the brain rhythms constantly change. At that level one doesn't find the self. At the non-empirical level one is truly a person, in one's own right one is an absolutely unique, individual person in God. At that level, we are ourselves through all eternity and we don't merge in God. That's the non-empirical, transcendental level of consciousness.

Could this non-empirical, transcendental individual conceivably go through different lives?

No. For the reasons explained: it will involve memories. This [self] is not in ordinary time. Memory means temporal succession. In fact, the main question for the Hindu is how such a self could be caught here. How could that self ever be caught in the wheel of births and rebirths. That is the unanswered question for Hindu metaphysicians. In fact, Hindus find it very awkward. Advaita and some systems simply dismiss the world as a kind of indeterminate shadow. The self is not in the shadow world at all. This is the reason a man like Iswarananda, an Advaitan, denies rebirth outright. Consciousness is transcendental. So this empirical thing is only a bioplasmic consciousness, he says. All life is connected. Consciousness pertaining to that is organismic, unitary. It is not transcendental at all. The way I look at it is, if you postulate these two levels, then the genuine self is transcendental, personal, pertaining to God. The question is how it could ever be caught in this fallen state, a question which is not answered. Of course, the Christian has an answer, the Fall. Here [in

Hinduism] too there is a fall in the sense of how it gets caught in this world. One can't understand it. Why it is caught here. The theists, since they cannot dismiss time, they have to admit change, the reality of time.

Turning to the empirical claims for reincarnation, what do you think of such claims, particularly claims of memories of past lives?

The empirical claim is never proven. The doctrine of rebirth is metaphysical. No empirical proof can be commensurate with a metaphysical doctrine. What persists throughout? The reincarnationist must have an answer. What persists? I have not found any clear answer. Some astral body? That's not the answer. Some say the "mind" but what kind of mind?

Many people do not remember. And even when they remember it's a kind of flickering. These children [with memories of past lives] don't always remember. In the seventh year their memories vanish. Why? It is very unstable, flickering. My point is that a metaphysical claim can't be proved empirically. Immortality is neither provable nor falsifiable in science. It's not falsifiable. It's not provable either. Reincarnation is a metaphysical claim. Strictly speaking it's not provable in science. What could science prove?

What connects the different lives? Consciousness? But what kind of consciousness when there is a loss of memory? Is it universal? Are all people reborn? is a relevant question. After all, only a section of humanity is supposed to remember. Even in India, we don't all remember. I don't remember anyway.

To what would you attribute these claims of memories of past lives?

One is cultural, the other is psychical. This flickering, empirical consciousness is open to invasions. At an empirical level it is very much open to influences. Parental influences, social influences. It is open at another level as well, a psychic level: telepathy, past lives. It is open to psychic influences coming from the past.

Whose past?

Other people's past, not our past. A person dies but the memories can invade a soul in the present. It is open and the boundaries are not fixed. The empirical consciousness does not have fixed boundaries. It is open at the empirical level just as it is open to noise, information, all kinds of disturbances.

Some psychiatrists say that in the case of adults, claims of memories of past lives are derived from some historical fantasy the claimants may have read and then identified themselves with.

There is proof of this, of what is called cryptomnesia. I have myself studied a case in detail.

You have done a number of studies of claims of past lives.

Yes. Several of these have been published. Cryptomnesia is one source but I am not thinking of that source here [but of] telepathic contagious influences coming from the past. The empirical consciousness does not have fixed boundaries. The boundaries are fluid. So [the influences] can very well intrude, as in double personality cases. The only thing is that this is not an abnormality. It is an openness, a psychic openness to receive influences from the past. In that way it can be successfully explained. In fact I'd like to know what cannot be explained in that way. Memories are unstable. A person [who claims to have memories of past lives] doesn't have these memories all through life, in [Ian] Stevenson's cases anyway.

This applies to memories [of alleged past lives] that are hypnotically revived. But how do you know they are your memories? Many hypnotists have published books in which the hypnotist has regressed into a person's past. But what I ask is, how do you know that it is this person's memories, in that sensitive state in which you have dipped into the historical past and you take what you find there and that invades your consciousness. Consciousness is very fluid. I find that quite consistent with the Hindu premise that this consciousness, the empirical consciousness as such, cannot be unique, personal, transcendental.

Am I correct in assuming that you deny that a person could go through more than one life?

It is a meaningless statement to me. Even for the orthodox [Advaitan] Hindu it is a meaningless statement since it is not in ordinary time. The question is, how did it ever get enmeshed in this cycle of birth and rebirth. The [Advaitan] Hindu doesn't answer that question. How did souls begin this business of getting involved in birth and rebirth, since they are non-empirical? Hindu metaphysics

finds it very difficult. There is never an answer. The monist denies
that this world is here. That's an easy way out: this process is unreal. The corollary of that is that there is no rebirth. Even Iswarananda
draws this conclusion (he is an Advaitan): this process is illusory,
there is no rebirth. He finds that the empirical consciousness supports his argument: biological, plasmic consciousness. It is not well-
defined, it is not individual, personal at all. The conclusion he
draws, of course, is Advaitic. But I am a theist and I do think that
doesn't follow. If you admit the theistic distinction between a non-
empirical personal level in which you are related to God and a more
empirical flickering level, then the reincarnation memories pertain to
the flickering state in which consciousness is psychically invaded.

*Is it meaningless to say that the empirical consciousness could
be reincarnated?*

Yes. Empirically it is meaningless because he [the person who is the
subject of the empirical consciousness] is dead and gone. Even in
Buddhism persons do not survive. Buddhism draws a strict logical
corollary. There is no rebirth.

*So you say it is conceptually impossible to talk of a person
being reincarnated?*

Yes. Which person? That [dead] person is gone. Then what do you
mean by saying he is reborn? Each person is different empirically.
How are the memories carried over?

*So you would explain these memories [of past lives] in terms
of telepathy, etc.*

Yes. Metaphysically. Of course, empirically also I would find supporting arguments. [Dr. Chari has made extensive critiques of claims
made by such reincarnationists as Ian Stevenson. In Dr. Chari's view,
Stevenson's "cases of people who claim to 'remember' former lives
are explicable by a combination of hidden and disguised normally-
acquired memories, extra-sensory tapping of the memories of other
people, and a strong empathetic identification with deceased persons. This explanation is not only feasible but actually illustrated by
the empirical data of survival research."]

*Does what you have written on genetics indicate that reincar-
nation is not feasible on empirical grounds?*

I think it is a very weighty objection. The empirical consciousness is the scaffolding, it seems to me, for the unfolding genetic process in which things are inherited in the stream. On that level again there could be no reincarnation – especially in modern genetics. There is an informational flow from the genes to the soma, to the body, the secondary level. There is no reflow from the body: genes are not modified. That is one argument against classical Lamarckian theory. Lamarck thought that a living being could modify the genes of its successors. A classic example is the giraffe. The ancestors of the giraffe learned to stretc.h their necks little by little and the successors acquired longer and longer necks. Lamarck explained evolution in that way. Biology even at that time cast doubts on Lamarck's theory. But today modern genetics has a conclusive objection: the flow of information is in one direction only, from this generation to the next, the genetic flow, then from the genes to the soma, the secondary level, but no reflow from the soma.

But in reincarnation habits, memories are all transmitted. How? They say it is through an astral body. But that would be the equivalent of a reversal of the informational flow. If memories are carried by the "astral body" even then it would contradict Crick's dogma, the central dogma of molecular biology: the flow of information is in one direction only. There is very impressive evidence for this. Long ago we found several proofs given by Lamarck were not proofs at all. He held that a person living in the tropics acquires a brown complexion and the children inherit that. They don't. The children are born fair if they are from the non-Eastern races. If you cut off the tail of an animal, succeeding generations don't inherit short tails. This doesn't happen at all. Many so-called proofs of Lamarckism were refuted long ago. But now modern genetics has impressive objections from its detailed study of the flow of information. So apparently even this [argument for reincarnation] is built on these empirical claims.

Each empirical consciousness is something new. The Hindu would have to say the transcendental self does not really become a self until its empirical scaffolding is furnished by this genetic stream. According to theistic Hindu theory there is a transcendental, non-empirical self distinct from God, related to God. What is gained from the temporal process? Reincarnation doesn't make sense because that self cannot simply be born or reborn in any sense. So what does it acquire from the stream? The [Hindu] theist believes that there is a real parinarma, an evolutionary process. What is God achieving in that? My answer would be that apparently an empirical scaffolding is very important for the transcendental self. It comes to selfhood only through this. It seems to me that this is a meeting place for Christianity and Hinduism.

The two levels of consciousness are somehow linked together, the empirical flickering consciousness and the non-empirical. This flickering consciousness is obviously not reborn. If this is not reborn, then what is reborn? What is the relevance of this temporal flickering?

The only viable form of Hindu theism would be one which admits an irreversible genetic stream furnishing a very important contribution to the non-empirical level. Until the empirical scaffolding is furnished, I don't see how the transcendental level of consciousness can work.

What is your assessment of Sarvepalli Radhakrishnan's case for reincarnation?

[In "Radhakrishnan's Interpretation of Rebirth", a paper in Volume 12 of the *Indian Philosophical Annual*, Dr. Chari wrote that Radhakrishnan was wrong on theoretical and empirical grounds in holding that one's acquired character determines the gene pool of the body into which one is reincarnated. This is wrong, he said, because it reverses the normal flow of biological information. Information flows irreversibly from DNA via RNA to protein, or unchanged (except for chance mutations) from the DNA of one generation to the next. But reincarnation involves the claim that genetic information goes from the protein of one generation to the DNA of a later one – and thus contradicts genetics.]

He tries to make as much sense as possible of the theory of reincarnation. Biologically he tries to provide for it by a form of Lamarckism. He wrote in the 1930s when Lamarckian theories were still going strong, before modern genetics took shape. He thought that some form of Lamarckism was needed, that habits, learning of one generation are carried over to the next generation. If that is the case why should not the habits of "x" be carried over to "y" who is reborn? He thought that. But that contradicts the genetic dogma of molecular biology in which informational flow can be in one direction only. Memories are secondary and they cannot be carried over by plasma. Radhakrishnan didn't worry very much about that question: how these memories are carried over.

Then he seeks some support in parapsychology. Though he thinks that parapsychology is not very reliable, there are still some clues of some kind of empiric, higher body. My difficulty is, how does that body carry the memories? How does it invade, at what point does it invade without contradicting biology?

Does the reincarnationist have a solution to this?

No. In the biological area it is impossible. At least [if reincarnation is true] there must be some tremendous kind of interaction [with the alleged "astral" body and if this is the case] practically all of biology is at a standstill.

What is the relationship between claims of memories of past lives and mediumistic possession?

My researches have uncovered another trap for the unwary in supposed cases of rebirth. Whether an Asian child's paranormal behavior suggests to the bystanders "mediumistic possession" or "reincarnation" depends very much on the kind of imaginative "reaching out" exercised by the child, which in turn is a function of the cultural setting. There are, in fact, no infallible criteria for "mediumistic possession" in the Asian area. Philosophers like C. D. Broad and C. J. Ducasse regarded "possession" as a kind of temporary reincarnation and "reincarnation" as a kind of permanent possession. Can any firm theoretical line of demarcation between these groups of phenomena be drawn, apart from the very terrene accidents of birth and death? If B's death follows A's birth, we decide it must be "possession." But if B's death precedes A's birth, how do we know which hypothesis holds the key? The late Somasundara Gnanasambandha Desika Paramacharya, the former head of an important Saivite center in Madurai, Tamilnadu, and the author of a popular book in Tamil on "spirit communication" which ran into two editions, was firmly of the opinion that all Stevenson's cases of the "reincarnation-type" could be explained in terms of "possession," keeping well in view the uniformly violent termination of the "former lives." The Paramacharya gave me a copy of his letter addressed to Stevenson in which the counter-hypothesis is stated vigorously.

Part III:

ARE RELIGION AND MORALITY SIMPLY AND SOLELY BY-PRODUCTS OF THE SOCIO-CULTURAL ENVIRONMENT?

PSYCHOLOGY, SOCIOLOGY,
AND RELIGIOUS BELIEF

Great Question 7: *Some thinkers hold that religion can be explained entirely in psychological and sociological categories. Can it?*

GERARD J. HUGHES

Freud argued that religious belief was a projection of the deep psychological need we all have for an ideal parent who can give love and stability and security to our lives. Yet a Christian might believe that God is indeed such a being. Augustine was happy to suggest that the human heart remains restless until it rests in God. The difference between Augustine and Freud, then, is not about the position that religion can occupy in the emotional life of the believer, nor about the psychological benefits that religious belief might bring. What is in question is the explanatory interpretation which should be put upon such psychological facts. In this connection I would wish to make just two remarks. I have already said that I do not believe that the religious experience of believers was in itself conclusive evidence for theism. The reason is that a Freudian explanation of such experience is possible. And if it is a possible interpretation, then it needs to be refuted by argument, and not simply rejected without discussion. On the other hand, while it seems to me that Freud calls attention to a feature of human beings which any believer might well accept, the believer cannot accept that a Freudian explanation of the psychological value of religious belief somehow discredits the Augustinian view of the matter. It is one thing to say that religious belief corresponds to deep psychological needs in ourselves, and quite another to say that God is simply an idealized projection of those needs.

This kind of Freudian argument highlights a more important point. We are able to fill out our concepts of "Father", "love", and "judge" as these are applied to God only by using our experiences of earthly parents, lovers, friends, and judges. If someone has

experienced only emotionally demanding, manipulative and author-
itarian parents, or possessive or unfaithful lovers, or a corrupt and
unfeeling judicial system, then those experiences will color their picture of God. Worse, the patterns of desires and devices they have
developed to cope with the destructive relationships they have had
will be distorted, unhelpful at best, deeply damaging at worst. If, as
Freud argues, we project our own deepest needs onto God, it may
well be that for such a person religious belief will compound the
damage already done. A healthy, undistorted religious belief requires
that someone has at least some experience of constructive human
relationships. As one of the biblical writers puts it, if we do not love
the people we can see, how can we possibly love the God we cannot
see?

Similar remarks apply to the relationship between religion and
social structures. That religion can be a powerful force to ensure the
stability and identity of a human society is surely true. But again,
any Christian would hope that the practice of the divine command
to love one another, and even to love one's enemies, will give us a
deep sense of our unity and interdependence as children of the one
God. It is quite another matter for someone to claim that the only
justification for religious belief is its contribution to social cohesion.

But here again, precisely because religion can be such a powerful
social force, there is the temptation to harness it to political ends
which have nothing to do with religion, and which are destructive of
human dignity. Historical examples, both past and present, abound.
The only antidote to such socio-religious manipulation is to ensure
that religious beliefs are constantly subject to criticism on the widest
possible grounds, scientific, moral, and psychological.

To establish that the existence of God is required as an ultimate
explanation of everything, including the existence of our religious
and social needs, is a much wider project, and not one which, in my
view, should be narrowly based on our religious experience, or the
social benefits of a shared religious outlook.

RICHARD SWINBURNE

Is the fact that individuals have the particular religious experiences
they do a matter of the way they are made psychologically, or the
way their society is formed? I think not, because I think humans
have free will and therefore their behavior is not to be entirely
explained in any categories, their behavior about anything. And

with regard to religion, although, of course, people's beliefs and behavior are much influenced – we don't have perfect free will, as I emphasized before – are much influenced by psychology and sociology, we do still have the power to resist some of these influences and, in turn, gradually to change the influences to which the next generation are exposed. So, no, it can't be explained fully in those terms.

We can make a difference to the world and we can decide to investigate new areas and reject fashionable views as a result of our investigation and therefore, the birth of religion is partly due to people rejecting the influences upon them. And they will reject those influences partly because arguments and experience have led them to suppose that the views of their society are mistaken in certain ways.

JOSEF SEIFERT

Certainly, religion, as the relation between humankind and God, can never be explained entirely in psychological and sociological categories. If God exists, religious acts and rites or sacraments objectively relate a human person, in worship, in praise, in prayer, etc. to God. Hence, if God exists, these religious relationships to God are never immanent and pure psychological or sociological phenomena. Thus to reduce religion to the psychological and sociological order is based on atheism and a thesis of the radical immanency and subjectivity of human consciousness and of its intentional objects as having existence only for humankind.

Moreover, a philosophy of religion could elucidate the fact that the specifically religious category of the holiness of God, as well as the nature of the religious acts, most of all of the act of adoration and of worship, by their very nature transcend themselves and relate humankind to a completely irreducible other reality, that of the absolutely divine and holy.

RIGHT AND WRONG

Great Question 8: *Can right be distinguished from wrong, good from evil? More fundamentally, is there an objective moral order and can human beings become aware of it?*

JOSEF SEIFERT

I think that right can evidently be distinguished from wrong. Already children can clearly grasp, if they are lied to by their brother or sister, or if something that has been given to them is taken away or destroyed by somebody else, that such actions are wrong. They understand with evidence that it is evil to torture some innocent person, to murder a child, etc. Already the child can comprehend, and often more keenly than adults, whose minds are frequently blinded by passions or obscured by confused theories, that this moral order is objective and not merely a matter of subjective preference or taste.

To recognize the objectivity of the moral order requires the evidence of value. For only because the human person possesses an inherent dignity and value that imposes moral obligations on us, can it be immoral to kill, murder, rape, deceive, etc., human beings. But this preciousness, this inherent goodness which raises a being out of the sphere of neutrality, is accessible to human reason with evidence.

We understand that to know is good and to be in error or ignorance is an evil. We understand that the truth of a judgment is a value and its untruth is an evil and that therefore to deliberately say an untruth, to lie, is morally evil. We understand that to be endowed with reason and understanding, with moral responsibility and love, renders to a being a higher dignity and value than a pig or a plant possesses. Thus there is a rationally accessible order of values and of goods (that is of beings endowed with value) which human reason can detect. No human can be so absolutely perverted, not even the most horrible criminal, that they will not understand any value whatsoever. Even murderers and mafia groups will recognize certain principles of loyalty, of justice of distribution, etc., as Sancho Pansa observes so well in Cervantes' *Don Quijote*, by pointing out to his master how justly the robbers had robbed different people and captured them, distributed the stolen goods among each other, exclaiming that justice is such an excellent thing that not even criminals cannot do without it.

Thus the evidence of the existence of objective values and of a moral order is undeniable and practically presupposed by anybody who denies it. And this evidence is a rational one.

In addition, however, we can understand the objective moral order also through faith and revelation, if we believe in the word of Christ, or also of the Church, and accept by faith what is right and what is wrong. Of course, what is believed by somebody in religious faith to be right or wrong can also be false opinion, if their religious faith is ill-founded.

Both of these sources of knowledge of good and evil do not contradict each other, as long as religious faith does not violate evident human knowledge of good and evil. The remarkable thing regarding Christian morality is precisely that it elevates natural morality, and that – without ever violating it – it contains all the natural insights into right and wrong.

Many philosophers have disputed the existence of such an objective moral order and particularly of actions which are by their nature intrinsically evil, and cannot be justified by certain consequences.

But if you understand morally relevant goods such as innocent human life, you will understand that actions that are directed deliberately at their destruction are essentially and intrinsically evil and cannot be justified by any further purpose. If we understand the dignity of a human person, for example, we understand that an act of rape or intrusion into the sexual privacy of another person by raping the other human being is intrinsically wrong, or that the reduction of a woman to a mere sex-object intrinsically violates the moral call to respect a person always for his or her own sake.

RICHARD SWINBURNE

We must start with what in morals, as with everything else, stares us in the face, and what stares us in the face is that certain things are wrong and certain other things are good. There are more difficult cases where we are not quite so certain whether an action is wrong or right but that doesn't mean to say that there aren't plenty of clear cases where we are, and philosophy must start from what is obvious and go to what is less obvious. What is obvious is that certain actions are wrong and certain actions are good and if a philosophical theory has the consequence that isn't so, then so much the worse for that philosophical theory.

Any theory that proves that there were no human beings would be obviously false and therefore to be dismissed. So any theory that proves there aren't any moral truths and therefore that it isn't moral truth that you want to have taught to children, any moral theory which had that consequence would obviously be false. So, yes, there is an objective moral order and human beings can become aware of it, because some of the aspects of it are just too obvious. And, of course, what it is will rather depend on other things, such as whether there is a God or not. If there is a God, then certain things become our duty which wouldn't otherwise be our duty, for example to worship God and do what He wants us to do. But the existence of God would only make a difference to the content of the moral order; it wouldn't make any difference to the fact of the moral order. If there is a God, there will be an awful lot of things which are right and wrong which would not otherwise be and, no doubt, there would be a depth and importance to their rightness and wrongness which otherwise they would not have. But still, God or not, there is clearly an objective moral order. What God makes a difference to, is just the content of that.

ALVIN PLANTINGA

Certainly; and deep in their hearts, most everybody else thinks the same thing. Different people may emphasize different things as right and wrong, but very few people think that there just isn't any difference at all between right and wrong. Those who are most enthusiastic about tolerance and who are reluctant to say that a given way of acting is wrong, also, typically, think it is wrong to be bigoted, to denounce somebody, or to disapprove of them. It is extremely difficult to be a normal human being and not think that some actions are wrong and some are right.

Is there an objective moral order and can you, indeed, become aware of it? Certainly there is an objective moral order. I think most other people think or presuppose that there is too and I guess we all think, then, that human beings can become aware of it. We think we do know of some things that are wrong and some things that are right. There may be a lot more to the objective moral order than we have a grasp of. If we were more perceptive, if our vision wasn't

obscured so much by the smoke of our wrongdoing, by sin, then perhaps we would see much more deeply into the objective moral order.
But certainly we all do see something of it.

GERARD J. HUGHES

Morality has to do with what enables human beings to flourish.
How humans can flourish will, as Aristotle pointed out, and as has
often been repeated since then, depend on the kind of beings that
humans are. What it takes for a human being to flourish will depend
on our common human nature and on the particular qualities which
each person possesses as an individual, and on the environment,
physical and social, in which that person lives.

If something like that picture is correct, it will follow that morality
will require us to treat different people in different ways, both because
of their individual differences, and because of the different settings in
which we encounter them. There will be no one single recipe for
enabling a person to achieve their optimum development. Morality
should reflect the complexity of human beings and their various physical and social environments, even when it can correctly be said that
these environments are far from ideal for humans to have to live in.

Unless morality is based upon accurate information about people's
abilities, and about the various ways in which they are affected by their
surroundings, it will inevitably fail to achieve its purpose. It follows
that our moral judgments will be no better than the factual information on which those judgments are based, and will have to be changed
in the light of new and more correct factual information. Moral principles cannot sensibly be formulated independently of our knowledge
of biology, psychology, economics, and the human sciences generally.
To the extent that our knowledge in these areas is incomplete or grossly inadequate, so will our grasp of moral truth be uncertain.

There is also a deeper reason why moral truth is difficult to attain.
The notion of human flourishing is, unfortunately, far from clear,
quite apart from the unclarities involved in deciding how that flourishing is to be brought about. We understand human nature sufficiently to be able to speak with reasonable clarity about physical
health, which is at least one aspect of human flourishing. We are much
less clear about mental and emotional health, and hence about the distinction between, for instance, flourishing eccentricity and mental
imbalance. More generally, though there are clear cases in which we
can say that the way a person is living is dehumanizing, and clear cases

where we can see that someone has lived a richly fulfilled life, there are many examples where such judgment is very hard to make.

We must carefully separate two kinds of difficulty, then; the difficulty in knowing whether a human life is a worthwhile human life or not; and the difficulty of knowing by what precise steps a worthwhile human life can be fostered. I suspect that, although the first difficulty perhaps presents more difficult philosophical problems, we are generally more confident of our ability to recognize when a life has been worthwhile, or when a way of living is dehumanizing. There are of course areas of uncertainty even here, and some controversies over lifestyle have become particularly acrimonious. Nonetheless, I think that, provided we really take the time and care to look and to understand, we are usually able to form a judgment with reasonable confidence. On the other hand, the second difficulty mentioned above is often much less tractable. Both with regard to individuals, and in connection with society as a whole, we often realize that we simply do not know what practical steps must be taken to achieve a situation in which people are fulfilled, even when we are largely in agreement about what "fulfilment" amounts to.

One might at this point simply throw in one's hand, and say that the truth is not to be found, or, worse, say that there is here no question of truth at all. That would be a mistake. We do have a reasonably good grasp of the ways in which our judgments on all these matters can be warped or misled or ill-founded. We know the kinds of information which would enable us to do better for ourselves and one another: information about biology, psychology, economics, social structures, and social psychology; better knowledge of precisely how we interact with the environment; and, on a more personal level, better knowledge of the talents, weaknesses, and needs of the individuals with whom we live and work. So we know in what direction progress in moral knowledge is to be made.

It is nevertheless tempting at this point to shortcut the painstaking road to better moral knowledge suggested in the preceding paragraph, and to appeal at once to religious revelation. But such a view is open to serious objections. Firstly, we need to be able to distinguish between alleged revelations and genuine revelations; secondly, we need to know how even genuine revelations apply to individual cases (for instance, even if it is accepted as a revelation that we ought not to kill, that still does not settle questions about the proper moral response to, say, irreversible coma). But to decide these questions, we need to use our minds, and our existing knowledge. In particular, we need to use our existing moral knowledge, which implies that not all moral knowledge can come from religious revelation.

To sum up, I would wish to say much the same about the relation between ethics and religion as I say about science and religion (Great Question 11). We should seek to ensure that our various moral beliefs are coherent with one another. If our existing moral beliefs and the content of revelation conflict, then both sets of beliefs must in principle be questioned. Revelation should be allowed to challenge our "secular" morality; and equally, our secular morality should challenge our understanding of revelation and its practical implications.

GEORGE F. R. ELLIS

Are moral principles relative to culture and society?

Do moral values have any real meaning, or are they purely relative to culture? Here is perhaps where the strongest disagreement exists: for example, I have been told how the anthropological ethic denies any absolute moral value system. I believe there is a misunderstanding underlying this statement, arising from that academic tradition which completely divorces analysis from useful application of analysis. It is clear that anthropologists or sociologists must suspend moral judgment as they study various societies, if they indeed want to learn how different social systems operate. This is not at all the same thing as saying that moral judgment is not possible. For example, there are traditional societies where firstborn children are slain (in Kenya); widows are burnt on funeral pyres at their husband's funeral (India); children are mutilated by having segments of their fingers cut off by their parents as part of a growing-up ritual (South Africa); cliterodectomy takes place (Egypt). While there may in each case be good reasons why these practices have developed, I resist strenuously the concept that they are all as morally acceptable as say the practices espoused by Ghandi. And the essential point is made above: one has to – explicitly or implicitly – make moral judgements whenever choices are made between competing policy decisions in the real world. Academics can if they wish divorce themselves from making such choices; this simply defines their own disciplines as of no practical use in terms of facing real-world problems. The reality of the moral choices to be made remains (and even the academic's own work contains value-laden assumptions, through the way they choose what to study).

If one truly accepts the relativist view of morality, one is bound to say there was nothing wrong with what Hitler did in the Holocaust, this was just one particular pattern of social behaviour among many which are morally equivalent, for there are no absolute moral standards. Or to bring the theme up to date, one must then maintain that the subjugation of women in many traditional societies is just as acceptable as the trend to women's liberation that has been evident in many Western societies in recent decades. I believe that whatever may be said about moral relativism in theory, in practice ethically aware people agree that there are practices that are simply unacceptable, or at least are at a lower ethical level than other practices; and this kind of view informs policy decisions.

On this view the disagreements across cultures are to some extent an expression of different degrees of moral awareness or development in those cultures; in fact there is a process of evolution of moral awareness taking place, that may be discerned in human history (for example, there is almost universal disapproval of slavery nowadays, as compared with its widespread acceptance a relatively short time ago). This is undoubtedly a contentious claim, but I believe it reflects what people in reality believe – as evidenced in how they behave – as opposed to what they may claim, on the basis of some theoretical system that is not in fact made manifest in the way they run their lives. To give a specific example: I believe most anthropologists and sociologists will fight for women's freedom in their own societies as if there is real meaning to this action, rather than just being an expression of their own culture which has no more justification than the attitude to women in societies where they are treated as slaves. Unfashionable as it may be, I propose that those societies where women are treated as equal to men are more advanced in their ethical understanding than those where this is not true. I understand that in so doing I am claiming precedence for my own particular (partly socially determined) moral understanding over rival views that are equally strongly held; nevertheless, I defend this position.

KEITH WARD

What do you make of the claims of evolutionary ethics?

Some proponents of evolutionary psychology claim that morality is nothing but a set of genetically imprinted behavior patterns which have been selected because they favored the survival of certain genes over others. This is a classic example of the aptly named "genetic fallacy", the mistake of thinking that to show how something developed is to show what it is. Of course morality uses as its basic data dispositions and behavior-patterns which have been selected through evolution. Appeal to natural selection gives an illuminating (but hardly exhaustive) explanation of how some of these dispositions have come to exist. It explains the mixture of lust, aggression, altruism, and submission which characterizes human nature.

Rational morality, however, supervenes on these dispositions, and asks questions about the consistency and universalizability of basic human goods, which no evolutionary account can answer. Insofar as morality is rational, it will not endorse acts just because they enable genes to survive, at whatever cost to personal happiness. Insofar as morality is genetically imprinted, it will not be amenable to reason at all, and seeking a rational morality will be useless. As Dawkins says, rational reflection "enables us to escape from the tyranny of our genes." But that is an admission that a solely genetic account of morality will always miss what is distinctive and valuable about human life.

If there is a creator God, one would expect that, in addition to purely rational considerations, there will be human discernments of the will and purpose of God which give to morality an ultimate authority which overrides self-interest, and a faith that moral commitment will not be in vain. Evolutionary ethics cannot support the supreme authority of morality, and it undermines any belief that the universe is oriented to the fulfillment of a moral purpose, which it is human destiny to cooperate in realizing. In short, evolutionary ethics denies what is, even from a humanist viewpoint, most distinctive about human existence, that which gives it dignity and sanctity, the capacity for moral reflection and action. From a religious viewpoint, it denies the deepest purpose of human existence, the free development of a relationship of joyful obedience to the will of God, within a community of justice, peace, and love. Human beings are certainly animals, but they are animals raised to the dignity of children of the creator God. In failing to see this, evolutionary ethics gives a drastically impoverished and grossly inaccurate account of human nature.

ATHEISM

Great Question 9: *Atheism – the rejection of the existence of God – is an intellectual option embraced by several thinkers. How do you explain atheism?*

ALVIN PLANTINGA

First of all, atheism goes back a long way. It is not an invention of, say, the Enlightenment, although it has been much more prominent since the Enlightenment. In the Psalms we read of the fool that said in his heart there is no God. And Jonathan Edwards, in the eighteenth century, talks at some length about atheism, about how it is much more prevalent now (then) than it was 200 years earlier.

How do you explain it? That is a really tough question. As I say, it is much more prevalent, prominent since the Enlightenment. But I don't know how to explain atheism. I think fundamentally it arises out of sin, although not necessarily sin on the part of the atheist in question. Atheism is a kind of blindness, a failure to see something that is very important in the world. Where does this blindness come from?

I think part of the responsibility has to be laid at the doors of Christians themselves. The spectacle of Christians, Protestants and Catholics, fighting, killing each other, carrying on as they did during the years of religious wars in the sixteenth and seventeenth centuries was an extremely unedifying spectacle. That turned lots and lots of people against Christianity. If this is what Christians are like, if this is what being a Christian entails or involves, they wanted nothing whatever to do with it. This spectacle of Christians at each other's throats is one partial explanation of atheism. And that these Christians were at each other's throats, I think, is in part a matter of spiritual pride. Catholics and Protestants should have responded to each other very differently; they should have seen that at a deep level they agreed. They agreed that there is such a Person as God and that He has this plan of salvation; they agreed that human beings were created in His image; they agreed on all the main features of the

Apostles' Creed and the Nicene Creed and so on. So why were they torturing and killing each other? They should have recognized that all the things where they had the right to be really sure were things on which they agreed; what they disagreed about were areas where the scriptures speak much less plainly. One's degree of belief should be tempered by that degree of plainness. One should believe the central elements of Christianity with maximal firmness; the degree of firmness should taper off as one gets to the periphery. There Christians can legitimately disagree. So, I think, one part of the rejection of the existence of God in modern society has to be attributed to the sin of earlier generations of Christians. But that is only a part. I would suggest that you take a look at Michael Buckley's *At the Origins of Modern Atheism* (Yale University Press, 1987).

RICHARD SWINBURNE

How do I explain atheism? Why are some people atheists? Well, I think the answer to that will depend on who they are and when they lived and what are the influences they were open to. But, if we are talking about atheists in our time, I'm sure that for them, as for all of us, part of the explanation of why they have the beliefs they do is the kind of intellectual environment they have been open to. But humans have the opportunity of going out and looking for the truth more fully than their environment has taught them and one explanation of atheism is, therefore, that although the persons concerned have been influenced by a certain class of arguments, they have not taken the trouble, or, alternatively, have not been fortunate enough to find the counter-arguments against atheism. Of course, it is not only a matter of argument. It is a matter of personal experience. Some people have been lucky enough to have an experience of the presence of God and others not so.

   Again, part of the reason why there are so many atheists around in our time is obviously is going to be a historical explanation. This will draw attention first to the great influence and prestige of science which has, mistakenly, led a lot of people to think that, therefore, there is less place for God in the universe. I give [in my answer to Great Question 11] my reasons for thinking that was a mistaken view of the relevance of science. But nevertheless it is a view that some people for wrong reasons have had, and has therefore led to atheism being more prevalent. Another reason, I think, why atheism is so prevalent in our time is because people came to think of the Bible, the, as it were, vehicle of Christian truth, as somehow shown to be false by the discovery that the world is older than four thousand years BC, or that various of the human authors of the Bible got certain historical or scientific things wrong. Therefore, people have concluded the Bible must be false and, therefore, since the Bible was so closely connected with the truth of the Christian religion, that must be false and, therefore, since that's the main form of religion people have been aware of in the West, therefore, religion itself must be false. Over-literal interpretation of the Bible, in particular in the centuries from the Reformation until the nineteenth century, has its share of responsibility for all this. Increasingly religious people tended to interpret the Bible more and more literally as we got to the nineteenth century. And then suddenly the discovery that the world was very old and some of the minor details of biblical history were not as the Bible recorded them had a tremendous effect on people's religious beliefs because they had interpreted the Bible in such a literal way. But if you look at the history of Biblical interpretation over the past two millennia, you find that this very literal way of taking the Bible is itself a product of fairly modern times and there was a long, long tradition, from the second century AD onwards until the fifteenth century, that a great deal of the Bible had to be taken not literally. There were rules which were devised by Origen and Augustine as to which passages you should interpret literally and which not. The basic rule was: "Take something literally if you don't know any reason why not to; but if you do have other reasons for believing that, if taken literally, it would be false, then don't take it literally, take it metaphorically in some sense." And it was on those grounds that Augustine and Origen argued that various things in the Bible which they believed to be false if taken literally (and they believed that on grounds of what they believed about science and history) should be taken metaphorically. So there was a long tradition of taking the Bible none too literally when it talked about science and history. That tradition tended to be forgotten. People by the nineteenth century thought, if the Bible says, or seems to say, in the first chapter (when this is taken in isolation from the rest of the Bible, and the tradition of the Church's interpretation of the Bible) that the world was created in seven days, it meant the world was created in seven days and, therefore, if somebody showed that it came into being over a much longer period, it followed that there was no God because literal interpretation of the Bible was closely connected with the central truths of religion. As I say, I think this was a great misfortune, this growing up of the over-literal interpretation of the Bible, and this has quite a share in the development of atheism in modern times.

GERARD J. HUGHES

In my view, there are two main reasons why people deny that there is a God. The first is that the intellectual case for the existence of God is not beyond all possible question. God is by nature quite different from any of the objects of our experience, with the result that our attempts to describe God are indirect and imperfect. To say that God exists is therefore to make a statement which is unclear in itself; and most religious believers will point out that God is in the end mysterious, beyond our intellectual grasp. Many atheists would see this unclarity as a sign of weakness. Moreover, the reasons for believing that there is a God are complex. Theism is a large-scale interpretation of our experience quite generally, and the data can quite plausibly be "read" otherwise. The evil in the world is the most obvious feature of the universe which might make an atheistic interpretation seem intellectually attractive, clear where theism is at best mysterious, unpretentious where the claims of religion seem over-ambitious.

A second explanation of why atheism is an attractive view is that many, perhaps all, religions have supported views which are demonstrably false and practices which are superstitious or immoral. While it would of course be argued by believers that these mistakes do not touch the essential core of religious belief, it is not difficult to see how other people conclude that religious belief is simply a combination of bad science and indefensible conduct. In contrast, atheism can be presented as a means of liberation from the infantilism of religion and the tyranny of dogma, and as the essential framework for a human race come of age.

I give [in my answer to Great Question 11] my reasons for supposing that religion and science need not conflict. Dissociating theism from bad science should not in principle be at all difficult. It is rather more difficult, I suspect, to ensure that religion is not used to support immoral practices, from mass murder to psychological manipulation, or superstition. Religious beliefs can be very powerful, and the temptation to harness this power for ends which have nothing to do with religion is likely to remain strong. Where religion is thus abused, atheism will always have its principled defenders.

Of course, just as there are religious bigots, so there are atheists with equally closed minds and inflamed crusading passions. They deserve one another. The proper response to principled atheists, on the other hand, is for religious believers to be equally principled, equally intellectually honest, and equally open to rational argument.

HUGO MEYNELL

Why are many thinkers atheists? Well, we are back at the problem of evil; that is a good reason why people deny the existence of God. Again, some tend to think or assume, as Wilfred Sellars puts it, that science is the measure of all things, of what is that it is, and of what is not that it is not. Of course, if you take these restrictions in a narrow sense, then they lead to atheism; taken in a broad sense, I have already argued that they do not. Also it is thought by many people, including the majority of contemporary philosophers, that none of the arguments for the existence of God are sound. Some philosophers have even claimed that it is strictly meaningless to say that God exists; though it is much less fashionable than it was in the heyday of logical positivism fifty years or so ago. The reason alleged was, roughly, that one couldn't conceivably see or hear or touch God. But you can't touch or hear or smell electrons or positrons, or for that matter the thoughts and feelings of other people; but they are there all the same. In general, apart from the problem of evil, I think that it is partly scientism, partly positivism, which has made atheism seem convincing to so many. I find it useful to divide atheists into two overlapping types, theoretical atheists and what you might call existential atheists. Existential atheists are people like Karl Marx and Friedrich Nietzsche, who rightly inveigh against the harm that is so often done to people in the name of religion, but wrongly (though all too understandably) regard theism as incompatible with a fully actualized human life. The complaints of existential atheists have to be taken with the utmost seriousness, because I am sorry to say that there is almost nothing so nasty, that some religious believers will not get up to in the name of God. In the Epistle to the Romans, St. Paul talks about believers making the name of God stink among the heathen. When you think of some of the abominable actions by representatives of the churches which have come to light recently, and the ingenuity and social ruthlessness displayed by them and their colleagues in covering them up, you can see that the existential atheist has a lot going for her.

JOSEF SEIFERT

The intellectual option of atheism has many roots. Some of these reasons we touch upon in discussing the problem of evil [Great Question 12]. There I try to point out how the choice of atheism is quite comprehensible in the face of evil, but nevertheless irrational and objectively not justified by the existence of evil.

But atheism has many other roots: the pride of people who do not want to accept their total dependence on God, and who wish to assert their own character as supreme in the universe; the wish that there not be any moral order and supreme judge but that we can live according to the arbitrariness of our own desires and wishes, etc.

But there are also countless intellectual errors such as materialism, determinism, etc., which can lead a person to adopt atheism.

Yet, none of the countless reasons and grounds for atheism can be justified rationally, as follows from the discussion of the arguments for the existence of God [Great Question 10].

Part IV:

IS THERE A GOD?

THE EXISTENCE OF GOD

Great Question 10: *The existence of God has been one of the most hotly debated issues in the history of human thought. What are your own conclusions on the question of God's existence and on what basis do you affirm or deny the existence of God?*

RICHARD SWINBURNE

I affirm the existence of God. I do so on the grounds that the hypothesis that there is a God can explain everything which we find around us.

Scientific theories aim to explain, each of them, a limited range of data, some of them quite a big range of data, but limited all the same. Quantum theory, for example, aims to explain the stability of the atom, the photoelectric effect, the Compton effect, the distribution of black body radiation, and so on and so forth. And we accept such a scientific theory on the grounds that, if the theory is true, we would expect to find the data which we observe; we wouldn't expect to find them otherwise; and the hypothesis is a simple one. The extent to which these three criteria are satisfied – first that, if the hypothesis is true, you would expect to find the data; second, that you wouldn't expect to find the data in the normal course of things; and third, that the hypothesis is simple – to that extent, the data provide evidence for the hypothesis, they make it to that extent, to the extent to which those criteria are satisfied, likely to be true.

Now, I think that theism doesn't explain merely a limited set of data but it explains all the observable phenomena we find, of the more general and of the more limited kinds, and that it satisfies well those three criteria for good explanations. It explains the existence of the universe, its conformity to order, in two senses, in the sense that it has simple scientific laws, and in the sense that there are, within the universe, animals and human beings, that is to say, particular loci of order; it explains the phenomenon of consciousness; it explains the facts of reported accounts of miracles, in particular those associated with the origin of Christian religion; and also the phenomenon of religious experience. I have selected a range of very general facts which we can all observe and more particular facts within the universe and each of these, it seems to me, are such that we wouldn't expect to find them in the normal course of things. If there is a God, we do expect to find them and the hypothesis of the existence of God is a simple one.

For example, the fact of there being a universe at all, how very odd it is, how unlikely a priori it is that there should be a physical universe. But if there is a God, in the sense of an omnipotent, omniscient, perfectly good, perfectly free, etc., center of being, then He has the power to bring about the universe and He has reason to do so in that a universe is a good thing and provides a theater in which finite creatures can develop, can mold their own characters, and can contribute to the world. And the hypothesis of theism is a simple hypothesis. Let me say why. The God whose existence we are considering is, by definition, omnipotent, omniscient, perfectly good, perfectly free, and so on, and I think that the various essential properties, the properties that make God God, really boil down to three: He is all-powerful, omnipotent, that is to say there are no limits, apart from those of logic, to what He can do; He is perfectly wise, He is omniscient, there are no limits, apart from those of logic, to what He knows; and He is perfectly free, that is to say, nothing from without influences Him as to how He will choose. Other properties, I believe, like perfect goodness, derive from those three essential properties.

Now, in postulating a personal kind of being who is infinitely this, that and the other, we are postulating one being, not many beings, and we are postulating the simplest kind of person there could be. A person is an individual with a certain amount of power over the world and with a certain number of beliefs about it and a certain amount of freedom to do things in it. But the persons we come across are persons of limited power, just so much and no more, limited knowledge and so on. But science always seeks to postulate simple properties in the objects which it postulates and a simple property, one very obvious kind of simple property, is of a zero or infinite degree of some quality. A scientist in his hypothesis will always postulate that something has zero rest mass or infinite velocity or qualities like that if it can, that is to say if such a hypothesis is consistent with the data. So theism is postulating just one being, not many beings but one being of the personal kind, but the simplest kind a person could be because the personal qualities are present in this being to an infinite degree. Put another way there are zero limits to them and, therefore, this is the kind of zero-infinity character of properties which science values.

So the theist can explain the existence of the universe by postulating one being which brings about the many bits of the universe. His existence makes it likely there will be a universe, one wouldn't ordinarily expect to find a universe, and it is a simple hypothesis. And likewise with the other things which provide the evidence of theism. The universe is an orderly universe. Things behave in accordance with simple scientific laws. If there is a God, He has reason to make it that way because simple laws mean that things behave in simple ways and the universe will therefore exhibit a certain beauty. Above all, if there are simple laws governing the behavior of material objects, then finite human beings can understand those laws and use them to mold the world. If, for example, it is a consequence of laws of nature that, if I sow seeds and water them, they will produce plants, then if such a law governs the world, human beings in the world can understand that law and use this regularity, this law, to produce plants.

But if the world is just chaotic, then people, limited beings, will never be able to learn about it and use it to mold the world. So if God is interested in creating limited, finite beings who can contribute to the world and grow, He needs to make the world an orderly place, with the sort of order that finite beings can understand. So if we find that the world does have that sort of order, then that is reason to suppose that the world was made by God. And so on with more and more detailed phenomena of the world. The fact of the world, its general orderliness, the existence of conscious beings, the particular phenomena of history, above all, the central phenomena of the events of Christ's life, death and reported resurrection. All of this is well explained [by the existence of God] going down to the most private and small-scale phenomena of individual religious experience. In all of these cases, my suggestion is that here we have a simple hypothesis which is such that you would expect to find these phenomena if the world is sustained and guided by God. You wouldn't normally expect to find them. Therefore these phenomena, these data, these bits of evidence, are evidence of theism.

So, in summary, I think the theistic hypothesis can explain the whole range of phenomena we find around us, including all those that science deals with, that is to say things being ordered by scientific laws, including the general phenomena of history and including some rather special phenomena to which religion draws our attention.

The divine attributes are omnipotence, omniscience and perfect freedom and such properties as perfect goodness, I think, derive from them.

ALVIN PLANTINGA

The existence of God has been hotly debated, although there have been literally millions, maybe billions, of people who have accepted belief in God without any debate or any argument at all. It is not primarily a topic of debate, except among a certain kind of intellectual constituency in the Western world and substantially since the Enlightenment. But taken in itself, it is a whole lot like, say, belief in other minds. Philosophers have argued about other minds too, about whether it is reasonable to believe that there are other minds. But all human beings, apart from philosophical discussions, do believe in other minds; and the vast majority of human beings, while perhaps they haven't all believed specifically in God, have certainly believed in something like the theistic God, somebody who controls nature, someone to whom they are obligated, to whom they owe allegiance and obedience and so on.

As to my own conclusions on this question: I certainly do believe in the existence of God, but I don't believe by way of conclusion from arguments or because I think the probabilities point in that direction. It seems to me that I experience God. I experience God in a variety of ways, just as lots and lots of people do: in church, in reading the Bible, in nature, in human relationships, in a thousand different ways. And so my reasons for accepting theistic belief, belief in God, are reasons more like my reasons for believing in other people, or that there is an external world, or in a memory judgment. It is not a conclusion from an argument. It is something more immediate, something much more existential and experiential.

GERARD J. HUGHES

Any philosopher who claims, as I do, that there is a God, has to reply to the arguments advanced by Hume and Kant, both of whom, albeit on rather different grounds, would dispute that we can have any good grounds for saying that God exists. They accurately pinpointed the key issues.

The classical and medieval tradition had confidently asserted that, if there exists anything at all rather than nothing, there must exist a being whose nonexistence is impossible; and that being can properly be identified with the God of the Judeo-Christian tradition. But Hume saw no reason to go further than simply to accept it as a brute fact that the universe exists. We have no knowledge, in his view, of any causal necessity in the world, and no means of reasoning from the existence of one thing to the existence of anything else. For all we know, events can simply happen, things can simply be there. Nothing is required for anything to exist other than the mere fact that it does. So we should beware of projecting our desire for explanation and intelligibility on to the world. The world is simply given, and its patterned regularity might well be nothing more than coincidence.

I find this position simply incredible. The ordered regularity of the universe is too all-pervasive to be sheer coincidence, and the success of scientific inquiry is surely best explained on the assumption that the universe consists of beings with stable natures which causally interact with one another in largely determinate ways. Events in the universe do not just simply happen, they are caused to happen.

With that much, Kant would have agreed. What he would not accept is that we can ask about the universe as a whole why it is there at all, and expect to discover the answer. To ask for a cause of the universe is to ask for something which quite transcends our experience. We have no possible way of showing that the universe as a whole might not itself exist of necessity, rather than because it is caused by some other, transcendent, being. In short, Kant accepts that the question "Why is there anything rather than nothing at all?" must be answered by saying that there must exist something whose nonexistence is simply impossible; but he can see no way of showing that this necessary being might not simply be the universe itself.

There is no simple counter to this position. Still, the classical tradition did advance reasons to show that any being whose non-existence was impossible must be quite unlike the universe of our experience; in particular, it must be timeless, unchanging, and not structured as the kinds of things in our universe are, simply because they are things of such-and-such a kind rather than some other. These arguments are highly technical, and a detailed exposition of them is not possible here. I believe, however, that despite their difficulty the classical arguments are basically sound, and offer a reasonable basis for belief in God.

If these arguments are valid, it becomes impossible to identify God with the world in any pantheistic fashion. While I can see the attraction of identifying God with the universe as a whole, with the consequence that we ourselves are parts of God, I would myself find it difficult to reconcile such a position with any form of the more traditional belief that God is to be worshipped.

In saying that the ultimate basis for my belief in God is to be found in some difficult philosophical arguments, I am well aware that these grounds are remote from the ordinary everyday experience of religious practice. I think such remoteness is almost unavoidable when one is speaking of the ultimate grounds for any of our beliefs, about God or anything else. I would, of course, not wish to deny the importance of many other features of religious living; notably, the experience of prayer, of the moral life, and the widespread human conviction that our lives must find their meaning beyond the grave. These features of human experience have always been, and remain, important elements of religious belief. My own view, however, is that while they can be legitimately invoked as part of an overall picture once the philosophical position has been reasonably established, they cannot provide an adequate substitute for a proper philosophical grounding. I take the same view of revealed religion quite generally. That any experience or event can properly be regarded as embodying a divine revelation seems to me to depend on our having already shown that it is reasonable to suppose that there exists a God from whom such revelations might come.

BRIAN LEFTOW

Some people expect philosophers to try to "prove" God's existence, and assent to it only if some hulking brute of an argument drags them kicking and screaming through the church door. But arguments cannot do that. Arguments do not compel our assent. They merely appeal for it. A proof is not an argument so compelling that one cannot reject its conclusion, but one so worthy that an ideally rational person would accept its conclusion. Suppose I show with impeccable logic that if 2+2=4, then God exists. If you understand the argument, and grant the connection between premise and conclusion, you still have a choice. You can grant that God exists, or you can avoid this by denying that 2+2=4. The argument does not force you to do either. It just sets up the choice. Which choice you make depends on which seems more implausible – that "2+2=4" is not true, or that there is a God.

Some propositions seem implausible due to arguments, or thoughts we can put into argument form. But it cannot always be so. Eventually, we hit bedrock. Some things just do seem implausible to us, and others do not. These perceptions can change. Arguments can help to change them. But while we have them, they and not arguments are the final arbiters of our beliefs. As this is so, I do not think that philosophic argument can ever move someone to theism – or atheism – unless that person is also prepared on another, more intuitive level to make the move.

To each of us, the world *looks* as if there is a God or as if there is none. It either does or does not seem that a hand is guiding one's life, or that one's life has a purpose which is not one's own invention. Those one loves do or do not seem too wonderful to be products of sheer accident. The world seems a fundamentally good place, despite its evils, or a bare neutral fact, or a horror. The religious people one knows seem good and kind, or evil and hypocritical; those whose goodness most impresses one are religious or irreligious. Or perhaps all this is just ambiguous. At first one may not associate the word "God" at all with these feelings or perceptions. All the same, if the world seems good, meaningful, purposed, etc., it seems to be such as a God would make it, and if the world seems neutral or evil, etc., it seems not to be such as a God would make it – and when we meet the idea of God, we realize this. It is possible that a good argument may get us to believe (or disbelieve) in God despite the way the world seems to us. But a good argument may also convince us by helping to change the way the world seems to us, or helping us see that the world does seem a certain way to us, and even the best argument will have a hard time retaining our conviction if it does not eventually bring some change of perception.

For me, two things made the difference. One was a sense that the New Testament got good and evil right. It would be hard to overstate the force of my feeling here: it seemed to me that if I was wrong about this, then I could see nothing about good and evil at all, and so would never know any truth about them.[1] The other was a thought I would now put this way: the Christian moral outlook is not separable from the Christian metaphysic and worldview. It would be surprising if Christian ethical claims were true and yet the worldview on which they rest were wholly false, for the way the world really is determines what is really good. Again, if only those who believe in God see good and evil entirely aright, this is reason (if there are truths about good and evil) to think that the theism which helps them see so clearly is true. For it would be remarkable if holding a set of false metaphysical beliefs were the best route to learning true moral beliefs.

So I became a Christian and a theist because I was drawn to the
Christian vision of the good. This does not seem to me an unusual
route to faith. Such writers as Augustine and Aquinas see the will as
more active in coming to believe that God exists than it is in coming
to believe that there is a cat on the mat. They do not mean that believers in God just decide to believe in God, in default of convincing evidence for or against God. Both Augustine and Aquinas see the will as
an appetite, a desire or love for the good as best we can understand
it. So when they emphasize the will's role in faith, their point is that
in large measure, one comes to believe in God because the goodness
of God as presented in some stories about Him draws one's love.

This is not to say that philosophical arguments for God's existence
have no role in faith. They can *help* move one to belief. They can also
help confirm one's beliefs. Tragedy may make the firmest believer
doubt; philosophy may remind the believer that such doubt should
not extend to God's existence. Good arguments for God's existence
can also show that a basic part of theist belief meets the strictest standards of belief-worthiness. This lends credit to the rest of one's religious beliefs. If it is "provable" that there is *some* God, it is the more
reasonable to have an opinion about *which* God there is.

Arguments for God's existence also reassure by letting believers
answer unbelievers' challenges. Some charge that belief in God is
irrational. If there are good enough arguments that God exists, the
charge of irrationality falls on the atheist, not the theist: it is irrational to deny a conclusion one ought to accept. Even if there are
also strong arguments that God does not exist, good enough arguments that God exists are strong reason to call theism rational. For
they are reason to suspect errors in the arguments against God, and
if one has such reason, one has reason to maintain one's own theism.[2] Some charge that belief in God is an emotional crutch, or an
instrument of domination by capitalists, white males, or other
bogeymen. They seem to think that one should not believe in God
because one abets something bad by doing so. A solid argument for
God's existence lets one dismiss these cavils. For if one shows that a
proposition is true, one shows that one has a right to believe it –
period. If one believes in God because theism is comforting or useful, that may show that one is not good or wise, but does not show
that one ought instead to be an atheist. That we should not believe
the *way* we do or for the reason we do does not imply that we
should not believe *what* we do.[3] The truth deserves believing, just

because it is true. The question of motive becomes irrelevant in the presence of good arguments.

I think there are in fact some very good philosophical arguments for God's existence.

JOSEF SEIFERT

Concerning the first part of your question, I affirm the existence of God both on the grounds of human reason and on those of faith in Jesus Christ and in Divine Revelation. I thus not only reject atheism but also pantheism as well as the "dialectical theism" by which, for example, John Macquarrie in his Gifford Lectures in the 1980s sought to replace "classical theism" and meant to offer a position "in-between theism and atheism."[4]

While I do think that traditional philosophy of God and theology ought to develop more genuinely personalistic metaphysical categories and abandon certain elements of a Greek metaphysics of God which risk to lose the sense for the entire newness of "being-a-person" and seek to define the divine perfections in an inadequate way, I basically defend the arguments for the existence of God along the lines of classical theism. Yet I seek to establish theism also philosophically on firm metaphysical and personalistic grounds. Thus the certitude of conviction that God exists, if it is thus founded, is totally opposed to atheism in any conceivable form.

This sounds simple and obvious enough but we have to recognize that most philosophers today have adopted in one way or another the epistemological subjectivism or at least the radical critique of classical and medieval metaphysics which German Idealism, British and Austrian empiricism and positivism have launched against the very foundations of a philosophy of God, and thereby also against the foundations of any religion which recognizes a God who exists wholly independently of history and human consciousness and about whom one can know more than that He is an X (or a *Umgreifendes* in the sense of Karl Jaspers).

These foundations lie chiefly in epistemology and metaphysics. Any proper philosophy of God requires and presupposes necessarily a realist epistemology which recognizes the ability of the human mind discovering realities that exist independently of human subjectivity.[5] And it rests on the foundation that the human intellect cannot just penetrate into those attributes of the world that are directly accessible in experience but can reach a radically different, transcendent, and divine being, given and accessible to our intellect "through the mirror of the world." Both of these grounds of a philosophy of God have been shaken in modern philosophy.

And thus not only atheism flourishes in a thousand open and even more camouflaged forms, but also many philosophical defenses of the existence and attributes of God move only on the levels of linguistic or phenomenological analyses which deny that their results truly reach the transcendent being of God and divine attributes which belong to Him, entirely independently from our subjective ideas. Therefore many of the attempts to defend God over the last century have been cryptoatheistic.

Even in some of the best philosophies of God in the twentieth century, which move within a classical realm, we find both traditional and new personalistic categories, when applied to God, confined to a non-metaphysical, psychological, historical, or linguistic sphere. Hand in hand with abandoning the categories of classical philosophy of God and of theology, also the applicability of the notion of personhood to God is often defended today on non-metaphysical grounds, claiming with Martin Buber that "the concept of personal being is indeed completely incapable of declaring what God's essential being is, but it is both permitted and necessary to say that God is also a person."[6]

I tried to revive a truly metaphysical and objectivist philosophy of God, which holds that indeed God's essential being, and it alone, is fully and perfectly personal, good, just, knowing, living, etc. Such a metaphysics of God is both in line with the perennial contributions of philosophers of the past and with modern phenomenologist realism and personalism.[7]

As a philosopher, I occupied myself with many different demonstrations of the existence of God which I deem to be cogent and conclusive. I recognize a great number of very different arguments that demonstrate the existence of God, both singly and most of all in their unity. In fact, I think that some of these arguments (for example that from causality or contingent existence) need others in order to be complete and not only to demonstrate the existence of a necessary and uncaused being, but that of God as an infinitely perfect being. Let me summarize some of these arguments in a sketchy form:

First, there is the series of classical cosmological arguments [outlined in 1–4 below] which proceed from the existence of the world and which possess a well-known expression in the "five ways" of St. Thomas Aquinas. I recognize their validity although I believe that they need to be reformulated and rethought, to avoid certain mistakes in their conception, and to base them on more ultimate metaphysical foundations than those that are apparent from St. Thomas's texts.

1. *The argument from motion and temporality to an eternal being*: The first of these arguments starts from the nature and existence of motion, which I interpret as comprising all change and temporality in the world. This argument recognizes that a continually changing and temporal being, which always moves from moment to moment of its existence, and whose very being is constantly renewed and receives new actuality in time, cannot account for itself. For it can neither explain why it continues to exist and to re-emerge from nothingness always anew, nor why it came to be (since no being that moves in time can be beginningless and actually infinite in duration), nor from whence it receives its always new present being. Neither its past being, which is no longer, nor its future being, which is not yet, nor its present being, which flees in a flash into the nothingness of the past, can contain the source of an ever renewed presentiality of being-in-time. From understanding this we grasp three further metaphysical facts: (1) Only an eternal being that possesses its entire reality in an everlasting present can account for itself, not a temporal one. (2) Therefore, the eternal being alone can also contain the sufficient reason for temporal being. (3) Moreover, the absolute and eternal Being cannot produce the temporal world by any necessity rooted in its eternal nature (which would make the world eternal and could not give rise to time and change, as Parmenides and many other philosophers saw) but only through freedom. Thus this argument ascends from a changing, temporal world to the existence of an eternal and everlasting, self-explanatory, omnipresent, and free being.

2. *The argument from causality to an uncaused first cause*: A second one of these arguments takes its starting point from the existence of causal relations in the world and from the evident principle of causality.

This principle neither implies that *all* beings possess a cause, which (absurd) formulation of the principle of causality would contradict the existence of God as an uncaused cause, as Hume correctly saw, nor that each event follows upon another one according to a law (a general rule), which both contradicts freedom and leads to an antinomy, as Kant pointed out. Above all, the evidence of the principle of causality in its inner necessity says nothing of that sort.

Rather, the principle of causality states that all changes and all contingent beings require[8] an efficient cause, i.e. a cause through the power and agency of which they are brought about and sustained in being. Therefore, no change and no contingent being can possess the sufficient reason for its being or for its being brought about in itself. It follows that an uncaused being alone can possess the reason for its being within itself (namely in its own necessary being and essence). Hence it alone can both account for itself and for all contingent being and change, as well as for all causality in the world. For an endless chain of causes, each of which would be dependent on another one, could never explain causality. Only an absolute beginning of efficient causality that is not dependent on antecedent causes can provide such an explanation. Moreover, only a free agency – which alone does not require further causes for its acting and can explain contingent beings – can originate the contingently existing world and especially free agents in it. Consequently, only a free and uncaused being can explain the ultimate origin of efficient causes and of the world of change and contingent beings. This argument thus arrives at an uncaused being and first free cause, which alone can originate the contingent world and the changes in it, as well as all causality in the finite world.

3. *The argument from contingent existence to a necessary being*: A third one of these arguments is based on the observation that all real beings in this world exist contingently. We can understand, both from the fact that we came into existence and from the non-necessary limitations of all our attributes, that we do exist but could also not exist. But we can understand also in another way – sketched by the young Thomas Aquinas in *De Ente et Essentia* – that all beings in the world exist contingently. For of any of them (for example, of human nature) there can exist other individuals of the same kind which do not in fact exist but are merely possible (for example, other human beings). But no such being which could be multiplied and exist in other individuals which are not yet existent or never will exist, even if it actually exists, exists by necessity. Hence all beings in the world, since their nature can be multiplied in other individuals, exist non-necessarily.

Now it is evident that any being that could not exist or that could not have existed (as all beings in the world) cannot account for itself in the last analysis: for it has no sufficient reason within itself for being rather than not being. Clearly, the non-necessity of existence, the fact that all beings in the world, while they do in fact exist, could also not be at all, is linked to the evidence that no being which exists in a non-necessary manner, can account for its own being. For the existence of all entities in the world does not flow with necessity from their nature and therefore cannot be explained from any principle within those contingent beings or the world.

From thence it becomes evident in a supreme sense that only a being that exists by necessity, and that could not possibly not exist, can both account for itself and contain the sufficient reason for the contingently existing world.

But it can do so only if it is a free, and hence a personal being. For if it acted not by the unforced spontaneity of freedom (which is a perfection that alone can explain, as its correlate, non-necessary existence), but by the necessity of its own essence and existence, the world would have to be divine and itself necessary – which it is not. Ergo the necessary being must cause the contingent one by a free choice.

4. *The insufficiency of the preceding arguments and the fourth way from imperfect beings to "that greater than which nothing can be thought"*: All of these arguments, which prove only an eternal, uncaused, necessarily existing and free origin of the world, are not yet properly speaking proofs of the existence of God; for God is above all the *id quo maius nihil cogitari possit* ("that greater than which nothing can be thought"), i.e. the infinitely perfect being. Without this infinite perfection, He would not be God at all but some other absolute being which, if it were evil, would be more a demon than a god. Therefore, in order to demonstrate the existence of God as possessing the innermost divine attribute of infinite perfection, these three cosmological arguments need to be completed by a fourth one which proceeds from the imperfections and gradation of all good qualities of beings in the world.

Thus the other cosmological arguments are valid only in conjunction with another argument that proves the infinite perfection of God. This applies also and most especially to the fifth cosmological argument which discloses more than the bare existence of God. Like the fourth one, it contains a natural and rational revelation of divine perfections in a more specific form. It proceeds from the empirical and concrete meaning, beauty, value, and all other order and perfection in the world, and infers that so much sense, meaning, order, finality, and beauty, as exist actually in the structure of organisms, in nature and in the human body, as well as in all the wonders of the universe, cannot have come about by accident but require a rational and understanding supreme intellect who is the origin of the world. Also this argument would only demonstrate a supremely intelligent origin of the world but, especially when we think of all the evils in the world, not God as infinitely perfect being. Precisely this, however, can be achieved by the argument from the limited perfection in the world to an infinitely perfect being.

Let us then turn more closely to our fourth cosmological argument that constitutes a new development of Thomas's fourth via. This argument recognizes that any essentially limited perfection (such as all species of being in the world) as well as any accidentally limited perfection, which is limited only in all its embodiments in the world (such as limited life, justice, being, consciousness, freedom, power, wisdom), but in whose essence (*ratio formalis*) we find no limitation, can never answer the Pascalian question: "Why is this being not more or less perfect than it actually is?" In other words, any limited perfection is contingent *in its limits* and thus also in its essence, not only in its existence. Hence a being of limited perfection cannot possess within itself the sufficient reason for its own being and for its own limits. These must be bestowed upon it from the outside. Hence, only an infinitely perfect being, "that greater than which nothing can be thought," can both explain itself and be the ultimate and free cause of the world.

Let us look more closely at this argument which proceeds from the limits of all perfections in the world. All goodness, all consciousness, all life, being, and knowledge in the world are limited. Of all such perfections as goodness, knowledge, life, justice, etc., man and any other being in the world possesses only a limited share. And as Pascal pointed out that no being that is limited in space and time can explain why it is here, rather than there, why it has this measure of its size rather than any other one in the infinite scale of possible mores and lesses, so no finitely perfect being can explain why it has exactly these limitations rather than any others.

Here we note an extremely important difference which St. Anselm of Canterbury discovered[9]: some good qualities or perfections, as that of being gold or all the species of animals and plants, are essentially and intrinsically limited; they do not admit of infinity and are always of finite goodness, most frequently incompatible with each other. To be gold excludes being silver or alive – and is also essentially limited by excluding higher perfections such as life or intelligence. On the other hand, there are many pure perfections: their *ratio formalis* (essence) is such as to make their possession, absolutely speaking, better than their non-possession for any reason. They admit of infinity and one cannot be greater than them without possessing them. Consequently, they must be all compatible with each other, for it contradicts the nature of that, which is absolutely speaking, better to possess than not to possess to exclude any other such perfection. Otherwise, a logical contradiction would arise in that it would be simultaneously better to possess perfection A (a pure perfection) and not to possess it (because it would exclude another pure perfection B). Being, goodness, life, knowlege, consciousness, happiness, intelligence, freedom – these and countless others are such pure perfections of which we can comprehend that they have no in-built limit and that, as long as they are finite, they are not fully themselves.[10] Since they are thus in a certain way "greater than which nothing can be thought," the being which is absolutely speaking "that greater than which nothing can be thought" – God, if He exists, must possess them in their plenitude, while He could not possess any "mixed," any essentially limited, perfection, except in the super-eminent way in which it is included and simultaneously surpassed in God's pure perfections.

Thus from the inexplicability of any finitely perfect being which cannot account for the non-necessary limit of all its perfections and thus also not for its contingent existence, and from the understanding of the pure perfections, our intellect can arrive at the conclusion that only a being of infinite perfection which could not have any less or more of any of its pure perfections, but possesses all of them without any limit, can possibly explain its own being. Likewise, only an absolute being which exists by necessity and through himself, can provide an ultimate explanation and answer to the question why there is something rather than nothing, why the contingently limited beings exists, rather than not. Hence, since there exist finitely perfect beings, an infinitely perfect being must exist.

There exists also a close connection between the fourth and the third cosmological argument: The non-necessity of existence is intimately connected with the imperfection of all beings in the world and with the contingency (non-necessity) which is inseparable from any finitude of perfection, because no finite being can ever answer why it did not receive a greater or lesser share of any of its perfections.

Thus we see, in the "mirror" of the necessary connection between contingency of existence and of limits of perfection, that the divine attributes of infinite perfection and of necessary existence are the only ultimate foundation and explanation of being. Moreover, any being who, like ourselves, exists in such a way that it could also die or not have come to be at all, can never find the ultimate source and explanation of its being in itself or in another limited being but only in God, in a being of infinite perfection.

Furthermore, God, the infinitely perfect and necessarily existing being, can explain our freedom, as well as our contingent being, i.e. the non-necessity of our existence, only if He does not create or act by a necessity flowing from His own nature but by freedom. For only freedom can explain the contingent existence of beings which could also not exist. For the lack of necessity and inner determinism which only a free creative act possesses, constitutes the only explanation for the analogous non-necessity of the contingent existence and the non-necessary limits and measures of perfections in the world. Moreover, only being created by a free divine act can bestow freedom upon a contingent being. Only freedom can bring forth freedom, and only a free and non-necessary creative choice can create freedom in a contingent being.

From there we can also arrive at the understanding that all pure perfections, all those qualities of which it is absolutely better to possess them than not to possess them (such as being, unity, life, understanding, knowledge, power, omnipotence, justice, consciousness, blessedness, goodness of any kind) and which admit of infinity, therefore can and must truly be attributed to God. As a matter of fact, from a metaphysics of those attributes which are called pure perfections we can arrive at the conclusion that God must possess each and every one of these perfections most fully and wholly.

5. *The moral argument*: But I also recognize, and even find of superior value in certain ways, those arguments that proceed from specifically personal acts and personal phenomena such as the moral sphere and conscience: arguing that there is an absolute moral and simultaneously metaphysical necessity grounded in the nature of the moral sphere that the moral order be restored and justice be realized in the end. This in turn requires an absolute and eternal judge who

punishes and rewards, or shows mercy (which presupposes justice) and thus (1) must be omniscient in order to know all guilt and merit, (2) must possess all power with which nothing else can interfere by obstructing the execution of justice (he must hence be omnipotent), and (3) must possess perfect goodness in Himself without which He would not be morally able and justified to be the supreme judge.

Turning to the history of philosophy, Plato likewise develops such an argument in its fundamental lines. If we sever his moral argument from his subjectivist epistemology, Immanuel Kant has also defended this moral argument along the lines developed above.[11] He adds other moral arguments, such as the one from striving with moral necessity for complete holiness, which in view of the infinity of its potential progress can never be fulfilled in any finite time. We might add that this argument should not primarily be viewed in terms of the unending time that the reaching of holiness as the perfect harmony of the will with "the moral law" and with all morally relevant goods would take (a completely secularized and immanent conception of eternity and moral progress), but in light of the moral life's inner link to an eternity which is not merely endless but qualitatively distinct from the mere unending continuation of the present life.

I would also argue that the supremely perfect moral judge manifests himself also, and in a more direct way, in the "magisterial dictate of our conscience" – in this source of all religious consciousness, as particularly John Henry Cardinal Newman has seen. Here we have in a sense more than a mere "argument" for the existence of God; rather, we encounter some "natural revelation of God" as our lord and judge.

6. *The argument from truth*: I would also defend (among other arguments from the "ideal order" of *eide*, eternal ideas, possible worlds, etc.) the argument from the existence, logical unity, and perfection of truth, which in its infinite vastness transcends every human understanding and every mere being borne by those propositions that are actually thought or conceived of by human beings because these contain too many imperfections incompatible with their being the bearer of *the truth*.

For all these concepts are limited and our use of them confused, whereas truth itself is neither confused nor limited. In our unclear judgments often truth and falsity are mixed; in contrast, truth itself is free of any error, pure and of perfect clarity. In our judgments we fail to draw out all infinite logical consequences which are nevertheless objectively contained in *the truth*, and without whose being true any given proposition the truth of which we recognize could also not be true. Thus truth transcends anything that could be a mere property of those judgments and propositions which owe their origin to human thought.

Hence truth itself cannot, in the last analysis, be explained in a purely immanent and material universe, and even not in a universe which would be only populated by human beings and contain only those concepts and propositions thought by them.

But truth can also not be confined to a mere ideal sphere of logical meaning-unities (propositions as Bernard Bolzano's *Sätze an sich*). For the timeless and infinite order and perfection of truth itself calls for a living spirit who knows and thereby perfectly embodies, or is, the truth itself. Hence truth provides a proof, or at least a strong metaphysical indication, of an infinitely perfect intellect.

7. *The ontological argument*: The strongest argument for the existence of God, however, though also the most difficult to comprehend, is the following one, which is often neglected and more often misunderstood both by its critics and defenders: I mean the Anselmian and Cartesian argument:[12]

Besides the arguments that proceed from the contingency of existence and from the imperfections of all beings in the world, or from truth, the moral order, etc., there is the so-called ontological argument, which concludes from the uninventable inner necessity and infinite perfection of the divine nature and of all its attributes, to which the necessity of real existence belongs with the same uninventable necessity as all its other attributes, that really existing belongs indeed truly and objectively and necessarily to such a being in himself. In all beings besides God we find only essential necessities which apply to the existing order solely under the condition that they exist. Thus we find, for example, that a triangle, if it exists, must have a sum of the interior angles equal to two right angles, but we can never understand that it belongs necessarily to the nature of the triangle to exist actually. On the contrary, we understand that real existence does not belong to islands or bodies. In contrast, in the unique case of God we understand that it lies solely in this divine nature – which we discover and which is wholly independent of all our constructions or subjective ideas, concepts or opinions – that the inner intelligible necessity of the divine nature includes God's existence and in fact His necessary existence.

Many objections have been raised against this argument: that it jumps from the order of concepts to that of reality and thus commits any one of many logical mistakes (like begging the question, confusing nominal with real definitions or tautologies with synthetic propositions a priori); that we do not possess any knowledge of the divine essence; that existence is always contingent and cannot be included in any essence; that the perfection of "that greater than which nothing can be thought" does not have anything to do with real existence, which would be no perfection at all, as the real concentration camps and wars demonstrate, etc.

In my attempt to defend this deepest of all arguments against these objections[13], I had to show that four conditions are to be met by this argument:

1. that its starting point is not a mere definition, a subjective concept, or a language game (in this case the argument would be reducible to a non-informative or an analytical proposition, or make an illicit jump from the order of concepts to that of reality), but an intrinsically necessary and objective divine essence which we discover as being wholly independent of our minds;

2. that we possess a true, although imperfect, knowledge of the necessity and objectivity of the divine essence, *without presupposing already God's existence*;[14]

3. that real existence, and in particular, necessary existence, can indeed belong necessarily to an essence, namely exactly to one, and *only* to one essence: namely the divine essence, and that necessary existence is a real, albeit unique, predicate;

4. that the infinity of reality, intelligibility, and most of all of value-perfection, objectively includes and demands the real existence of God. And that therefore God really exists simply because He is God: that His own nature is proof of His existence: God as the ultimate criterion and proof of Himself (*Gott als Gottesbeweis*).

It is impossible to demonstrate or even to explain sufficiently in such a short space the givenness of all of these conditions of the validity of the ontological argument. Suffice it to say that I deem it to be the most sublime, the most comprehensive and the most lucid and ultimate of all the arguments for the existence of God.

RUSSELL PANNIER, T. D. SULLIVAN

God is a myth, some say. The evidence is overwhelming that the universe is a closed physical system.

Is this something we really know, or all but know? Is the game up for theism, except in diluted form, all symbol and sentiment, nothing supernatural, nothing real?

Of course we cannot in a few pages seriously consider the case against theism, but we can perhaps come to see how hard it is to construct a case that makes God's existence highly improbable. The basic reason is this. In order to establish the extreme improbability it must be shown that at least one of the following two propositions is false: (1) the physical world began to be; (2) whatever comes to be has a cause. For if both (1) and (2) are true, it follows that there is an extrinsic cause of the physical world, a creator.

Now consider (1). How could anybody know it is false that the physical world came to be? The standard cosmological position is that the universe is temporally finite. Of course for all we know (1) could be false. But we are not claiming that (1) is true; we are simply saying that no one has a good reason to believe it is false. Proposition (1) is at least as probable as the opposite.

So also is (2). In fact, all experience seems to speak for (2), nothing against it. Some philosophers have denied (2) on the grounds that the principle of causality is not self evident, that Hume has shown anything can come from anything or nothing at all, that quantum physics has overturned the causal principle, and that even if the causal principle holds for things in the world, there is no reason to believe that it holds with respect to the origin of the world itself. But these objections are too weak to render (2) suspect. For even if the causal principle is not quite as obvious as, say, some principles of logic, it is at least as obvious as a fundamental principle of physics such as the first law of thermodynamics. Everything we know about things coming to be indicates they have causes. In certain moods, even Hume seemed to feel (2) is undeniable, averring he never "had asserted so absurd a Proposition as that anything might arise without a cause."[15] As for quantum mechanics, there is nothing in the standard interpretations that requires us to abandon the idea that there are necessary conditions for the emergence of entities and states of entities. At most what is required is that we drop the idea that everything has necessitating conditions. Quantum mechanics leaves open the possibility, indeed appears to presuppose, that there are necessary conditions for the occurrence of quantum events. And it is exceedingly difficult to exempt the origin of the universe from the causal law while holding that the law applies to everything within the universe.[16]

It might properly be protested that nothing said so far shows that the existence of God is certain or even probable; at best what is established is confident atheism is unwarranted. OK, the probability of God is not zero or exceedingly low. But where does that get us? Atheism still might be the better bet.

True enough, if we have nothing else to go on. But of course there is more. And if we can come to see for the reasons just given that a creator's existence is not highly improbable, then when we add in the additional evidence perhaps the probability can be raised to more than .5. We have made progress because if we think that existence of God is an absurd rival to the scientific world picture, then other evidence will not be taken seriously. Reports of a resurrection of the dead will be dismissed out of hand. So will arguments based on the content of alleged revelations in Hinduism, Judaism, Christianity, or Islam. But if we believe that the existence of God is not highly improbable to begin with, then we are poised to give serious attention to these additional considerations, and to the evidence marshaled in what we call "The Mind-Maker Argument."[17]

The Mind-Maker Argument begins with a fact: We can grasp instantiable characteristics or universals, as they are usually called. Suppose for example that you think: *This is a neuron.* In grasping the complex thought, you grasp the constituent concept of a *neuron*. The characteristic neuron is an instantiable, i.e. there can be more than one instance of a neuron. The important point for our argument is that unlike particular instances of neurons, e.g. the neurons in your head that are firing now, the instantiable characteristic neuron has no spatial location. It is pointless to ask "Where is *neuron*?" The same is true of other instantiable characteristics such as *validity* or *consternation*. No one asks "How many meters separate *validity* from *consternation*?" Or "How wide is *equanimity*?" Now for any y, if y does not occupy a position in space then x is not spatially related to y. (If you are nowhere, Jones cannot be to the North of you.)

Furthermore, for any x and y, x is physically related to y only if x is spatially related to y. It follows that nothing is physically related to abstract instantiable objects of thought. But to grasp an instantiable your mind must be in some state at the time, say state s. Since nothing is physically related to an abstract instantiable, state s is not physically related to the instantiable object of thought. It follows that psychological state s, the state that puts you in cognitive contact with the abstract instantiable object of thought, does not physically relate you to the object of thought. This consequence is inconsistent with a physicalistic world-picture. Of course one can get around the implication by denying the psychological data, as some physicalists do. But there is no need to tell ourselves that we cannot perform familiar mental acts. After all, as we have already seen, there is no good reason to be confident about the physicalistic world-view.

HUGO MEYNELL

As to the reasons for believing in God, I think that if I had to choose between fideism, meaning you simply have to take God on faith, and atheism, I would choose atheism. One ought to have good reasons for believing in God, which don't presuppose what they have to prove. And I maintain that the best reason for believing in God is the fact that nature is open to our understanding in the way that it is. The universe has got to be intelligible for science to be possible. Some people say that the universe may not be completely intelligible, but I don't think this is properly thought through. When a scientific theory turns out to be false, scientists don't say that the matter in question cannot be explained at all. They look out for another theory. We have no real idea of what it would be to clearly and distinctly to affirm the existence or occurrence of a wholly inexplicable state of affairs. The essence of science is to move from description in terms of what is available to our senses to explanation in terms of theory, and so from knowledge of a world relative to us to that of the world as it is in itself. And a world to be known in terms of theory is an intelligible world. The divine intelligence is the ultimate explanation for the intelligibility of the world; the divine will for the particular kind of intelligibility that scientists progressively find it to have – in terms of oxygen rather than phlogiston, in terms of evolution rather than the special creation of species, and so on.

I think, in a way, Immanuel Kant is a remarkable witness to this. Kant points out that nature is in one aspect sensible, in another intelligible. But of course he ascribes the intelligibility to the operation of our own minds. However, if he is to escape total subjectivism, this leaves him with the puzzle, with the muddle rather, of unknowable things in themselves, which are neither sensible nor intelligible, and, as Hegel shows, these things in themselves really are not doing anything. If you remove all the sensible and intelligible properties from a cat, you are left not with a mysterious cat-in-itself, but with no cat at all. The only satisfactory conclusion from the success of science, I guess, is that we live in a really intelligible universe, where reality, as opposed to appearance, is intelligible as opposed to the sensible, as Plato pointed out long ago. And the best explanation for the intelligible fact which is the universe is something like an intelligent will as the basis of it. So that is my main reason for believing that there is a God.

There are two subsidiary arguments which may be worth mentioning. One was particularly sponsored by the Islamic theologians of the Middle Ages, especially Al-Ghazzali. He said that if anything comes into existence, there must be a cause for its existence. Now the universe comes into existence. Therefore there must be a cause for its existence, and that is God. Now his argument for the premise that the world came into existence does not seem to me to work. On the other hand, I gather that nearly all contemporary cosmologists agree that the universe started with a Big Bang, that the universe did come into existence fifteen to twenty thousand million years ago or whenever it was. So now Al-Ghazzali's dubious premise can be supported on a scientific basis. Furthermore, a new version of the argument from order to design has been developed recently, which has to do with what is called the Anthropic Principle. The universe seems to be set up on the basis of laws and initial conditions which are remarkably finely tuned to the production of life. I understand, to take one example among many which could be mentioned, that if the Big Bang had been a tiny bit less violent, too much hydrogen would have turned into helium; and if it had been just that bit more so, the galaxies wouldn't have formed. So there is one main argument for the existence of God, and two subsidiary ones that appear to show some interest.

An associated question concerns the train of thought which asserts that the universe cannot explain its own existence and that the existence of the universe leads us to a being which both explains the existence of the universe and explains its own existence. What is your view of this particular approach?

Of course, an old counter-argument to cosmological arguments for the existence of God is represented by the well-known child's question,

"Who made the universe?" "God, darling." "But, Mommy, who made God?" It seems to me that God's existence, if God exists at all, is self-explanatory in the following sense. If, indeed, there is something which conceives and wills *the whole of* the rest of what is, rather in the same kind of way that you and I conceive and will our actions and products, then that being cannot by its very nature be dependent upon anything else. So in that sense God's existence, if God exists, is self-explanatory. One doesn't need any kind of "ontological" argument – one which seeks to infer divine existence from the very definition of God – to supplement the line of thought which I have sketched.

What do you think of the principle of sufficient reason, in this context, as it applies to the existence of God?

Certainly, the principle of sufficient reason plays a part in these arguments. States of affairs are alleged to obtain; and God is invoked to account for them. We accept the principle of sufficient reason as a matter of course in other contexts; otherwise, as G. E. Moore would say, we would just have to give up. Without the assumption that what happens is subject to some explanation, we would not be able to cope with the world at all, let alone engage in the enterprise of science. The apparent problem here is, if sufficient reason is needed for the universe, sufficient reason is needed for God as well. I have already tried to meet the problem, by showing how God, while needed to explain the world, is to be conceived as self-explanatory.

RALPH MCINERNY

I'm guided by my Catholic faith so that I don't think up ideas of God or imagine them or invent them. I accept them. However, as a philosopher, I ask myself, what possibility there would be, independently of faith, of knowing that God exists. As you know, the whole notion of proofs for the existence of God has fallen upon hard times. One might say, who cares? If you have religious faith, who cares what the fate of arguments might be? Well, the Catholic position is that it makes a great deal of difference and for several reasons. One is that we take it that the epistle to the Romans makes it a matter of revelation that people can know God apart from revelation. The ancient Romans were held accountable for moral turpitude because they could know that God exists, and that obviously has moral implications. So the Church has always taken that text to mean that it is possible for human beings, independently of revelation, to come to a knowledge of God. And why is that important for the faith? It indicates that there is a kind of lingua franca possible about God between the Christian believer and the theist, and it also means that Christian faith is reasonable. Not that you understand the Trinity except as revealed. But that God exists can be proved. So, if some of the things that have been revealed can be proved, it is reasonable to think that the others can be as well or that the others are intelligible, rather, and that one day one will know them. So it protects one from fideism, the tenet that religious faith is simply unrelated to any other knowledge claims or any other facts about the world and it's just the Great Pumpkin or something. It is just accepted and there is no positive or negative connection with anything else. All those reasons, you know, first, it is my faith that guides me as to what I hold about God but among other things I believe that it is possible to know that God exists and so as a philosopher I have always been interested in the fate of the proofs of the existence of God. I myself think that there are sound and valid proofs for the existence of God, but no one has ever thought that they were easy, except maybe St. Anselm.

What do you think of the cosmological argument?

I would hold that there only are cosmological arguments as opposed, say, to the ontological argument. That is, that one can from the things that are made come to knowledge of the invisible things of God. The premises of the proofs are truths about the world, the cosmos. From these one concludes to a first efficient, final or formal cause, but they are the only proofs that I would recognize, cosmological proofs.

Do you think there is some kind of a fundamental insight shared by most of humanity through most of history that something cannot come from nothing, a sort of cosmological insight with respect to the existence of God?

I think it is hard not to believe in God. Far from thinking of it as the ordinary thing that disbelief is overcome by religious beliefs, I think, by and large, most people have an almost instinctive sense that there is a God. As to what He is and how He is and all that sort of thing, you get a lot of very strange conceptions. There is a sense of one's own finitude. People are either rendered fearful or wondering at the world. This tends to lead them to an acknowledgment that there is something that is at the bottom of it all. Newman argued that the very fact of conscience is a powerful proof for the existence of God, that people feel accountable and not simply to themselves or to other people like them but ultimately to God. He developed that.

Would you agree that the burden of proof is on the person who rejects the insight that leads us from the finite to the infinite?

Well, yes, it's true. You know someone can always say, "Sure people start off that way but maybe they are all wrong. So how do you know that for sure?" Whether or not one looks at it skeptically, which intellectuals tend to do, which I think is unfortunate, certainly one would ponder it thoughtfully and want to know more about it and want to know how you address certain difficulties that arise within one's own mind, not from outside. You know the impulse to want to know more and more does not come from skepticism. It comes from a confidence that we can know things and they are there to know. So I don't think we want to give too much aid and comfort to negative questioners because they are an anomaly really; or they are only of interest in so far as there are positive things we share with them.

BERNARD J. F. LONERGAN

[Bernard Lonergan's argument for God's existence is developed in chapter 19 of his famous work *Insight*. "The existence of God," he writes, "is known as the conclusion to an argument and, while such arguments are many, all of them, I believe, are included in the following general form. If the real is completely intelligible, God exists. But the real is completely intelligible. Therefore, God exists." It is assumed, notes F. E. Crowe, that the real and being are one and the same because the former is not merely an "object of thought" but also an "object of affirmation." From the fact that the human mind can know being through "intelligent grasp and reasonable affirmation," Lonergan infers that being is intelligible. Additionally, if the questioning dynamism of the mind is permitted in its entirety, it becomes clear that being is completely intelligible. Since "material reality" is not completely intelligible in itself it has to be grounded in something which has "an intelligibility that is at once complete and real." This complete and real intelligibility is identified "with the unrestricted act of understanding that possesses the properties of God and accounts for everything else."]

It's a question about questioning. Anything we learn is through questions and answers and where does the questioning come from? Really, the number of questions you can ask is unlimited. And consequently there has to be an intelligible world. You are going to know some things. What makes the world intelligible? What's the one basis on which you can assume that the world is intelligible? Not as a matter of fact.

Couldn't the atheist say that it is a matter of brute fact that it just happens to be intelligible and reasonable? It just happens to be so.

Yes, you can say that. But that isn't being intelligent or reasonable. "Merely a matter of fact" is "I refuse to think," "it feels good." That's all it means. That's the ground for being an atheist.

But if you do accept it as intelligible and ask why is it intelligible, what answer does that lead you to?

You are asking the questions. Why do you ask the questions? That's why. Are your questions intelligent or unintelligent?

Intelligent.

All right. You are presupposing there is something intelligible to be understood. Okay. It comes out of the blue. Who put it there? Who made you?

Who made me? It goes back to my parents and then back from there.

All this long stream of ancestors and so forth. What accounts for that?

In his debate with Frederick Copleston, the British agnostic Bertrand Russell said "the world is here and that is all." We shouldn't ask why it's here.

Except to be stupid. You don't need intelligence to say that.

But if you do ask why, you go backward to this series of ancestors, causes, etc.

No, no. You're setting up this indefinite series you don't know too much about. But why should there be such a series? What is the ground of that? What makes me intelligent?

The fact that you ask?

That's what you're presupposing when you ask.

Where do you go from there?

Well, you find yourself, live up to your lights. Simple.

A materialist would say "Matter has been here eternally" and we are just manifestations of matter.

Don't waste your time arguing. Arguing doesn't mean anything. The only argument that has a sure foundation is based upon your understanding yourself, your own consciousness, your own questions. They are your questions. You have to live with them and give them answers, honest answers. It's up to you to decide.

How do you know that your answers are the right answers?

What is the condition of a true judgment, the virtually unconditioned? You have your experiences, you have your understanding of your experiences and you have the experiences of finding the evidence for that understanding. This is the external world you are examining. Well, you never have the virtually unconditioned, you have the probably virtually unconditioned, as near as you can come. It's all hypothetical. But in regard to yourself, you know in your own experience, your intellectual experience, your original experience, your responsibility. There's a target. The immediate data of your own consciousness. And if that is what you are, you'll have the answers. It's up to you to decide what you are or don't want to be.

It would seem your argument begins with the fact that reality is intelligible and the condition of its being intelligible is that it is dependent on an ultimate reality which is the explanatory ultimate.

You're thinking strictly in terms of arguments. A scientist always thinks in terms of data and understanding and the success of his understanding to cover all the data. That isn't arguing. *Insight*: what is it concerned with: it is setting out an analysis of knowledge based on the immediate data of consciousness. That's what the book is about and gradually we have introduced people to the immediate data of their own consciousness. Examples from mathematics, examples from science, examples from common sense, examples of judgments. Trying to set everything out as a dialog with different people, and everyone saying, well, include me, that leads nowhere. Know yourself, that's the first step.

How do you explain the fact that some thinkers are atheists?

Well, there's such a thing as scotosis. In *Insight*, chapter 6, I talk of scotosis, the darkening of intellect, the effects of original sin, the weakening of will, the propensity to evil. These things have been around for a long time. The thing is, why did Adam sin? If there were a reason, not merely an excuse, but a reason, it wouldn't have been a sin. So, when you ask me why these people talk and think the way they do, I say: It's the darkening of intellect due to sin.

H. D. LEWIS

I find it very puzzling to say well, the world is here and there is nothing to account for it, it just happened. I mean, how did we come into being, not physically, but that we should appear at a certain stage in time and so on? I find there is a great lack of perplexity about the world and ourselves.

What is your approach to the existence of God?

I think my starting point is very secular: the impossibility of accounting for everything in a secular way. I think that is very much my beginning. It is not just in that instance but in other ways these can't be exhausted – finite explanations. They tell us these wonderful things about distances, new constellations, constellations far older than ours and so on. But it just doesn't make sense to me to say that it has always been – changing or not. I find it particularly difficult to make sense of what it means – "always." If you reflect, you just cannot, independently of any further implications, accept the idea of a totally random springing into being out of nothing. Can you avoid asking why the world is the sort of world we find that it is, independently even of its being wonderful in so many ways, if there was simply a random start with no sort of "before" at all? Why this sort of world, and why start when it did?

There are many mystifying features of the world as we encounter it and we should think correctly about that. That is why I am so anxious dualism and things like this should be boldly stated because they all lead up to something that remains unexplained and mystifying, and I don't think that people thought eventually they would find explanations exhaustively of these things and I don't think we ever will. We have got to take the world as we find it and some things in it are very bewildering, and out of that we can conclude to some reality altogether different in character from anything we can understand. It is not that we are not clever enough but that we don't have any hopes of understanding those sorts of things. So one has to recognize something transcendent or ultimate and I think that the Hebrew–Christian tradition and the Islamic is good on this. It makes a sharp distinction between finite and infinite and so on, and says that we are real finite creatures with a finite understanding, that there is some infinite beyond it all and then that gets read into history and religious experience and so on. What we have to say is that the entire finite world, as we understand it, is rooted in some reality altogether beyond finite existence, an ultimate, and for us irreducible, mystery.

Why do philosophers like Professor Antony Flew and Sir Alfred Ayer reject God's existence?

Well, I don't know. I think that, in the case of those two people, I think their philosophical attitude is pretty inhibiting. They are both confirmed empiricists and if you start off with an empiricist supposition to begin with, then you can't possibly get beyond it, beyond what you observe. And if nothing makes sense for you beyond that, and it doesn't for Ayer, he would say, "it is all fantasy, all rubbish," it just didn't make sense to him. Actually, Ayer and I, years and years ago, had a fine broadcast discussion on this.

Is there any way to bring empiricists to an awareness of the transcendent?

I don't think so. They have got to abandon their empiricism.

What is your response to the empiricist claim that your quest for an ultimate explanation stems from a psychological problem?

I don't think it is psychological. There is no special reason for wanting to be comforted or something like that. It is just that it seems to me inescapable in itself and I think it is hard to think of the world being just a going concern and that it happened somehow. It is hard to think that this all came about just by chance. I also stress this comparison of other minds because we don't know another person's mind as we know our own. I know what I'm thinking and talking about. I know what you are thinking because I hear what you say or watch your behavior or something of this kind, but obliquely, and I think it is the same with our knowing the being of God.

And you describe this as a fundamental insight which you either have or you don't?

Yes, I think so, and I don't know how to explain why some people have it and some don't any more than the problem of evil or something like that.

In these fundamental assertions, you are remaining true to common experience and so would you agree that the burden of proof is really on the atheists and the empiricists because their denials fly in the face of what is commonly perceived?

Yes, to some extent, I think it is. They don't realize it and don't acknowledge it. Some of them are ruling out the fact that their minds are real. I don't for a moment think that I am just my brain. I know that if something went wrong with my brain, I would be ill and couldn't do things but it doesn't make any sense to me to think that I am my brain. I know I am having all these experiences, I know my thoughts, I know myself, I know what is in my mind. But there is this pre-conceived notion among so many contemporary philosophers that if you believe anything with a bit of mystery in it, you are being emotional or unfair or affected by your own desires or something like this. I don't feel that one little bit. I am completely unshaken by anyone who would suggest the sort of line that "I believe these things because I want to or something." I feel that must be the truth of it and I have no interest, whatsoever, in a religious practice or affirmation that doesn't claim truth.

Is the best approach to materialists one of drawing attention to their own thoughts and experiences as being non-material?

Yes, very much so. I don't understand these physicalists, some of them very clever people, and proud of their achievements and so on. If it is just all physical why should they be proud of it? And look at the standards they have. Gilbert Ryle, the editor of *Mind*, was a very atheistic sort of person but he wouldn't let anything get into *Mind* that wasn't of the very highest standard and wasn't in proper English or something like this and would be very scornful of something that wasn't up to the proper standard. How can those things matter to them if it is all bodily and nothing else? I think we have got to get people to understand that to begin with, then bring them on from there.

WILLIAM P. ALSTON

I think the idea of a cumulative case that's been spelled out by various people, including Basil Mitchell and others, is very important. A lot of the argument over the existence of God concentrates on one particular possible basis for this and one supposes that if you dispose of that, that settles the matter. But, of course, belief in the existence of God has a large number of different sources, for example the traditional philosophical arguments for the existence of God, many of which I think have substance to them, although I don't think any of them constitute, by themselves, a conclusive case by any means.

The cosmological argument for example certainly has weight: if there is a being that exists necessarily and has the power to bring other things into existence and sustain them in existence, then that provides an explanation for the existence of what we see around us and provides an answer to the question, "Why is there something rather than nothing," an explanation that we don't have otherwise, and so that definitely counts in favor of the existence of such a being.

Of course, people will say that this doesn't give us everything we're interested in about the nature of God. That is true; it doesn't tell you anything about the goodness of God or divine laws, and it certainly doesn't give you any details of Christian theology. But that just goes back to the point that you can't expect one of these sources to do the whole job. Consider recent versions of the teleological argument, in terms of the fine tuning of various physical dimensions, fine tuning that's required for there to be life. The range is quite narrow; if these variables deviated from their actual magnitude by even a little bit, the necessary physical conditions for life wouldn't have existed. I think that is a significant reason for supposing that there is a being with a mind that is arranging things to achieve certain purposes, that's responsible for the whole thing. That's another bit of the picture.

I think the ontological argument has a certain degree of force, especially in the version that was developed by Alvin Plantinga. As

Plantinga acknowledges, people can question the credibility of some of the premises but that is a familiar situation when you try to reason about fundamental issues like this and, as Plantinga says, at least it's not unreasonable to accept the relevant premises here and, therefore, this shows at the very least a certain degree of reasonability in believing in the existence of God. And, of course, the ontological argument gives you a whole lot of stuff you don't get from these other arguments, because in the ontological argument you start with the concept of an absolutely perfect being. So, depending on what is or isn't more perfect than what, you're going to get a being that has anything that you regard as a mode of perfection in the highest possible degree, and we couldn't ask for more than that.

But these philosophical arguments for the existence of God are only part of the picture and that's not what looms largest in actual theistic religions like Christianity. We have to think about people who don't engage in philosophical reasoning of this sort and ask whether they can have and do have some basis for believing in the existence of God. I think they can and do, and also people who engage in philosophical reasoning can and do have other sorts of bases for believing in the existence of God. What this is, to put it in a nutshell, is their experience of God at work in their lives. This can take a variety of forms. The more direct forms involve a direct experience of the presence of God to them and God doing various things with respect to them and their engaging in interaction with God. It's the sort of thing you find in its most highly developed form in the mystics, but I don't think it's confined to mystics at all. It's very widely dispersed in the population in milder forms, less dramatic forms. There have been a number of surveys in the last few decades, most recently by the Gallup organization and earlier by various sociologists. The findings are pretty consistent. It depends, of course, on whether you are surveying the population generally or whether you are restricting yourself to church members. If you're talking about Christian church members, something like two-thirds report having had some direct experience of the presence of God and that really shakes a lot of people up. It runs strongly counter to a fairly widespread supposition, especially with intellectuals, that the experience of God is something very unusual, really weird, and confined to a few fanatics or people that may not be completely mentally balanced. And so far I'm just talking about the most direct form of the experience of the presence and activity of God in one's life. We must also remember that the whole involvement in the Church and the whole religious way of life is properly construed as involving an awareness of God and is construed in these terms by people who are really into it. No doubt, there are a lot of more perfunctory church members who just go through the motions or think of the Church as some sort of social club. But the people who are really into it experience all aspects of their involvement as constituting or as involving an awareness of God in their lives. For example, they take themselves to be engaging in dialogue with God in prayer.

Indeed, I think many people experience everything they do, everything that happens to them, as being experienced or done in the light of the continual presence of God to them, and this ties into another main basis for belief in the existence of God, which is a religious tradition. The Christian tradition as embodied in the scriptures and elsewhere, in the history of the Church through the ages, is a record of people's encounters with God, their interactions with God.

Of course, you can say, "Well, that's just the way it seemed to these people. Why pay any attention to that?" But I think this again indicates that we've got multiple supports here that depend on each other. So if you wonder why you should pay any attention to what the biblical writers think about what they take to have been encounters with God, what they take to have been God at work in their lives or in the lives of their communities, then you can think about what seem to you to be your own encounters with God, if you think you have had any, or you can think about the philosophical arguments for the existence of God. The philosophical arguments provide some basis for thinking that the sort of being these people thought they were encountering really exists. And if you get doubts about the philosophical arguments, you can reflect on the fact that there are various people who thought they actually encountered a being like this. That sort of lends additional weight to the arguments for supposing that there is such a being. I think these things mutually reinforce each other. My book called *Perceiving God* is primarily concerned with supporting the thesis that what seems to people to be an experience of God often actually is a genuine perception of God at work in their lives. But in the last chapter of that book, I talk about the way in which that fits in with all these other kinds of supports for belief in the existence of God, how they interact and how they mutually support each other.

Would you say the cosmological argument entails an approach of going from the notion of everything having an explanation for its existence to the conclusion that you either have an infinite chain of such explanations or a being which explains whatever exists?

Yes. It doesn't have to be put in terms of stopping an infinite regress, but that's a way in which it has often been thought of. If you are thinking in terms of an infinite chain of explanations, that certainly doesn't tell you why there is something rather than nothing.

This means you are talking about a being that would explain itself as well as everything else.

Yes, that is definitely what the argument points to. I don't know whether "explain itself" is a good way to put it. I would say, "exists necessarily."

Though we can't see why?

Well, maybe we can and maybe we can't. The ontological argument claims to give an insight into why. But even if you reject the ontological argument, still the supposition that there is a being that exists necessarily, gives you an ultimate explanation in a way that you don't have without that.

NOTES

1. I did not then take it as a live option that there is no real truth here. I have since learned how good a case one can make for this option, and yet it still seems to me that there are in morality truths of the most robust sort.
2. Of course, atheists can likewise say that their good arguments that God does not exist render atheism rational, and give reason to suspect error in theists' reasoning. If so, perhaps both theism and atheism can be rational. This is plausible, for even if "God exists" and "God does not exist" cannot both be true the very fact that smart, knowledgeable, rational people embrace both suggests that there are good reasons on both sides of the debate. Some might say that if there are roughly equal arguments pro and con the existence of God, the most rational view is not theism or atheism but agnosticism. But this is so only if there are no pressing reasons of other sorts to choose between theism or atheism. Buridan's Ass had equally good arguments for eating the bale of hay on the left and the one on the right. The need not to starve was reason enough to find some non-argumentative way to decide which one to eat. There may be pressing reason to have some positive opinion as to

whether God exists. Again, the option between theism and atheism may not be one on which it is practically possible to be neutral: perhaps agnostics are atheists in practice. Finally, as the text notes, if one has reason to think that arguments that P are sound, one has reason to think that arguments that not P are not sound, even if one cannot see flaws in them. If so, one has reason not to be agnostic about P.

3. This needs a slight qualification. Suppose that a proposition P is true, and so ought to be believed. But suppose too that we are just not able to believe P in a way we ought to believe it, but can only believe P in ways we ought not. Ought we then to accept or to reject P? If "reject" is the right answer, then good arguments do not make all thoughts about motive irrelevant. But I suspect that the right answer is: it depends on whether the value of having the truth about P outweighs the harm accepting P does to one's overall habits of belief, i.e. outweighs how much accepting P promotes habits of belief-formation which tend overall toward false beliefs. So if there are any cases of "necessarily tainted belief" – which is not at all clear – it may be that not all or even most really do make motive into a serious obstacle to the rationality of belief.

4. John Macquarrie, *In Search of Deity – An Essay in Dialectical Theism* (New York: Crossroad, 1985).

5. On an extensive development of such an epistemological realism cf. Dietrich von Hildebrand, *What is Philosophy?*, 3rd edition (London: Routledge, 1991); Josef Seifert, *Back to Things Themselves. A Phenomenological Foundation for Classical Realism* (London: Routledge, 1987).

6. Martin Buber, *I and Thou* (T&T Clark, 1959), p.135. See also John Macquarrie, ibid., pp. 247ff.

7. Cf. on this my *Essere e persona – Verso una fondazione fenomenologica di una metafisica classica e personalistica* (Milano: Vita e Pensiero, 1989).

8. Among other causes such as final causes or formal and material causes, of which the principle of causality does not speak.

9. Anselm of Canterbury, *Monologion*, ch.15.

10. Cf. Wolter, Allan, *The Transcendentals and their Function in the Metaphysics of Duns Scotus* (New York: Franciscan Institute Publications, 1946); *Essere e persona*.

11. Due to his subjectivist epistemology, however, he can interpret them only as subjective moral postulates from which one cannot derive the objective metaphysical truth that the order of morality will be fulfilled.

12. It was first developed by Anselm of Canterbury (11th century) in his *Proslogion*.

13. In *Gott als Gottesbeweiss – Eine phänomenologische Neubegründung des ontologischen Arguments* (*God as Proof of God's Existence. A Phenomenological Foundation for the Argument for the Existence of God from the Necessary Divine Essence*). (Heidelberg: Winter Verlag, 1995)

14. This can be shown from a philosophy of eidetic essential necessities independent of the human mind, which I tried to bring to evidence in the book *Back to Things Themselves – A Phenomenological Foundation for Classical Realism*.
15. *The Letters of David Hume*, ed. J. Y. T. Greig (Oxford: The Clarendon Press, 1932), vol. I, 187.
16. For a defense of this claim see T. D. Sullivan, "Coming to Be Without a Cause," *Philosophy* 65 (1990), pp. 266–268 and "On the Alleged Causeless Beginning of the universe: A Reply to Quentin Smith," *Dialogue* XXXIII (1994), pp. 325–335.
17. The details are worked out in Russell Pannier and T. D. Sullivan, "The Mindmaker," *Theos* (New York: Peter Lang).

GOD AND MODERN SCIENCE

Great Question 11: *What bearing, if any, does science have on religion – particularly with respect to the questions of God's existence, the origin of the universe, and the possibility of miracles?*

RICHARD SWINBURNE

My answer would be fairly obvious there. Science certainly has bearing on religion, drawing our attention to the fact that the world is ordered by simple scientific laws: that is something very extraordinary we wouldn't expect to find in the normal course of things. Saying that some laws of nature, say Newton's laws, govern things is just to say that things in the world behave in the orderly way that Newton's laws codify. Yet how extraordinary it is that everything in the world behaves in the same simple ways as does everything else: every electron in every part of probably infinite space and time behaves in exactly the same way as does every other one. Science tells us of this, and in telling us draws attention to an enormous coincidence which provides the grounds for an argument of very considerable strength from the operation of these scientific laws to the existence of God. Science is very good evidence, as such, the general fact of scientific laws governing the world is very good evidence for the existence of God. Though note that in recent years the kind of science which has developed has quantum theory as its central plank and although quantum theory, like all previous scientific theories, draws our attention to the immense orderliness of the universe, it is an orderliness with a certain amount of gaps in it. According to quantum theory, the regularities which are evinced by objects are only of 99.9 per cent regular behavior and therefore, as it were, there is possibility within the orderliness of the universe for humans to exercise free will and for miracles which do not necessarily involve the breaking of scientific laws.

The origin of the universe. Well, I don't think that the doctrine that the universe has a beginning is a crucial theist doctrine. God is the creator and sustainer of the universe but it doesn't very much matter, as regard to that doctrine, whether the universe is infinitely old or of only a finite age. If it is infinitely old, then God has been keeping the universe in being for infinite time; if it is finitely old, then for finite time. So the particular details of physical cosmology, which might suggest that the universe had a beginning with the Big Bang or that it didn't (perhaps a new theory will come along which will suggest that), do not seem to matter very much either one way or the other as regards religion.

HUGO MEYNELL

In the nineteenth century, a very popular view was that as we become increasingly rational about the universe, as we apply the principles of reason to it, so God retreats more and more. But now we have the postmodernists and deconstructionists, who have no more use for reason than they have for God, and so in principle are just as hostile to science as they are to theistic religion. I think these people have grasped the extremely important point that, in the last analysis, theism and belief in the rationality of the universe, such as makes science possible, belong, as it were, in the same basket. In the long run, to reject God is to reject reason, and to reject reason is to reject God.

As to miracles, there is a dictum of Leibniz, which I think is very fine, that God brings about miracles not in the order of nature but in that of grace. Miracles aren't a matter of God correcting shoddy workmanship, but of God communicating with sensitive and rational creatures. I think that Hume's highly influential definition of a miracle, as a violation of the laws of nature, is misleading, and obscures discussion of the subject, whether one believes in miracles or not. Augustine's definition is much better. He says that when God carries on in the ordinary kind of way, we call it nature; but when God acts in some strikingly exceptional way, for our instruction and admonition, we call it a miracle. Now, if you take the miracles attributed to Jesus in the New Testament as standard cases of what is meant by miracle, it is obvious that they are characterized by these two features pointed out by Augustine. All of them are significant; they form a part of a kind of divine language in which God is supposed to talk to human beings. But also, of course, they stand out just as events; instantaneous cures of decades-long paralysis or blindness from birth, or walking on water, are not part of the ordinary course of things. The Crucifixion is a good example of an event which, of course, is of enormous significance to Christians as part of the divine communication with us, but is not exceptional just as an event. It thus has one feature essential to a miracle, but not the other; regrettably, there was nothing particularly exceptional in those days about people being crucified. Now there is an amusing passage in Matthew Arnold, where he is running down those who set store by miracles. He supposes that someone is giving a learned or pious discourse, and announces that in order to confirm what he says, he will hold up his pen and it will become a pen-wiper before the eyes of their audience. Even if it does turn into a pen-wiper, comments Arnold, nothing whatever is added to the significance of the discourse. Of course, the miracles related in the canonical Gospels are not at all like that; they are profoundly symbolic of the divine action and intentions for humanity. This is made particularly clear in John's Gospel, though it is pretty obvious from the other ones too. In John's Gospel, Jesus turns the water of traditional ritual into the wine of his presence, is the living bread without which we starve, is the light without which we stumble in darkness, is the life without which we die, and so on; and he shows all these things by miracles that he performs. The canonical Gospels, of course, are in utter contrast with the apocryphal Gospels in this respect. In the apocryphal Gospels, you get a story about the child Jesus, where another little boy bumps into him and promptly falls down dead. Or the child Jesus makes birds out of clay and they fly away.

As to the relation of miracles to the laws of nature, it seems to me that there is some evidence that paranormal events quite regularly occur in the presence of great sanctity, and also in the presence of outstanding evil. St. Teresa of Avila seems to have levitated, and found it a great nuisance and embarrassment; apparently, too, people are apt to levitate when they go through various yogic techniques. I would guess that paranormal events regularly, and one might say quasi-scientifically, take place in conjunction with special spiritual development according to laws which are so far unknown. (This is one reason why Hume's definition is so misleading.) These considerations shed light, I think, on the insistence by the Catholic Church on some miraculous events associated with saints when she comes to canonize them.

GERARD J. HUGHES

Since the Enlightenment, it has been commonplace to suggest that religion and science are somehow competing ways of making sense of our lives and our world. Secular scientists have on occasion been happy to suggest that their discoveries, for instance about the history of the universe or the origin of humankind, have somehow replaced religious beliefs with truths that are more securely grounded; and, on the other hand, some fundamentalist religious believers have seen science as endeavoring to contradict their most cherished convictions. Both these positions seem to me radically mistaken.

From the point of view of the theist, scientists gradually discover what kind of a universe it is that God has created, what its history is, and how it works. They do this by discovering the causal connections between things, thus enlightening us about their natures and the ways in which they interact. When cosmologists extrapolate backwards in the history of the universe and postulate a moment at the beginning of time when all the energy/matter in the universe was concentrated in one unimaginably dense original 'singularity' (as the jargon goes), they are, to the best of their ability, working backwards from the present using the scientific laws which have been discovered. What they are not doing is answering the philosophical question about the status of the reality whose working they seek to unravel. Present speculation suggests that space/time/matter simply came into being, with no previous physical cause. But the philosophical issue, whether the universe is inherently dependent upon some non-physical cause which might properly be described as God, is not something which can be settled one way or the other by scientific inquiry, because God's causal activity is not on a par with the causal activities of the things in our universe.

Religious fundamentalists are equally mistaken, though in a different way. They typically take one description (usually a traditional and hallowed description) of God's relationship to humankind to be a literal account of God's methods and procedures. In so doing they ignore the literary genre of their own sacred texts, and hence misunderstand their meaning and point. The opening chapters of the book of Genesis, for instance, are not, and were never intended to be, a scientific description of the origin of the universe. Among other things, those chapters set out to deny the view that the universe depends on two creators, one good and one bad, and seek to provide an alternative explanation of the evil and sufferings which characterize human existence. They never set out to provide an account of the process of creation which could be made to compete with scientific accounts.

Obviously, the progress of the sciences down the centuries has often led believers to revise their understanding of God and of God's creation. Indeed, that is how things should be; the content of religious belief must, if it is to be intellectually honest, be compatible with whatever we take to be true in any other area of human inquiry. Just as in earlier ages our views about the physics or human psychology involved mistaken beliefs, so earlier religious beliefs may also have involved mistakes. On the other hand, just as religious believers must be prepared to correct some of their views in the light of truths discovered in other areas of human inquiry, so too, I would suggest, we must be open-minded enough to allow other beliefs to be challenged on occasion by religion. Take, for instance, belief in miracles. By this I do not mean those events which have perfectly standard this-worldly explanations, but which a believer might regard as expressions of the providence of God; I mean events which are of religious significance and for which there is no foreseeable explanation in terms of the laws of nature. Of course it is true that the credulous will claim that some occurrence is miraculous when there is a perfectly ordinary explanation, or where it seems likely that such an explanation could be forthcoming. Of course, too, it is possible to conclude that there is no possible natural explanation simply because our grasp of the workings of nature is in some way quite deficient. In such cases, the belief that an occurrence is miraculous may be reasonable, and yet false. But I see no way of excluding altogether that there might occur events which are brought about by God, and for which there is therefore no possible natural explanation. We should be sufficiently open-minded to recognize that the sciences can, by definition, study only those things which are accessible to scientific methods of investigation. There is no reason to assume that such methods must be all-encompassing.

In short, I see philosophical inquiry, religious belief, and the human and natural sciences as complementary attempts on our part to make sense of ourselves and our world. Honesty requires that we should try for coherence between all the beliefs we hold; and open-mindedness requires us both to be prepared to modify our beliefs, religious and scientific, in the light of new arguments, new evidence, or unfamiliar lines of inquiry.

JOSEF SEIFERT

Considering philosophy as the supreme science, and also allowing for a theology which interprets divine revelation and Church teaching to be a divinely inspired science, I have already addressed indirectly the role of each of these sciences with regard to the question of God's existence and with regard to God's actions.

Philosophy can also explain the origin of the universe in a free act of divine creation (which already Plato postulates in his *Timaios* long before Christ) and the *possibility of miracles*, proving both the infinite power of God and the non-necessity of the events and natures in the world, which are two conditions for the meaning and possibility of miracles.

Theology, based both on reason and on faith, knows the existence of God's creation of the world and of miracles from a new source (the Bible, God's Word, and His free self-revelation).

As far as natural and empirical sciences are concerned, they bring us into contact with the wonders of the physical and chemical world, and above all of the living bio-cosmos. They can thus broaden our experiential basis for knowing this concrete world of ours, and contribute to opening our eyes for the impossibility that a thoughtless cause of the universe could have brought it about.

John Locke observed very well in his *Essay Concerning Human Understanding*, that a mindless cause of the universe could never have brought about knowing, conscious, free, living, meaningfully structured beings. For that reason, a properly philosophically understood natural science can provide many arguments for the so-called teleological proof for the existence of God: that meaningful, ordered, intelligible, and yet not necessary structures of the world, as we admire them in each living cell, in each species of plants and animals, and most of all in the human body and the unity of body and mind, could never have been the result of chance or of unconscious blind purposes of nature.

Thus the world, as it is explored by science, reveals in a thousand ways the existence of a supremely intelligent cause of the universe. This argument cannot be a pure matter of natural science as such, however. It always involves philosophical knowledge. Furthermore, neither natural science as such nor its philosophical interpretation in terms of meaning and teleology, can cope with the problem of evil. Therefore, in my opinion, this argument from the meaningful structure of the world that is strengthened by science, requires some other and more metaphysical proof of the existence of God to be wholly convincing.

Against such a philosophical background, however, some contributions of modern science, such as the discovery and theory of the statistical character of the microphysical laws, and others, provide also empirical arguments for the possibility of miracles. Other scientific discoveries, such as of the expansion of the universe and of all the cosmic bodies fleeing from an imaginary center at a very high speed, when properly interpreted philosophically, show the temporal beginning of the universe. Therefore, these results of astronomy and physics indirectly prove that eternal being that is necessary as the cause of the universe, because the temporally limited being of the universe cannot come from nothing. When properly understood in the light of the philosophical insight that no temporal being, no being-in-time, can be beginningless, the same scientific results also prove that the cause of the physical universe cannot coincide with the world but must be an extra-worldly being and cause.

Another fascinating discovery of astronomy is known under the name of the anthropic principle, which proves that the arising of man and even of infra-human life in the universe was bound to innumerable and highly complicated conditions of the physical and chemical universe. The arising of exactly these conditions, given the innumerable chances of conditions hostile to life, could certainly not be assumed to be the mere effect of chance.

In these, and in many other ways, modern science, when joined to good philosophy, constributes much to our knowledge of God. But it can do so, and even form the concept of God, only by using methods and borrowing concepts taken from other disciplines: from philosophy and theology.

ALVIN PLANTINGA

Take the last, the possibility of miracles. Some people claim that science shows or suggests that miracles aren't possible; but that's utter baloney. Science doesn't show any such thing. Some scientists, perhaps, think that it is a presupposition of science that there aren't any miracles, but that seems to me quite wrong. Science requires that the world be regular and orderly, that there be no massive irregularities. It has to be reliable. One has to expect that if I, say, discover the half-life of radium, it is not going to be the case that in ten years it will be quite different, or that ten years ago it was something different. If things were like that, science would be impossible. But of course it isn't required that there be no miracles; it isn't required that God could not or would not do things differently on a given occasion if He wanted to. One wants to know, for example, what the chemical constitution of wine is; and a necessary condition of this being a decent, soluble question is that wine not change its constitution every day. But it doesn't follow from that that God couldn't, on a given occasion, change water into wine. So, I would say, the possibility of miracles has very little to do with science.

The question of God's existence? Science seems to me not to address questions of that sort at all. It doesn't address the question whether there is such a person as God. On the other hand I do think there is a connection between religious belief and science. It seems to me the proper way for science to be conducted (at any rate, one good candidate for the proper way for science to be conducted) is along the lines suggested by Augustine, but also by Abraham Kuyper, who was the last prime minister to be a great theologian (or the last great theologian to be a prime minister); he was prime minister of the Netherlands around the beginning of this century. Kuyper argued that there are really two sciences. And what he had in mind was this: if you propose to treat scientifically such things as human beings, for example, then a lot will depend, with respect to the kinds of conclusions you reach, on what sorts of things you think human beings are. You may think they are creatures created in God's image; alternatively, you may think they are creatures cobbled together by an evolutionary process in which there is a very substantial chance element. You may think they can be understood fundamentally in terms of relationship to God, or you may think they are to be understood, rather, in terms of their evolutionary origin. This seems to me to make a great difference.

So, for example, if you think the second way, the naturalistic way, then you might be inclined to come up with conclusions like those of Herbert Simon. In an article in a scientific journal in 1990, he addresses the question of the right understanding of altruism – the fact that people like Mother Teresa, the Little Sisters of the Poor, the Methodist missionaries of the nineteenth century, and the Jesuit missionaries of the sixteenth century appear willing to sacrifice their own interests for others. Indeed, all of us, to some degree, sometimes go out of our way, sometimes compromise a bit or a good deal of our own interests in order to help somebody else. Well, Simon says, how do we understand that? And, of course, he thinks this is a question because he says the rational thing for a human being to do is to try to increase his or her fitness, where fitness is a measure of the probability of one's genes being widely disseminated in the next and subsequent generations.

That is the rational thing to do. Someone like Mother Teresa is not following the rational course. So the question is why does she do what she does? His answer is that she does what she does because of two things: greater than ordinary docility, on the one hand, and then, on the other hand, limited rationality or, not to put too fine a point on it, stupidity. That is why she does these things. But if you thought of human beings instead from a Christian perspective, you couldn't possibly think that was a decent answer to the question why people like Mother Teresa do what they do. Rather, the right answer has to do with the fact that she is reflecting, in her limited human way, God's great love for humanity displayed in the Incarnation and the Atonement. So how you do science may very well depend, to some degree, on how you think about human beings.

Of course this is a very complicated question. You might say, "Well, what Simon does is not really science; it is something else, perhaps some combination of science and theology." This was something insisted upon by Pierre Duhem (who was a contemporary of Abraham Kuyper); he said the right way to do science is to make sure that no metaphysical presuppositions intrude into it, where the kinds of metaphysical presuppositions he has in mind are ones that divide us. His idea was that we should all be able to do science together – Catholics, Protestants, Buddhists, Muslims, atheists, everybody. That is the great thing about science, it is a common, cooperative venture. That is an interesting and worthy suggestion. There is some question as to how far science taken that way can go; furthermore, from, say, a Christian perspective, science taken that way would have to be supplemented by something else, something that took account of all that we know in trying to figure out the answers to scientific questions. But it is still an interesting and worthy suggestion. Of course, if we do think that is how science should go, then enormous chunks of what presently goes under the name of science wouldn't really be science; they wouldn't be Duhemian science.

For example, much of what goes on in cognitive science takes utterly for granted that human beings are material objects – takes materialism for granted. But this is, of course, a metaphysical assertion or assumption that not nearly everybody accepts. So, if we were to do science in a Duhemian way, taking materialism for granted would be just as much out of order, as would be, say, doing biology starting from the presupposition that God created everything. And furthermore, scientific enterprises like Simon's, on altruism, would also not be Duhemian science. Vast stretc.hes of evolutionary and biological thinking take it for granted that human beings and biological systems in general have a sort of *chance* origin, aren't designed, aren't created, and so on. Again, that wouldn't be proper Duhemian science, since the assumption that these biological systems aren't designed is not one that we would agree upon. Christians think they are designed.

But, of course, some Christians or theists hold that there are certain evolutionary mechanisms but that these mechanisms were divinely designed.

Yes. So what is improper from the Duhemian point of view would be the assumption that biological systems are not designed, that they originate by chance, with chance mechanisms like random genetic mutation together with natural selection.

Couldn't the naturalist apply some version of Ockham's Razor in arguing against the need for any divine design in a scientific discussion? How does this relate to your contention that belief in God is properly basic? Is the burden of proof on the theist?

Well, I was just talking about the Duhemian science. I was saying that Duhem says that the way to do science is by not importing any metaphysical assumptions of any kind, either theist or naturalist. I was talking about things under that heading. You ask about how Ockham's Razor fits in: clearly, if you are already a believer in God and you're doing science, you're not going to refuse to take advantage of what you know about God, just because of Ockham's Razor. Just as I am not going to refuse to take advantage of what I know about your actually sitting there talking to me, just because of Ockham's Razor. That would be a complete misuse of Ockham's Razor. The Razor has to do with the sort of situation where you have two hypotheses, that is, two propositions or explanations of a given range of data. To say that they are hypotheses is, among other things, to say the warrant they get is a function of how well they explain the data in their range. (Of course different things will be data with respect to different hypotheses.) Ockham's Razor comes in in this way: if both these hypotheses explain the data equally well and one of them calls on more and different entities than the other one – postulates more and different entities than the other one does – then the first one is so far forth the better hypothesis. But that has nothing to do, it seems to me, with the existence of God, or the existence of other minds, or of a material or of an external world. It is not the case that I believe in God because I think this is a good explanation of the way the world is. I don't believe in the Atonement or in the Trinity or believe that God has a plan for our salvation because I think it is a good explanation of some data. Not at all.

What is your view of attempts to postulate God's existence in the context of explanation such as in the work of Richard Swinburne?

One way to understand what Richard Swinburne is doing is this: He is saying, "Whether or not belief in God is for most of us an hypothesis, nonetheless one can give a good hypothetical-type argument for the existence of God by noting that the existence of God can certainly serve as an explanation of all sorts of things that are hard to explain otherwise." This might give someone who didn't have experience of God a reason for believing in God. Even if one does believe in God on other grounds (grounds other than these argumentative grounds), the existence of these arguments is very worthwhile, interesting, and important. It serves to confirm belief in God, and it also unearths interesting connections between belief in God and the sorts of phenomena that are appealed to in describing the premises of the arguments in question.

RALPH MCINERNY

Well, I think science can mean either science in the narrow, modern sense of a very definite technique whereby we try to explain natural phenomena by way of hypothesis and working out theories and discarding this and that and the other thing, or it can mean more broadly the knowledge that we have of the sensible universe, of the world around us. Obviously we have knowledge of that world prior to doing science. So call it prescientific, call it the natural standpoint, whatever: it seems to me that is much more important for religion than specifically scientific knowledge, for this reason, that there is so much advance and change and shifting in scientific theories that it would be very unwise for people to link religious beliefs to the current theory. Then it would have the fate of that current theory. But every theory about the world presupposes these pre-scientific convictions about the world around us and that is sufficient, I think, for purposes of religion. That doesn't mean that one is disinterested in science but I think most of the great scientists have had a very modest

conception of what science is able to achieve or how final its positions can be and that seems to me to be a very attractive thing,
because, you know, if you just take astronomy, over my lifetime, the
advances in knowledge are just unbelievable. And yet astronomy is
the oldest science. The first thing that people wondered about the
planets, about eclipses and all the rest of it, and many of their theories, of course, looked kind of weird to us but maybe our theories
will look weird to somebody too.

*Do you think a traditional faith would preclude life on other
planets?*

Do you mean human life or just life?

Any kind of conscious life.

Well, I don't see why it would. The only real thing that seems to me
to be precluded would be that there would be other human beings,
and for a lot of reasons: the whole unity of the human race and the
whole story of salvation yields a geocentric universe as far as the
human race goes. I don't mean we are the center of the universe. I
think from the point of view of ontological value the earth is the center of things, so, you know, to think that there would be a human
race elsewhere is almost incoherent. They would be people who
would have the same parentage we do only they don't have the same
parents we do. So I think it would be very difficult to know just what
the problem would be. But, as with this thing on Mars, it seems to
me there is an awful tendency on the part of people to go far beyond
what they can to sort of downplay the importance of Earth. It's the
strangest thing. You get that very often when people talk about
astronomy: they are almost gloating over the fact that the Earth is
this little speck. Yes, but you are on that speck talking about the
whole thing. That is rather amazing, isn't it? So, it seems to me to tell
against itself. Here you've got these specks on this speck which somehow, in our minds, can comprehend the whole and that is truly amazing. That is much more amazing than physical space, it seems to me.

OWEN GINGERICH

*As a scientist, on what basis do you affirm or deny the exis-
tence of God?*

As a scientist, as someone who has looked very much at the structure of science, I realize that science does very little of its operation

by proof; mostly it is a system of coherence: how things hang togeth-er and how things make sense. And it seems to me from my own point of view, looking at nature, looking at scripture, looking at human relations, it makes sense to me to accept the existence of God. This provides for me a coherent structure. In other words, I am one of these people who refuses to believe that human consciousness is a capricious accident of nature. I believe in purpose and I believe that we are part of the purpose of the universe. That is for me a view that I cannot prove, but I would defend it from the point of view of making sense.

Would you construe the existence of regularity and order in the universe as evidence for a creative mind behind the universe?

I do not find that order as such is a compelling kind of argument. But the intricacy of design is very powerful to me. We can see such an enormous amount of fine tuning in the way the universe is con-structed. It seems to me that it calls for a superintelligent designer.

Do you find the argument from design, in some modified form, to provide a plausible basis for affirming the existence of God?

This is the plausibility argument that I accept. It is not a proof. I realize that the arguments from design have been thoroughly exam-ined and found wanting as a strictly logical deductive system. But nevertheless it strikes me as making more sense to believe that nature is ultimately purposeful rather than merely accidental.

Would you say that one reason for affirming God's existence is that from a probability standpoint it seems to be a plausible explanation for a universe showing such intricate design?

I would hesitate to say that I am deciding this on the basis of proba-bilities because probabilities have a very technical meaning. While I would say that I am choosing the more probable route, I would pre-fer to say that on the whole I am taking the more coherent picture, the one that holds itself together and makes sense. I want to avoid some-body coming to me and saying, can you use Bayesian probability to confirm your position? I'm not prepared to argue it on that level.

Ultimately, then, it comes down to the fact that this would seem to provide a more coherent explanation?

Exactly.

What kind of attributes would you postulate for God?

If one identifies God merely as a great transcendence, as Milton Munitz argues in his book *Cosmic Understanding*, then we derive a kind of unknowable God. However, there is a logical contradiction in that: If God is unknowable we cannot be certain that God is unknowable, that is to say, there is always the possibility of God making Itself known to us. I would accept the statement in Genesis 1:27 as being the fundamental meaning of that first chapter: God created man in His image, male and female created He them. This suggests to me that we have certain God-given attributes including the possibility of understanding the divine, of being ourselves creative, having conscience and consciousness.

I believe that, therefore, part of the nature of God is to be on the one hand very subtle and on the other hand not entirely secret, so that we have the possibility as rational, thinking beings to gain some understanding of this infinite mystery that surrounds us. And just because we are doing it by human thought does not mean that this is a fiction or a fantasy any more than our constructing the scientific theories of the beginning of the world, of the nature of atoms and quantum mechanics, and so on. It is, I think, a part of the God-given attributes that we have the possibility of understanding the divine in some small way. It is a continuing search for each of us who are theologically inclined. It is a lifetime quest to try to understand this better, and it is a quest of the entire human race.

Would you see God as being distinct from the cosmos?

I would accept God as creator and therefore something different from being the cosmos itself. I think it's almost a tautology to identify the cosmos itself with God. I accept God as a transcendence who continually works within creation yet also in a profound sense stands beyond creation.

What bearing, if any, does science have on religion – particularly with respect to the questions of God's existence, the origin of the universe, the origin of life, and the possibility of miracles? Do you think science can tell us anything in those areas or are these outside scientific discourse?

The Judeo–Christian tradition has, of course, believed fundamentally in *history*, that there is a changing universe, a kind of stage in which God acts. And it is amazing that modern science, unlike the Greek view of things, shows a universe with creation, with evolution, and with a fundamental pattern of change. Part of that evolution of the universe is preparing for the possibility of life, that is to say, the atoms that are required for life are not present in the Big Bang. They come about much more slowly over the long eons that follow.

Now I don't find that the Bible is a scientific textbook. I would very strongly endorse what Galileo said, that the Bible teaches how to go to Heaven, not how the heavens go. So I would take issue with the Creationists or people who want to make a literal scientific textbook out of the Bible. On the other hand, I think that science and discovery does tell us something about the framework, the stage on which God acts. If you think back to the time when the Middle Ages were coming to a close, there was a very distinct sacred geography in which God was not all that far away. You could measure in miles how far away God and Heaven were beyond the sphere of fixed stars. And that is something that science has forced us to abandon. So there are interactions between science and our religious beliefs. I think we've come to a much more sophisticated level of sacred geography now that is very far different from the conception in the Middle Ages and early Renaissance.

Now you ask about the origin of life. It seems to me science is by its nature looking for mechanistic explanations. That includes mechanistic explanations for the origin of life. This doesn't mean that science is anti-God or atheistic. But it simply means that the rules of how we do science exclude the hand of God as an explanation. I can hold an apple in my hand and let it go; it falls to the floor, and you could say that is because of God's action in the universe causing the apple to drop. And in a certain sense, as a theist, I believe in God as a continual sustainer of the universe from one moment to another and one moment to another in the trajectory of the apple. But that's not science. When Isaac Newton gives a law of gravitation that enables us to describe mathematically how the apple will drop as it falls (and it doesn't refer to the hand of God), that is a different kind of thing than our theistic understanding of the universe. And I would say that's the same with respect to the origin of life. We cannot distinguish scientifically to what extent the hand of God was involved in this, whether the hand of God is only in the initial design that has all the potentialities of different life-forms of which some of them get realized because we can tell in looking at the incredible complexity of the genetic structure of human beings that there are fantastically more possibilities than the human population can ever achieve. Not all genetic possibilities will ever be realized. But some are. And the same can be true with life itself.

How about the origin of the universe? Is there an ultimate mystery here that lies beyond science? If we attribute the origin or existence of the universe to certain laws of physics, then we can still ask how these laws came to be.

The laws of physics are in some fashion designed, and that is where I feel that God's creativity is at work. Even if it were shown that in some way the universe existed forever, that there was no moment of creation, I would say that does not eliminate the need for a Creator because in my view of the universe the Creator in the sense of the designer of the physical laws is still required.

And this would apply even to notions such as Stephen Hawking's no-boundary proposal in his A Brief History of Time?

That's right. There's a curious kind of conundrum in this book and it was seized upon by Carl Sagan in writing the introduction, where he pointed out so dramatically that Hawking asks, "What need then for a Creator?" Sagan did not reflect on the way in which Hawking, in fact, ends the book with this sense of mystery about where the laws themselves come from. It is an interesting and strange kind of mathematical transformation that Hawking has accomplished, in which he has no moment of beginning or no moment of creation and yet he has a universe with an age and a history. Therefore for all practical purposes there is still an emergent universe.

We return to the question of what bearing science has on the possibility of miracles.

It's certainly the case that the universe after the twentieth-century revolutions in physics is a far differently conceived place than it would have been, let us say, in the aftermath of Laplace and his intense determinism. It seems to me that there is a kind of openness in the universe at its very basic structure that would allow for the operation of God's will in a way that is undetectable with respect to physical experiments. So I am very open on this question, just as I think the universe itself is open. I think there is a possibility of miracles in the universe. Therefore there is meaning in the efficacy of prayer. These are difficult theological questions, which I don't feel that I'm particularly well-positioned to discuss in a philosophical way.

GEORGE F. R. ELLIS

What do we know from modern cosmology about the origin of the universe and at what point does the origin problem move from physics to metaphysics?

The universe has expanded to its present state from a hot Big Bang, whose physics is well understood back to the time of element formation (but is rather speculative at earlier times than that). The Cosmic Microwave Background Radiation examined in detail by the COBE satellite is relic radiation from the hot early phase of the evolution of the universe.

The study of this expansion and evolutionary development is the subject of physical cosmology. The first set of problems, then, are those arising in this study. These are basic observational difficulties, additional problems due to horizons, and the limits of possible physical verification.

BASIC OBSERVATIONAL DIFFICULTIES:

Our ability to directly determine the geometry and distribution of matter in the universe is restricted by many observational difficulties, including the faintness of the images we are trying to understand. We can only detect distant matter by means of particles or radiation it emits that travels to us, receiving most of our information from light. (Here it is understood that light is a generic term for any form of electromagnetic radiation by which we can see distant objects: radio waves, infrared radiation, ultraviolet radiation, and x-rays as well as ordinary light). There are therefore fundamental limitations on the region of the universe we can see, because the radiation conveying information travels towards us at the speed of light (and any massive particles travel slower than this speed). As we look out to further and further distances, we are necessarily looking further and further back in time (for example the Andromeda galaxy is a million light years away; this means we see it as it was a million years ago). We are therefore seeing the sources at earlier stages in their evolution. This makes it very difficult to disentangle the effects of physical evolution of the sources observed, from geometrical evolution of the universe. This is the main reason we are unable to tell directly from observations of the rate of change of redshift with distance if the universe will recollapse or not.

The expansion of the universe is well evidenced by the redshift-distance relation for galaxies, but we have trouble in identifying accurately the size and age of the universe, determined by the Hubble constant. While redshift can be measured accurately, it is rather difficult to measure the distance of distant galaxies. We cannot easily use astronomical objects as standard candles because we do not understand their evolution – how have they changed with time. Equally we have great difficulty in even estimating how much matter there is in the observable region of the universe, because of the problem of dark matter: it is possible that most of the matter in the universe is not radiating very much and so is almost indetectable.

These problems are aggravated by the fact that as we look to sources at further distance (and hence higher redshift), the amount of light we receive from them rapidly fades away – an inevitable consequence of the nature of redshift (photons lose energy as their wavelength increases). Thus at larger and larger distances, the universe fades away. Modern detectors can to some extent compensate for this – and we are presently receiving remarkable images of objects at enormous distances from the Hubble Space Telescope; nevertheless what we can tell fades rapidly away on our past light-cone (that part of the universe we can see to), and so what we can deduce off the past light cone fades even more rapidly.

Furthermore, there is an absolute limit to what we can detect by astronomical observation at any wavelength. This is because as we look back into the past and the temperature of the background radiation rises, it leads to ionization of matter at a redshift of about 1000; and then the universe becomes completely opaque. We cannot see to earlier times because radiation cannot penetrate the hot, dense primeval plasma that existed at those times. No improvement of technology will change that situation. The COBE images of microwave background radiation temperature fluctuations are images of the most distant matter we will ever be able to see by electromagnetic radiation, that is, by ordinary telescopes, whatever their wavelength (neutrino or gravitational wave telescopes can theoretically see to earlier times; but they too – if ever developed sufficiently to produce images of meaningful quality – would also each encounter a similar barrier at earlier times).

HORIZONS AND LIMITS OF VERIFICATION

However, there other fundamental restrictions on what we can observe.

The particle horizon: Because the universe has a finite age, light can only have traveled a finite distance since the origin of the universe. This feature implies that we can only see out to those particles whose present-day distance corresponds to the age of the universe; the particles beyond cannot be seen by us no matter what detectors we may use (light has not had time to travel to us from them since the creation of the universe). The effect is the same as the horizon we see when we look at distant objects on the Earth: there are many further objects we cannot see because they lie beyond the horizon. In the case of the expanding universe, we call the horizon separating those particles (which later will become galaxies) that we can have seen, or indeed have had any causal contact with, from those we cannot, the *particle horizon*. Actually we cannot even see as far as the particle horizon, because the universe is opaque at early times (before decoupling), as just explained. In reality we can see only as far as the *visual horizon*, corresponding to where the universe becomes transparent; this lies inside the particle horizon, and corresponds to looking back as far as the matter that emitted the cosmic background radiation (at the time of decoupling). To fully understand these limits one should look at the associated space–time diagrams.

It is because of these limits that we are able to say very little about the universe on scales bigger than the *Hubble size* (the distance we can have seen since the beginning of the universe, roughly ten thousand million light years). Thus we cannot observationally distinguish between universe models that are strictly homogeneous in the large (implying conditions are the same at a distance one million times the Hubble size away from us, as they are here), and those that are not. If the universe has finite spatial sections, there are at least as many galaxies outside our view as within it; while if it has infinite spatial sections, we cannot see an infinite number of galaxies, so what we can see is an infinitely small fraction of all there is. Any statements we make about the structure of the universe on a really large scale (that is, many times the horizon size) are strictly unverifiable.

Small universes: There is one exception to this generally pessimistic situation. It is possible (even if the universe is a low-density universe) that the large-scale connectivity of space could be different from what we expected, so that the universe is in fact a small universe, spatially closed on a scale smaller than the Hubble size. Then if one could go in an arbitrary spatial direction at constant time, one would eventually end up very close to where one began (as in the case of a sphere, torus, or a Mobius strip). If this were the case we would be able to see right round the universe several times; so we could see each galaxy (including our own) many times through images in different directions in the sky, a relatively small number of galaxies giving a very large number of images.

The effect is like being in a room whose walls, floor, and ceiling are all covered with mirrors: you see a huge number of images of yourself fading away into the distance in all directions. Similarly in a small universe, despite its small size we would see a large number of images of each galaxy fading away in an apparently infinite universe. In this case (and only in this case) there would be no visual horizon, and we can in principle determine the geometry of the whole universe by observation, for all the matter that exists is accessible to our observation (in contrast to the usually considered situation, where only a small fraction of that matter can be seen). Furthermore, in this case we would be able to study the history of our own galaxy by optical observations, as we would be able to see it at different times in its history in the different images that would be visible to us.

Now it is possible we live in such a small universe, but if this were true then observationally proving this to be the real situation would be difficult; and there is no solid evidence that this is indeed the case. Thus the working hypothesis is that we do not live in a small universe, but we should keep an open mind on this matter.

Limits to verifiability: Overall, what we can say with any degree of certainty is strictly proscribed by observational limits. We can in principle observationally determine (a) a great deal about the region we can observe (which lies inside the visual horizon); (b) a little about that which lies outside our visual horizon but inside the particle horizon (we might be able to tell something by use of neutrino or gravitational wave telescopes, some day when technology has developed sufficiently, but this is decades into the future); (c) nothing about that which lies beyond the particle horizon: this region is unobservable by any method. In a small universe there are no visual horizons, but the real universe is probably not like that. The implication is that when our models give predictions of the nature of the universe on a larger scale than the Hubble radius, these are strictly unverifiable, however appealing they may be.

LIMITS OF PHYSICS VERIFICATION

In trying to understand the early universe, we also come up against major limits in terms of our ability to test the predictions of our proposals for physical laws. Even if we could build a super-collider as large as the entire Solar System, we could not reach the kinds of energies that come into play in the very early universe, so we cannot test the behavior of matter under the relevant conditions. This puts major limits on our ability to test whether our theories of those times are right or not. For example, while it is commonly believed that inflation – a period of very rapid expansion – took place in the early universe, we have been unable so far to detect in experiments on Earth the field responsible for inflation, and so cannot confirm that the proposal for the underlying mechanism is correct. Similarly the proposals as to how synthesis of protons from quarks took place in the early universe cannot yet be confirmed because we have not seen the relevant particles, and measurements of the decay rate of the proton contradicts that simplest theory that could underlie the proposed mechanism; we do not know which of the more complex possibilities (if any) may be correct.

Indeed the early universe is the only place where some of the laws of physics come fully into play (apart from what happens to matter in the final state of collapse in a black hole; but that is completely inaccessible to observation); consequently the situation is reversed from what we might hope, in that instead of being able to take known laws and use them to determine what happened in the very early universe, we may have to proceed the other way round, regarding the early universe as the only laboratory where those laws can be tested. This has led to an important discovery; comparison of element abundance observations with studies of nucleosynthesis in the early universe determined that there are only three neutrino types, rather than four, before this question had been tested experimentally on Earth. Results from the accelerator at CERN later confirmed this conclusion.

However, this type of reasoning only works when there are a few clearcut alternatives that make clear observational predictions, and depends on the assumed cosmological conditions being correct.

When we consider the really fundamental questions, whose understanding is the Holy Grail of theoretical physics, even the broad kind of approach to take is not clear. One is concerned here with the unification of our understanding of all the known forces into a single theory that, at a fundamental level, is a "theory of everything," combining together the features of gravity, electromagnetism, the weak force, and the strong force in a way compatible with relativity theory and with quantum theory.

Various proposals have been made, of which the recently most popular is superstring theory, representing fundamental particles as string-like rather than as point particles. However, this has not yet been formulated in a fully satisfactory way. Some such kind of physics probably controls the very earliest phases of the expansion of the universe; we can reject some of the theories on the basis of their cosmological predictions, but cannot in this way select a particular one as being correct, nor can experiments on Earth distinguish between them. We certainly cannot use this broad class of theories to determine a unique history for the very early universe. Thus the practical limit of testing of physical laws, in particular, testing the nature of fundamental forces, are major limitations in determining what happened at very early times (fractions of a second after the Big Bang).

Physical origins: This problem occurs a fortiori in considering the origin of the universe, which set the conditions determining what exists today. The Big Bang theory outlined previously makes it clear that at a very early times there must have been an epoch where the ideas of classical physics simply did not apply; Quantum Gravity (a theory unifying general relativity with quantum theory) would have been the dominant factor at these times. There are a number of different theoretical approaches to this topic, none of which is wholly satisfactory, so we do not even know for sure what basic approach to use in such theories; and there is no way we can test these different options by Earth-based experiments. However, it is these theories that underlie what we would really like to know about the nature of the origin of the universe.

Despite this uncertainty, we can claim that major features of quantum mechanics, such as the underlying wave-like nature of matter, must apply here also, on this basis we can make quantum cosmology models with claims to correctly represent the results of the as yet unknown theory of quantum gravity, when applied to the very origin of the universe.

Various such theories have been proposed to explain the origin of the universe in terms of quantum development from some previous state (a collapsing previous phase, a region of flat space–time, a black hole final state, some kind of "pre-geometry"). Such approaches can provide a whole series of alternative proposals for the origin of the Hot Big Bang which has led to our existence, but of course simply postpones the ultimate issue, for one can then ask, what was the origin of this previous phase? This remains unanswered.

Tied in to this is our lack of resolution of some of the fundamental issues at the base of physics: notably the arrow of time problem, and the nature and consequences of Mach's principle. There is no time to deal with them here.

The no-boundary idea: One rather unique and intriguing proposal sidesteps this problem neatly. This is the Hartle–Hawking suggestion that the initial state of the universe could be a region where time did not exist: instead of three spatial dimensions and one time dimension, there were four spatial dimensions. This has a great advantage: it is then possible there can be a universe without a beginning, for (just as there is no boundary to the surface of the Earth at the South Pole) there is no boundary to this initial region of the universe; it is uniform and smooth at all points. Much is made of this proposal in Hawking's book *A Brief History of Time*, for it does indeed describe a universe without a beginning in the ordinary sense of the word, although time does have a beginning (where there is a transition from this strange "Euclidean" state to a normal space–time structure). Attractive as this is, one must be concerned about its foundations.

Firstly, such proposals suppose unraveling some of the underlying conundrums of quantum theory that have not yet been solved in a fully satisfactory manner (specifically, the related issues of the role of an observer in quantum theory, and what determines the collapse of the wave function, which is an essential feature of measurement in quantum theory). These do not arise as significant problems in the context of laboratory experiments, but become substantial difficulties in the context of applying quantum theory (which is usually applied to submicroscopic systems) to the universe as a whole.

Second, we certainly cannot test the Wheeler–de Witt equation underlying quantum cosmology: we have to accept it as a huge extrapolation of existing physics, plausible because of its basis in established physical laws but untestable in its own right. Even some of the underlying concepts (such as "the wave function of the universe") have a questionable status in this context (for they are associated with a probabilistic interpretation which may not make sense when applied to a unique object, namely the universe).

The issue of initial conditions: Thirdly, and irrespective of our resolution of the previous issues, we are tackling here the problem of initial conditions for the universe: we are trying to use physical theory to describe something which happened once and only once, and for which no comparable happenings have ever occurred (or at least, none are accessible to our observations). The notion of a law to describe this situation faces considerable difficulties. If a "law" is only ever applied to one physical object, it is not clear if the usual distinction between a physical law and specific initial conditions makes sense. That "law" certainly cannot be subject to empirical test in the same way as other physical laws.

Whatever "law" we may set up to describe this situation, we have one and only one test we can do: we can observe the existent universe and see if it is congruent with the predictions of that "law." If it passed this test, this supports that law but not uniquely, for there will in general be several laws or underlying approaches that give the same result; these cannot be distinguished from each other on the basis of any experimental tests. We can obtain strong support for one particular view (such as the Hartle–Hawking "no-boundary" proposal) only by utilizing criteria for good theories that are metaphysical.

Whatever explanation we may give for them, unique initial conditions occurred at the origin of the universe. They determine both the initial structure of space–time, and its matter content.

The matter we see around us today is the remnants of that initial state, after it has been processed by non-equilibrium processes in the early universe and then in a first generation of stars. Thus we understand the role of initial conditions; however this analysis does not answer the ultimate issues of origin and existence, in particular why the initial conditions had the form they did (even if the Hartle–Hawking proposal were correct, or a steady-state universe description, for that matter, there are alternative possibilities; we would still face the issue, why does that particular prescription describe the real universe?).

We know a great deal, indeed an astonishing amount, about the structure and evolution of the universe in the large; but there are also major limits on what we can know scientifically about these issues, in the sense of being able to test them observationally, when we go to the limits of what can be observed and the underlying question of the uniqueness of the initial state (whether it is a singular state or not). These are unsolved by physics itself; they inevitably lead to metaphysical issues and questions.

Much has been made in recent years about the anthropic principle – the remarkable coincidence of the relative strengths of the forces of nature, the properties of elementary particles, etc., that made human life possible at all in the universe. What bearing does such "fine-tuning" have on the metaphysical question of origin?

The major question that one is concerned with here is, What is the role of life in the universe? Certainly on a physical scale life is quite insignificant in the immensities of galactic and inter-galactic space; but physical size is not necessarily a measure of importance.

The point is that a great deal of "fine tuning" has taken place in order that life be possible; in particular, various fundamental constants are highly constrained in their values if life as we know it is to exist – there are many relationships imbedded in physical laws that are not explained by physics, but are required for life to be possible. How has it come about that the universe permits the evolution and existence of intelligent beings at any time or place?

THE ISSUE OF FINE TUNING

Significant alteration of either physical laws or boundary conditions at the beginning of the universe would prevent the existence of intelligent life as we know it in the universe. If physical laws were altered by a remarkably little amount, no evolutionary process at all of living beings would be possible; so these laws appear fine-tuned to allow the existence of life.

We can easily consider universes where life would not be possible. There could be a universe that expanded and then recollapsed with a total lifetime of only one hundred thousand years; evolution could not take place on that timescale. The background radiation might never drop below 3000 K, so that matter was always ionized (electrons and nuclei always remaining separate from each other); the molecules of life could then never form. Black holes might be so common that they rapidly attracted all the matter in the universe, and there never was a stable environment in which life could develop. Cosmic rays could always be so abundant that any tentative organic structures are destroyed before they can replicate.

Thus there are many ways that the boundary conditions in a universe could prevent life occurring. But additionally, we can conceive of universes where the laws of physics (and so of chemistry) were different than in ours. Almost any change in these laws will prevent life as know it from functioning. If the neutron mass were just a little less than it is, proton decay could have taken place so that no atoms were left at all. The production of carbon and oxygen in stars requires the careful setting of two different nuclear energy levels; if they were just a little different, the elements we need for life would not exist. Perhaps most important of all, the chemistry on which the human body depends involves intricate folding and bonding patterns that would be destroyed if the fine structure constant (which controls the nature of chemical binding) were a little bit different.

To understand the import of this, one must appreciate the complexity of what has been achieved. The structure and function of a single living cell is immensely complex. However, a human grows to an interconnected set of ten thousand billion cells, all working together as a single purposive and conscious organism in a hierarchically controlled way (the *organization* issue), put together according to instructions in the DNA molecules that are read out and executed in an order that depends both on time and position (the issue of *development*), able to function continuously all the time as the number of cells increases coherently from one to ten thousand billion in a highly organized fashion, passing through different stages of maturity (the issue of *growth*), all of this happening in an interacting set of organisms of a similar levels of complexity within a hospitable environment (the *ecosystem* issue), this system itself developing from single cell to the level of complexity we see around us today (the *evolution* issue), all the while remaining functional. And all of this is possible because of the nature of quantum mechanics (essentially the Schroedinger equation and the Pauli exclusion principle) and of the forces and particles described by physics (essentially the electromagnetic force acting on the proton and the electron, together with the strong force binding the protons and neutrons in the atomic nuclei), which together control the nature of chemistry and hence of biological activity. They all fit together as required because of the precise values taken by the fundamental constants that control the strengths of physical interactions, which happen also to allow the functioning of stars as required to produce the needed elements, and allow development of the solar system (which is made possible through the force of gravity), with a hospitable surface for life on the Earth (one of the key elements here being the remarkable properties of water, which again would be different if the fundamental constants were different).

The nature of this achievement is truly awesome. And the modern moves towards determining a unified fundamental theory of all forces could make this even more amazing, because if physics ever achieved its aim of determining a single theory with essentially no free constants, then these extraordinarily complex structures would be the result of the action of that unified theory: in effect, the nature of the unified fundamental force would be preordained to allow, or even encourage, the existence of life.

In summary, to allow life to occur, we require the existence of heavy elements; sufficient time for evolution of advanced life forms to take place; regions that are neither too hot nor too cold; restricted value of fundamental constants that control chemistry and local physics; and so on. Thus only particular laws of physics – and particular initial conditions in the universe – allow the existence of intelligent life. No evolution whatever is possible if these laws and conditions do not have a restricted form, which will not be true in a generic universe.

Thus the universe provides a hospitable environment for humanity. Why is this so? Because of the deep connections between physical aspects of the universe, this is not an issue related to only one aspect of the structure of the universe; it refers to the total interrelated organization of the laws of nature and the boundary conditions for those laws, that fashions the universe as we know it. Thus the profound issue arising is the anthropic question: Why have conditions in the universe been so ordered that intelligent life can exist?

THE WEAK ANTHROPIC PRINCIPLE

There are two purely scientific approaches to the anthropic issue. The first is the Weak Anthropic Principle (WAP), based on the comment: it is not surprising the observed universe admits the existence of life, for the universe cannot be observed unless there are observers in it. This seemingly empty statement gains content when we turn it round and ask, at what times and places in the universe can life exist, and what are the interconnections that are critical for its existence? It could not, for example, exist too early in the present expansion phase, for the night sky would then have been too hot. Indeed from this viewpoint the reason the observed night sky is dark at night is that if it were not dark, there would be no observers to see it. Furthermore one can deduce various necessary relations between fundamental quantities in order that the observers should exist, so that if, for example, the fundamental constants vary with time or place in the universe, life will only be possible in restricted regions where they take appropriate anthropic values.

Hence this view basically interprets the anthropic principle as a selection principle: *the necessary conditions for observers to exist restricts the times and places from which the universe can be observed.*

This is an interesting and often illuminating viewpoint. However, it is also a conservative approach, avoiding the main issue under discussion.

THE STRONG ANTHROPIC PRINCIPLE

By contrast, the Strong Anthropic Principle (SAP) tackles the issue head on, claiming that it is necessary that intelligent life exist in the universe; the presence of life is required in order that a universe model makes sense.

Considered purely scientifically, this is clearly a very controversial claim, for it is hard to provide scientific reasons to support this view. The most solid justification attempted is through the claim that existence of an observer is necessary in order that quantum theory can make sense. However, this is based on one of a number of different interpretations of quantum theory; the nature of these quantum foundations is controversial, and probably falls within the untestable category of issues discussed above. Furthermore, if we were to suppose this argument correct, then the next step is to ask, Why does the universe need quantum mechanics anyway? The argument would be complete only if we could prove that quantum mechanics was absolutely necessary for every self-consistent universe; but that line of reasoning cannot be completed at present, not least because quantum mechanics itself is not a fully self-consistent theory (apart from the logical issues at its foundation, it suffers from divergences that so far have proved irremediable in the sense that we can work our way round them to calculate what we need, but cannot remove them).

Neither argument by itself gives a convincing answer to the anthropic question. They attempt to relate to issues of meaning which physical cosmology, and indeed science, is unable to address. They require a metaphysical explanation.

What are the metaphysical questions that underlie science?

To focus this issue, one should turn to the metaphysics of cosmology, and the three major questions one finds here:

1. Why are there any laws of physics?
2. What determines their form?
3. Why does anything exist at all?

These issues lie at the foundation of cosmology, which – like all science – assumes at its very start existence of space–time and matter, and that some laws of physics exist and determine what happens to them; and considers the consequences of those particular laws which happen to have been actualized in the existent physical universe. Then it is important to realize:

Science itself cannot resolve the metaphysical issues posed by questioning the reason for (i) the existence of the universe; (ii) the existence of any physical laws at all; or (iii) the nature of the specific physical laws that actually hold. These require a different kind of explanation than a purely scientific approach can provide.

The point here is that science assumes as its ground the existence of laws of nature. It cannot by itself investigate this issue of why laws exist – there is no experiment we can use to do so. Again one of its central concerns is what the laws of nature are; but it cannot in a serious sense ask why the laws have the specific nature they do (for example why does gravity exist?) – that is again a metaphysical issue. We cannot devise experimental tests that will answer such questions.

Thus science itself cannot provide a metaphysics that relates to the issues of meaning that are expressed in "Why" questions; it cannot tackle the issue that the person in the street wants answered: What underlying meaning may there be?

When supposed science attempts to answer this question, you may be sure you are dealing with pseudo-science rather than science.

Science itself cannot, by its very structure and nature, answer questions to do with meaning – with the kinds of issues that are our concern in living our daily lives.

In what way does our moral experience suggest the existence of God?

There are really only two viable standpoints here. The first is that this moral strand is simply a result of our evolutionary heritage, broadly arising through socio-biology processes and adaptation of the mind to the necessities of survival. I believe this is an inadequate proposal, for a number of reasons. Firstly, it seems highly unlikely that such an evolutionary approach can lead to high levels of moral behavior – not least because evolutionary pressures have no concern for the individual – they are concerned only with survival of populations. They would favor survival of the fittest at the expense of the weak rather than behavior patterns that make a virtue of looking after the weak, who will always be a burden on society, for example by looking after Downs Syndrome children. Secondly, if this were indeed the only basis for our inbred ethical tendencies, then once we realized this was the source, that realization would remove the moral standing of our highest ethical experiences – for it removes the incentive to higher behavior, replacing it by in effect stating that the highest good is survival of the species. This understanding would remove legitimate concern for the individual. It would provide the foundation of fascist ethics. And thirdly, it completely underestimates the major problem for such theories arising from the fact that nothing we think or learn affects in any way the genes we pass on to our children. That genetic heritage is determined the day we are born, and is unaffected by any experiences we undergo.

The second option is that in the end none of this makes sense unless it is real: that this moral path is inbuilt into the foundation of the universe, along with the laws of logic and of physics. There is an ethical underpinning to the universe as well as a physical one. Our moral understanding does indeed proceed through a slow process of adaptation both of the brain and of culture; but these are of the nature of a discovery of the way things really are, rather than of creating a convenient set of behavior patterns from nothing.

The key point, then, is which is the more fundamental: the physical or the moral and ethical strand in the foundation of the universe? It seems clear that there is no way that the physical by itself could ever lead to these kinds of ethical concepts. However, despite what may be said about the so-called naturalistic fallacy, the ethical could lead to the physical if we adopt the traditional Christian view, in the following form: Fundamental assumption: there is a transcendent God who is Creator and sustainer of the universe, and whose purpose in creation is to make possible high-level loving and sacrificial action by freelyacting, self-conscious individuals.

On this view, this aim is what underlies all physics and indeed the universe; it gives the rationale and foundation for cosmology and thereby explains some of its major features. This leads to a coherent view based on top-down causation where theology is indeed the queen of the sciences as it shapes the nature of physical laws. It ties in with religious experience which is taken by those experiencing it to be self-validating.

In essence the argument is that morality is real, and we know it is real through our everyday experience (which is indeed data about the nature of the universe). The only genuinely viable foundation for true morality (as opposed to attitudes and behavior necessary for a society to function relatively smoothly, which is just utilitarianism) is that this morality has an independent and intrinsic existence of its own – just as the laws of physics and of logic do. And the most obvious viable foundation for that existence is through the moral nature of a creator.

KEITH WARD

On what basis do you affirm the existence of God as opposed to the rival options of chance and necessity?

The whole of modern science is based on the fundamental presupposition that the universe is intelligible, that it can be understood by the human mind, that events do not just occur for no reason. The natural sciences have achieved their enormous success by discovering underlying laws which describe measurable regularities of relationship between basic physical forces and the fundamental particles upon which they operate. The question, "Why do these events happen as they do?" has unfailingly had an answer, which observation and imaginative theorizing together have uncovered.

What this suggests is that there are underlying connections which necessarily obtain in the physical realm. But the basis for that necessity remains obscure. As cosmologists trace the laws of nature back to their space–time origin, it seems as if only two basic options suggest themselves. One is that in some way the fundamental laws and initial conditions of the universe are necessary. They have to be what they are, and if one could understand that necessity, one would have answered the most fundamental question of all, "Why does the universe exist as it does"? The other is that the fundamental laws just exist by chance. There is no objective necessity in nature, and there is no basic reason why things are as they are. Explanation has to come to an end, and we have to say, "Finally, it just happens!"

The appeal to chance must be the last resort for a scientific mind. It is simply giving up on the attempt to find an explanation. It seems odd, even though it is not self-contradictory, to say that there is an explanation for everything, except for why the whole system is the way it is – when that is the very thing we most want to explain. So necessity is the more attractive option for a scientist. But this universe just does not seem to be necessary. It seems to be a contingent universe, one that could very easily have been other than it is, in many ways.

Still, in some way its basic laws and processes might be necessary. Maybe the basic equations of quantum theory only permit one consistent set of solutions – but why should those equations be the way they are, or how can they give rise to a physical universe, if they are only mathematical equations, and thus apparently abstract?

The ideal situation would be if one could find something that is necessary and yet also really existent, something that could select the basic equations which govern this space–time universe, and also bring about the basic forces of nature over which those equations could operate. That is precisely the traditional idea of God in classical Judaism, Islam, and Christianity. One can find it in a paradigm form in Anselm and Aquinas. According to this view, God is a being which, uniquely, exists by absolute necessity. There is no alternative to God's existence, since God exists in every possible world, as the basis of that world's (possible) actuality. God, having knowledge of every possible state of affairs, conceives of all mathematical truths and can select an elegant subset of them to govern a physical universe. God, being self-existent, does not depend on anything else for its existence, but possesses the power of being in itself. So God has the power to bring material forms into existence, over which the selected laws can operate. God, it seems, is just the hypothesis that science needs to provide a finally satisfying explanation for why the universe is the way it is. God is that necessary being which answers every "why?" question by showing the reason why the ultimate laws of the physical universe are as they are.

But how can a necessarily existent God give rise to a contingent universe? Are we not reduced to the empty bluster that the universe is the way it is just because God arbitrarily wills it? Not at all. God, on the hypothesis, exists by necessity, and possesses the essential properties of the divine nature (those without which God would not exist at all) necessarily. Among those properties God is necessarily omnipotent. That is, God is able to bring about any state of affairs consistent with the divine nature, which cannot itself be other than it is. Among those states of affairs are many contingent universes. So it is necessarily true that God can bring about one, or many, contingent universes. In other words, it is necessarily true that God can act contingently, by free choice.

If God does so, that does not make God's acts arbitrary. That would once again reduce explanation to mere chance. The crucial point is that God always acts contingently for a reason. That reason lies in the distinctive goodness, or value, or intrinsic worthwhileness, of the states produced. So now we have the ultimate explanation for the universe, its laws and basic physical states – there is a being which exists by necessity, and which necessarily selects the basic laws of the universe for the sake of the good states that the universe will realize. God is a supremely elegant ultimate explanation, because God unites both causal and purposive explanations in one simple integrating hypothesis.

The hypothesis of God is far superior to the hypothesis of chance, because it offers an ultimate explanation for the universe, in terms of a necessarily existing cause and a purpose of intrinsic goodness. It is superior to the hypothesis of blind necessity, because it locates necessity in an actually existent being with the power to bring into existence a physical universe, and it accounts for the contingency of the universe in terms of its freely and consciously chosen goodness.

The God hypothesis will only work if this universe does realize distinctive and worthwhile forms of goodness, if it is overwhelmingly better that it exists than not, and if the goods it realizes could not otherwise exist. These are, I think, plausible axioms, and if they are accepted the strongest hypothesis which justifies the success of science and the complete intelligibility of the universe is that of one necessarily existing creator, capable of free action for the sake of goodness.

What is your assessment of the relevance of the quasi-theological interpretations of recent studies in cosmology (found, for instance, in the works of Stephen Hawking and Peter Atkins) to the question of God's existence?

Recent cosmological attempts to give a thoroughgoing explanation for the universe are remarkably similar to traditional theological theories about God and creation, though they embody a number of misunderstandings of the theological traditions. The chief misunderstanding is that theists posit a disembodied person who arbitrarily starts the universe going, but then lets it run largely on its own. They then protest that the existence of such a person would need explaining, and they sometimes try to show that the universe could originate on its own, without any creator.

I have pointed out that the traditional idea is that God is a necessarily existing being, incapable of being brought into being or of being destroyed. Anyone with complete understanding would be able to comprehend the necessity of the divine being, and see how and why the universe originates by a combination of necessity and of free divine decision to realize distinctive values. This would be a truly ultimate explanation.

Quantum cosmologists cannot provide such an ultimate explanation, since they must leave the initial quantum states and the very complex laws governing their behaviour (which they sometimes, very misleadingly, call "quantum fluctuations in a vacuum") unexplained. The vacuum in question is not, of course, absolute nothingness, but an array of electrons in their ground-states. The fluctuations are subject to a law which realizes possible states serially and exhaustively, on the theory – a law whose existence and effectiveness itself needs explanation.

If appeal is made to the relative simplicity of the initial states and the elegance of the basic laws, such theories are quite near to the theistic postulate of a necessarily existent being, selecting basic laws for the sake of goodness (elegance and beauty is one important sort of goodness). It is important to note that, although the existence of God satisfactorily explains initial conditions and basic laws, the divine nature is not knowable in itself by human minds. Thus the ultimate explanation, though it exists, is knowable only by God. For humans, the ultimate explanation of the universe must remain a postulate, an asymptotic goal of enquiry.

When Hawking says that, if there was not a first moment of time, there would be no need for a creator to start the process going, he misses the point that it is the process as a whole that needs explaining. Whether or not time had a first moment is irrelevant to the question of creation, since God must be creating (holding in being) the universe at every moment, not just the first moment. The postulate of creation asserts that the whole universe exists through a combination of necessity and conscious choice. In pointing out the extremely finetuned, complex and elegant structure of the universe, modern cosmology shows it to be the sort of universe a being of vast intelligence and power could create, and so makes the postulate of creation highly plausible.

What is your view of the relation of theories of evolution and natural selection to the existence of a creator, with particular attention to the approaches adopted by Charles Darwin and Richard Dawkins?

The postulate of theism most basically differs from that of nontheistic cosmology in assigning a purpose to the universe, making its existence not a result of blind necessity, but of conscious intention. A purpose, most generally, is a state of intrinsic value, usually reached by a process well-designed to achieve that state. In many cases, the process itself, not just the final state, can be a part of the purpose.

Cosmic and biological evolution appears to be a process which follows simple and elegant laws to move from an initial state of blind unconscious energy (the Big Bang) towards a state of highly complex, integrated, conscious existence with the ability to comprehend and redirect the process itself towards the existence of consciously created, shared and appreciated values. Such a movement from primordial undifferentiated energy to sentient life appears to be purposive. It strongly supports the hypothesis of creation, the dependence of the whole universal process on a conscious act of God.

Darwin's presentation of the theory of natural selection overemphasizes the extent to which mutations in genetic material are random, exaggerates the extent to which nature is a ruthless struggle for survival in a hostile environment, and overlooks the progressive nature of evolution from primitive cells to conscious rational agents. Contemporary neo-Darwinians, like Dawkins, update Darwinian theory by supposing that it is genes, not organisms, which replicate, mutate, and compete for survival. They regard bodies as machines for carrying genes, and insist that the evolutionary process is a blind competition of selfish genes to replicate more efficiently. Human beings are the by-product of that process, the slaves of the genes, the hidden masters of evolution.

This whimsical fantasy gives us a wholly topsy-turvy view of life. Genes, little bits of DNA, become devious plotting agents, and human beings become robotic slaves of their plans. But genes are unconscious chemical codes, whose function is to build proteins into organic forms, and eventually into the bodies of conscious human agents. We may as well say that we are the servants of our electrons, and that they decide what we are going to do. It is much more sensible, as well as realistic, to say that electrons and genes form the material substratum which makes conscious life possible. They are the necessary conditions of the sort of life we have, but as far from being its goal as it is possible to get.

For the theist, the atheistic presentation of the data of evolution – which Darwin did not share – is based on a number of misperceptions. Mutations are not "mistakes" in copying DNA. They are carefully planned variations, finely tuned to produce viable organisms, through a nondeterministic process inevitably producing disadvantageous mutations which will tend to be self-destructive. Mutations are not truly random or necessarily blind, since they follow from physical laws which are elegant and largely predictable in their macrocosmic consequences.

Nature is not a ruthless war of each against all, but a realm in which dependence and cooperation are essential to the construction of coherent organisms from proteins. Genes are not selfish, in the sense of seeking to perpetuate themselves by any means. On the contrary, they are very altruistic, devoting their short lives to building bodies, cooperating with other genes to do so, and always hoping to get mutated into more efficient recipes. The survival of genes is of no ultimate importance. What matters is the formation of conscious agents, and genes are only important because they are instrumental to that end. There is competition and extinction in nature, but one should note the cooperation and creativity which are just as important in the story of evolving life.

Finally, a theist cannot see the evolution of humans as an improbable freak accident, against all the odds. Since organisms are selected by the environment, and God designs and sustains that environment, it is plausible to see humans as the goal of the whole evolutionary process, and carefully controlled mutation and selection as the means by which they come to exist.

Indeed, the hypothesis of God makes the evolution of rational sentient life from inorganic matter much more probable than blind natural selection alone. On blind natural selection, the existence of human life is almost infinitely improbable. If God creates the material universe, the evolution of conscious beings, capable of knowing and loving God, becomes virtually certain. Since the best hypothesis in science is the one that makes a given process more probable, and since conscious agents have evolved, the hypothesis of God is much the best explanation of evolution.

A wise and powerful creator might well choose to create rational agents through a long evolutionary process, which would enable them to be the means of shaping the material world itself, of which they would be an integral part, into a fuller expression of spiritual purpose. Such agents could evolve through mutation and natural selection. But one must remember that the laws governing mutations and the environments doing the selecting are both sustained and shaped by God, and are therefore far from being blind.

THE PROBLEM OF EVIL

Great Question 12: *The problem of evil, the problem of reconciling the existence of evil and suffering with the existence of an all-good, all-powerful God, has puzzled believers and unbelievers. What solution, if any, do you see to this problem?*

RICHARD SWINBURNE

The problem of evil. Yes, indeed, this must be the central difficulty always for theism and the doctrine that there is a God. I think that the problem is a soluble one but it is a difficult problem.

The basic solution is that all the evils we find around us are logically necessary conditions of greater goods, that is to say that greater good couldn't come about without the evil or at any rate the natural possibility of evil. That is obvious in one or two fairly simple cases. For example, it is a good thing that humans have free will, in the sense that they can make choices which have an influence either for good or for ill, choices which are independent of the causes affecting them; they can choose independently of the influences which act upon them. It is a good thing that such agents, in particular humans, should be the source of the way things go, for good or evil, that they should be mini-creators having to some extent the divine power of molding themselves and other people in the world for good or evil. It is good for them that they should have this sort of responsibility. But, of course, if they are to have this sort of responsibility for the way things go, either for good or evil, it is possible that they may promote evil or negligently allow it to occur. So if there is to be the good of significant free will there has to be the possibility, which may be actualized, of evil. That is the core, I think, of any solution to the problem of evil.

But, of course, not all of the evils in the world are caused by human beings. There is much disease and suffering which humans have no responsibility for and much suffering of animals before ever there were human beings. So we can't account for all the evils of the world in terms of human bad choices but I think that the other evils of the world nevertheless play a subsidiary role in making possible the kind of free will which the free-will defense says to be a good thing. For example, if we are to have a choice between good and evil, we must know how to bring about different good states and how to bring about different evil states, and how do we get that knowledge? Well, we get that knowledge, rather typically, by observing how things behave in the natural world, by observing the processes which produce good states and the processes which produce evil states and then, having learned what those are, we are then in a position either to encourage the one process or encourage the other.

Let me take a rather trivial example to illustrate this. How am I to have the opportunity of poisoning somebody? Well, only if I observe what kinds of food cause people to die and what kinds of food gives them nourishment. And if I observe that somebody eats some berry and then dies, this gives me a bit of knowledge, the knowledge of how to poison them by giving them the berry, the knowledge of how, through negligence, to allow them to die by allowing them to eat the berry or a knowledge of how to save them from that sort of poisoning by destroying the berry. So the natural processes which produce good and evil give me the kind of knowledge I need in order to have the sort of free choice which the free-will defense describes as such a good thing. Now the berry example is a very trivial and artificial example but it does illustrate the more real-life case that it is only through observing natural processes that we learn what are the possibilities open to human beings for good or evil. Take a real life disease case, rabies. Rabies in dogs leads them to bite human beings and give human beings a terrible death. We observe that, and having observed that we now have the power to stop that disease by killing dogs who have rabies or, alternatively, not to bother, in which case to allow the risk of people getting rabies. And, in general, all the natural processes which produce good and evil give us a greater range of knowledge and a greater range of possibilities for good or evil.

I think there are all sorts of other ways in which the evils in the world provide us with greater possibilities of choice for good or ill. For example, if somebody is suffering through no fault of their own, no fault of anybody's, nevertheless there is the possibility of other people reacting sympathetically to their suffering. Sympathetic reaction is a good thing but it is only possible if there are people suffering to whom that reaction can be shown. Now it is very natural to respond to this sort of example by saying "Well, although sympathy is a good thing, it is not as good a thing as the suffering, which it is a reaction to, is a bad thing." But clearly no God would multiply suffering infinitely in order to give us infinite opportunities for sympathy. But there is a case for saying that the world is better for having a few pains and a bit of opportunity for people to be involved with others at their deepest level when they are suffering and lonely and in need of other people. It is a good thing that there should be some opportunity for that sort of involvement which will only be possible if there is some sort of suffering to be involved with.

Of course, there must be a limit to the amount of suffering which people are allowed to cause to others for the sake of their own free will and, generally, there must be a limit to the amount of evil which a good God is going to allow to occur for the sake of the goods of human knowledge, human freedom, human involvement with others, which that makes possible. But, if you take all evil away from the world, people don't have serious choices, people don't know how to make differences to the world, people aren't involved with others at their deepest level. And I think what God has given us is a world with significant possibilities for us making it one way or the other and significant possibilities for involvement and responsibility for each other and that is not possible without a bit of evil. I think the solution to the problem of evil is along those lines, but it needs a lot more detailed showing with respect to each kind of evil how that makes possible a greater good. And I think that is possible for all the kinds of evil we find around us, which are after all limited, finite-term evils.

GERARD J. HUGHES

The experience of human suffering, and the often terrible impact of human malice, pose a serious problem for any theist who believes that God is the creator of all, and that God is good. The crux of the problem is the sense that God could, and should, have done better than create a world in which such things seem to be woven into its very fabric. I do not think, for the reasons I shall give, that there is any clear way in which the theist can hope to show that the problem is a false one. There just is no simple answer. Still, it is possible to give some arguments to show that the evil in the world does not make belief in a good God intellectually impossible, or even unlikely to be correct.

Let me begin with some disclaimers. I do not think that the theist should accept the burden of proving that every case of suffering, or every act of malice, always turns out to be for the best, in the sense that with hindsight we can always see some point to it, some benefit from it. We cannot, and that is that. Again, I think it would be unwise of the theist to take refuge too quickly in some version of "God's ways are not our ways," though there is no doubt an acceptable construction which might be put upon those words. For, however inadequate our concepts of "person" and "moral agent" and "benevolent" when they are used to describe God, unless these are, at least in some sense, appropriate ways for us to think of God, it is difficult to see why we would consider God to be worthy of our worship, still less of our love. True, if God cannot properly be thought of as a moral agent, the problem of evil would lose its bite; for the whole point of the problem is to suggest that God has acted wrongly. But to solve the problem of evil thus at a stroke is to do so at a cost which the theist must refuse to pay. As will appear, I think a degree of agnosticism in this whole area is entirely proper; what I take to be useless is to appeal to the transcendent otherness of God as a way of refusing to make any intellectual effort whatsoever to try to lessen the force of the difficulties.

A prefatory remark of a rather different kind is also required. The problem of evil cannot even be stated unless it is assumed that it is proper to speak of moral truth; and it cannot be stated with much force unless it is assumed that moral truth does not simply depend on human conventions which could well have been quite different. Why? Because the problem of evil depends upon there being moral standards which, it is alleged, God has violated; and if these standards are no more than accidental human conventions, or ways in which we project our own emotions on to the world, then, while there would no doubt be a psychological difficulty for us in having to accept that God need not be bound by our conventions, that is much less of a problem than having to accept that a good God has violated moral standards which are part of the fabric of the world He has created.

One facet of the problem of evil is the assumption that it would clearly have been possible for God to have created a better world than this one. Such a response to the evils of this world is, of course, a very natural one. It does not require an over-fertile imagination to fill out the details of what such a world might be like; a world in which harvests never failed, in which animals and humans were immune from the manifold sufferings which currently afflict us as a result of our interaction with the forces of nature; a world in which people freely choose to behave to one another with sensitivity, justice and kindness, and so on. The fertile imagination, however, is not really much of a guide to what is actually possible. Science fiction is full of tales about time-transportation, all but effortless intergalactic travel, people being removed from one location and unproblematically reconstituted somewhere else almost in an instant. It seems fairly clear that at least some of these exotic events and states of affairs are simply incompatible with the most basic laws of physics which characterize the workings not merely of this planet but of the universe as a whole. We must not be led by the seductions of pure fantasy into supposing that a more idyllic version of this planet would be possible within the laws of physics. Indeed, chaos theory suggests that even some minor changes in the starting conditions of the universe would not have produced the world more or less as we have it, but with selective improvements. On the contrary, a universe which started only slightly differently from this one would have been quite unpredictably unlike ours by now. The assumption that God could have produced a broadly comparable planet differing only in the ways we would wish to specify is an assumption for which there simply are no good grounds.

Of course, for all we know to the contrary, God might well have created a totally different universe, based on totally different physical laws; or a universe of purely spiritual beings in which there were no physical laws as such at all (though there presumably would be some laws to describe the ways in which the minds of such beings worked). But such an incomparably different universe is not one which we are in a position to compare in any respect with our own. We simply cannot say whether it would be better or worse than this one. What possible standards can there be for comparing utterly disparate worlds?

In short, we have no reason to suppose that God could create an improved, but comparable, version of this world; and no reason to suppose that a radically different alternative world, if such were possible for God, would be in any intelligible sense better (or worse) than this one. This is not to say that this is the best possible world. Rather it is to say that, for all we know, it might be; and that in some cases the very notion of "best," or "better" is so far as we are concerned an entirely empty one. That we can readily imagine such a world does absolutely nothing to establish the crucial assertion in the formulation of the problem of evil, that God could have done better. What the problem of evil gratuitously assumes, the theist is entitled equally gratuitously to deny. Such a denial is emphatically not a solution; but neither is the contrary assertion an adequate justification for saying that there really is an insoluble problem.

The fact that much of the evil in the world consists of immoral human decisions raises a particular set of questions. Let us assume that human beings could have chosen not to act immorally (on which see Great Question 8. Is it then the case that any blame for our immoral behaviour is entirely ours and not God's?

Even in the cases where we are fully responsible for the wrong we do, it does not, I think, follow that God is in no sense responsible. God did, after all, create a world in which such choices could be made. Could he know in advance that some immoral choices would be made? If our choices are genuinely free, I see no way in which God could know which way any individual choice would be made, as it were independently of his eternal knowledge of the choice that is actually made. There is no basis on which such knowledge could rest. On the other hand, it might nevertheless be that God would know "in advance" that, as a matter of statistics, if any given choice might be made well or badly, some will certainly be made badly. In which case, God is surely responsible for creating a world in which this would happen. But whether a world in which no such choices were even possible would be overall better than the world we have is a question which I think simply cannot be confidently answered one way or the other. So even in this case it does not seem that there are any conclusive reasons for asserting that in creating our world God acted wrongly.

ALVIN PLANTINGA

Many philosophers have claimed that there is a contradiction between the existence of an all-good, all-powerful God, all-knowing God, on the one hand, and evil on the other. This seems to me to be demonstrably wrong, and, as a matter of fact, at present, not very many people do affirm that there is this contradiction.

But lots and lots of Christians and others are still deeply puzzled by the existence of evil. Why is there so much evil if God is really good, if God is what we think He is? Why does He permit things like the Holocaust? Why does He permit ethnic cleansing? Why does He permit people to kill each other and savage each other in a thousand different ways? The newspaper is full every day of horrifying stories about what human beings do to each other, how they treat each other. Why does He permit that? I think the right answer is, one doesn't know; God hasn't told us why.

And the right attitude, I think, is outlined in the book of Job. First, there takes place a transaction between God and the members of the Heavenly Host; then as a result of this transaction God permits Job to be afflicted by Satan. Job doesn't know anything about the Satan connection. He doesn't know why he is being afflicted; he also knows he is no worse than the next guy, in particular, he is no worse than his comforters, his friends who come to see him: Bildad the Shuite, Eliphaz the Temanite, and Zophar the Naamathite. They come and tell him he must be a really wicked man because he is being afflicted in this way. He replies that he is no worse than they are. He keeps saying to them and to God, that he doesn't think he is any worse than others, and winds up, in the middle of the book, telling God that he thinks that God is mistreating him, that God is not being just. He goes on in that vein at some length, and then finally God speaks to him. And what God says substantially is this: "Job, you can't figure out what my reason is for permitting you to be afflicted. And from that you infer that I probably don't have a reason. But that is where you are wrong. You are extremely limited with respect to knowledge. You know very little. Were you there when the morning stars sang together and all the sons of God shouted for joy? I probably couldn't even explain to you, without changing your nature, what my reason is for much of what goes on, including why it is that you are suffering. What you should do is recognize that I am, in fact, very good, and trust me." And then Job sees that is what he should do; he realizes he spoke where he had no knowledge and at the end of the book he says, "I don't know why God permits this, but I will, nonetheless, trust Him." And that seems to me to be the right attitude for Christians and other theists with respect to evil in the world. As Psalm 119 puts it, "I know, O Lord, that your judgments are right, and that in faithfulness you have afflicted me. Let your steadfast love be ready to comfort me according to your promise to your servant."

HUGO MEYNELL

On the problem of evil, my immediate feeling is that it obviously puts the ball squarely in the theists' court. Is it not as clear a contradiction as could well be, that there is evil, or at least so much evil, in a world supposed to have been created by an almighty and omnibenevolent God? I have already said that I think there is good reason to believe that there is an intelligent will underlying the universe. Now in what sense and in what circumstances could such a being appropriately be called good? It is characteristic of theists, of course, that they believe not only that God has created the world, but that God is bringing the world to some kind of consummation in which those who have striven for the good may hope to share. God has brought into existence electrons and protons, physical matter and chemical elements on the basis of that, biological life on the basis of that, and intelligent biological life – as exemplified by you and me – on the basis of that. But intelligent biological life is unfortunately infected by sin; the characteristic Christian claim is that God through Christ is bringing about what St. Paul calls a new creation, where the effects of sin will be done away, and humanity will be brought to a state of unprecedented perfection and sharing of the divine life. (Teilhard de Chardin, a visionary rather than a systematic thinker, talks about a biosphere giving rise to a noosphere, and the noosphere giving rise to a Christosphere.)

That there are sufferings and miseries in the world, and that these are not just due to malign human agents, are things that most certainly cannot and must not be denied. One of the things that make atheists furious, and properly so, is when theists get complacent about or try to minimize the real horror of the pain and misery that there are in creation.

The theist may with some plausibility suggest that that the world is a "vale of soul-making" or "moral gymnasium" and point out that you can't have real courage or pity or generosity without pain and suffering, or indeed without at least the genuine possibility of cowardice or cruelty or meanness. Even if one concedes that, the sceptic may reply, is the game worth the candle? Is the cultivation of such virtues really worth the immense mass of animal and human suffering?

So where does all this leave us on the question of divine goodness? First, God has what one might call outstanding metaphysical excellence, just by virtue of being sole and eternal creator. God as eternal creator is not subject to the physical wear and tear, or the alteration of will and intention, which are essential conditions of physical and moral evil as we know them among creatures. Second, God is of supreme aesthetic goodness, as one might say, in that to enjoy God is the supreme delight available to rational creatures; of which we have the remotest glimpse in shared sexual rapture with a beloved partner, or contemplation of the mind of Shakespeare through *The Tempest* or that of Mozart through the Jupiter Symphony. Third, according to Christians and other theists, human beings, so far as they strive against sin and the evil and the falsehood that it brings in its train, are invited to share in this delight, in a future life in which those who suffer in the present are to be comforted, and in which all injustices are to be connected. If so, but hardly otherwise, I would say, there is some kind of cosmic justice, which is a necessary condition of God being good in anything like the sense of morally good.

Before we leave the topic of evil, I want to insist how important it is that people who are extraordinarily fortunate, like myself, should never gloss over the appalling misery that other people have to go through in the course of their lives. I once had to give a course about evil and suffering in the great religions. Very depressing it was. But it seemed to me that the only thing that they all had in common was a conviction that suffering be put to work, and some positive use could be made of it, in preparing oneself for a more fully realized life.

JOSEF SEIFERT

The problem of evil, of moral evil and of unjust suffering, is certainly the most powerful argument used by atheists against the existence of God. And yet, there is a remarkable metaphysical agreement between theists and atheists regarding evils: Atheism agrees with theism in its best forms that only an all-good, all-powerful God, who at the same time embodies moral perfections and thus perfect justice, can be properly speaking God. Any cruel, merciless, and unjust God would not properly be God.

Therefore, on this common ground, the question for believers and unbelievers alike is: "How is it possible that an infinitely perfect God would permit the existence of evil in the world?"

Here we can first recognize that if the truth of the existence of God is in itself cogently demonstrated, the difficulty of reconciling this truth with the horrors of evil must not lead us to deny it. For if God's existence is cogently known, the reality of evils cannot contradict it, even if you do not comprehend why not. Moreover, note a most significant epistemological distinction applying here: With respect to the reconcilability of the existence and permission of the occurrence of evil with God's goodness and power, we just lack comprehension, but we have no positive insight that the existence of the evil in the world disproves God. For there could be many reasons why God permits evil: such as punishment, trial, consequence of sin, of demonic influences on nature and history, etc. And there could be as many goods which we cannot even attain to fully in thought because they involve eternity, by which God could take away, heal, or recompense suffering. On the other hand, we have certain and most reliable reasons which teach us that God must exist. But the lack of comprehension of how evil can be permitted by God can never be an argument against the positive insight and demonstration of his existence.

Moreover, in order to cope with the problem of evil, one must first understand that the gravest and most horrible of all evils are not the sufferings of human beings or animals but the moral evils. As Socrates states so clearly: "It is better for man to suffer injustice than to commit it." The perpetrator of a crime is more evil, and in fact evil and shamefully ugly in a completely different sense than the sufferings of the victim are "evil." The disharmony which results from the moral evil, with its cosmic dimensions of offence of God, of sin and of guilt, is incomparable to the evil of death, which could also be brought about by a car accident.

These much more serious, moral evils are hardly ever mentioned by atheists, however, when they speak of the problem of evil, which they usually reduce to the problem of pain, probably because moral evils are primarily directed against God and offend God, rather than being primarily directed against man, as sufferings are.

The evils of injustice and of sin, however, are objectively the most difficult to explain because it is incomprehensible how an infinitely perfect God would allow that his creatures constantly turn against Him and offend Him. Thus the problem of moral evil (and of sin) is a theocentric problem of evil. Here, the mysterious silence of God lets us admire the patience of God and the ever new chances of moral conversion granted to creatures.

Quite distinct is the "anthropocentric" problem of evil and innocent suffering which Ivan Karamazov in Dostoyevski's *Brothers*

Karamazov formulates. Here we are horrified by the silence of God in the face of all the sufferings, tears and unjust oppressions of mankind, and particularly by the crimes committed against innocent human beings: against children who are mercilessly slaughtered, tortured, abused. In the face of these evils, it appears that God is merciless and unjust, permitting these evils to happen.

But to say it again: We must not think that we can understand, with our human reason, the absolute impossibility and irreconcilability between the infinite perfection of God and the permission of these evils. In fact, there could be many reasons hidden from our full comprehension, such as the punishment for the original sin of our ancestors, personal punishments, trials which should lead to the purification of the soul, unjust sufferings which later will be wiped away when the innocent will be restored to unfathomable dimensions of happiness, etc.

Moreover, the philosopher cannot refute, even if he does not believe in its truth, the most sublime and the most complete response to evil: the one Jesus Christ gave in taking upon himself freely the most bitter passion and the only absolutely innocent suffering. For by far the greatest evil of pain, and thus perforce the greatest mystery of the evil of suffering, reveals at the same time the compatibility of evil in the world with the love of God, if Christ is truly the Son of God: the passion and death of Christ himself. This greatest evil, the permission of which is the greatest mystery, is also an irrefutable demonstration that the existence of evil is not only compatible with the existence and mercy and love of God, but that this existence and mercy and unfathomable charity of God reveals itself precisely in the unjustest of all unjust sufferings. If God himself became man and died for our sins, and if this is the supreme manifestation of divine love, we can understand how the infinity of divine love and the deepest abyss of evil are reconcilable.

At least we must recognize that no scientist and no philosopher can disprove, in the face of the answer given by Christ's passion and death to evil, that the existence of evil is indeed compatible with divine perfection. This religious answer to evil has a philosophical side to it: philosophy and reason cannot refute its validity.

Nevertheless, in spite of all philosophical and religious answers to the question of pain and of other evils, the existence of evil remains a profound mystery for the human mind, a mystery which no human being can fully resolve. But again, we must distinguish clearly between our lack of being able to solve the problem of evil and any alleged insight of the atheist that the existence of evil disproves God. This is in no way given to us. Therefore, we have to embrace both truths: the existence of an infinitely good and all-perfect God and the striking reality of evil – even if we cannot fully reconcile both in our limited minds.

SANDRA MENSSEN, T. D. SULLIVAN

Can the world's evils be reconciled with the existence of a good God? The question has exercised almost every philosophically inclined nonbeliever; it poses what tradition has labeled "the problem of evil." Afflictions witnessed or experienced, and acts of malfeasance observed or performed, lead a person inquiring into the possibility of the divine to wonder whether there could be a creator of the vast oceans and the undiscovered stars who is good, whose goodness commands respect and love and worship, whose eye is on the sparrow, and the child in Zaire, and the baby in the next room.

Traditional discussions of the problem of evil go a long way towards identifying reasons God might have for allowing evil, and also towards showing that whether or not human beings can identify plausible reasons God might have for allowing evil, it's plausible that there are such reasons. The traditional account that seems strongest to us claims that the world as a whole is very good, that evils within the world are inevitable by-products of the laws that give the world its design, and that individuals benefit in uncountably many ways by being part of a world designed as our world is.

There are also, we think, several promising non-traditional lines of argument about evil. We will mention two here; both involve reflection on the best way of explaining the facts about evil and about good (it's a little surprising that attempts to explain evil so often are divorced from explanations about good). The first line of argument arises from consideration of whether there is a "criterion of goodness" for worlds, a standard that gives sense to the assertion that the world is good, or that determines which worlds are good and how they rank against one another.[1] It is, we believe, possible to develop an argument that nontheistic criteria of goodness for worlds (such as utilitarian or aesthetic or functional criteria) are problematic: some non-theistic criteria count as "good" worlds that people intuitively judge bad, and some count as "bad" worlds people think a good God could create. But theistic criteria – criteria that involve reference to

God's purposes or to God as an ideal or model to be imitated – do not suffer from these defects. Furthermore, one may argue that the traditional problem of evil implies that there is a criterion of goodness for worlds since under careful formulation the problem must refer to a lack of goodness in the world as a whole. This all suggests that when carefully formulated the problem of evil may dissolve.

The second non-traditional line of argument we want to note involves reflecting on a "problem of good" parallel to the traditional "problem of evil."[2] This second line of argument is especially effective for one who thinks the contemporary scientific evidence that there is a creator of the universe is plausible or intriguing. The argument goes as follows: If there is a creator of the universe, it's likely the creator is either maximally wicked or maximally good (it's not likely a creator of this world is amoral or has a mixed moral character). But asymmetries between the problem of good and the problem of evil make it impossible to even begin to construct atheistic solutions to the problem of evil that parallel some of the best known theodicies (for instance, there is no atheistic solution to the problem of good that parallels the theistic solution according to which evil is a privation of good). And in those cases where it may seem possible to begin to construct atheistic solutions that parallel theodicies, the atheistic solutions cannot get very far: both free-will defenses of a maximally evil Demon (which parallel free-will defenses of a good God) and "soul-breaking" defenses of a Demon (which parallel soul-making theodicies) are inherently less successful than their counterpart theodicies.

No theistic solution to the problem of evil will succeed, however, unless there's reason to believe in an afterlife of a certain sort, an afterlife in which God can compensate victims of horrendous earthly suffering, victims who (unlike the vast majority of those of us who suffer) have enjoyed no earthly goods that overbalance or defeat the affliction. Voltaire's *Candide* is a reductio of the claim that a good God could allow uncompensated horrendous suffering, even though it is not a refutation of Leibniz's surprising assertion that God has created the best possible world.

So is there good reason to believe there is an afterlife in which victims of suffering (at least) inherit some great good, enjoy some beatific vision or experience God's unending love? Without an evidentially justified revelation it's hard to see how we could have evidential warrant for belief in an afterlife. For there are serious flaws in many philosophical arguments intended to show that the human soul is immortal and that it will or can attain blessings in a heavenly existence. And even the best philosophical arguments for this conclusion are very difficult, long and complicated, involving concepts philosophers must work years to understand.

Ultimately, then, a theistic solution to the problem of evil will depend on whether there is an evidentially justified revelation, a message God vouchsafes to an individual or a group of persons, that includes the promise of an afterlife.[3]

RALPH MCINERNY

Well, I think one ought to start with the problem of good. Why are there so many good things, why do so many good things happen to us and so forth? I don't mean that in a chuckleheaded way but I think that evil is a negation. So if you don't have a lively sense of the good you don't know what evil is. I mean, it's an absence of something, but there is a lot more present than there is absent, so good outweighs evil many tons of times. I think we ought to start off that way and marvel at the goodness of our lives and of the universe and so forth before we start whining about the evil which is usually due to us anyway. I think it is an overblown thing. People pretend to be absolutely discombobulated because there was an earthquake in Lisbon or something and they have to write *Candide*. But most days there aren't earthquakes in Lisbon and maybe we ought to marvel at that.

In general would you say that the free will argument gives a satisfactory response?

Sure. We are responsible for moral evil certainly and physical evil may very well be a consequence of moral evil. Thomas Aquinas regarded the disorder in the universe as a consequence of original sin. We can't attribute any evil to God. That would be abhorrent because it is nothing and nothing is impossible to God. But, when you are talking about someone getting hit over the head or losing a child or something, to be told that evil is nothing, may seem to diminish the importance of such a terrible loss. It's the fact that there is a loss that makes it so terrible.

NOTES

1.   This line of argument is developed in detail in Sandra Menssen, "Grading Worlds," *American Catholic Philosophical Quarterly*:

Annual Proceedings of the American Catholic Philosophical Association, vol. LXX (1996).

2. This line of argument is developed in detail in Sandra Menssen, "Maximal Wickedness vs. Maximal Goodness: A Short-Cut Theodicy?", *American Catholic Philosophical Quarterly*: Annual Proceedings of the American Catholic Philosophical Association, vol. LXXI (1997).

3. In "An Alternative Approach to Belief in a Good God," in *Theos* (New York: Peter Lang) we argue that philosophers interested in the problem of evil should consider the role philosophy can play in an argument that there is an evidentially justified revelation.

PANTHEISM

Great Question 13: *How do you view pantheism, the notion that we are all "part of" God, that God can be identified with the world?*

RUSSELL PANNIER, T. D. SULLIVAN

Theists maintain that God acts in the spatio-temporal universe. What exactly do they mean? One way of understanding the positive content of a metaphysical assertion is beginning with its negative content – what it denies. We begin with the latter.[1]

One thing theists certainly intend to deny is the proposition that God is literally identical with the universe. This concept of literal identity can be explicated in terms of what we shall call "strict identity." Let "x" and "y" be referring expressions. To say that x is strictly identical with y is to say at least that, given a certain assumed semantical content, x and y designate the same entity. We can now be more precise about the meaning of the denial. Theists mean to deny that God is strictly identical with the universe as a whole, that God is strictly identical with any proper part of the universe and that the universe is strictly identical with any proper part of God.

We cannot set out here any of the supporting reasons. Suffice it to say that some very plausible arguments proceed from three assumptions about God's nature: (1) God is an ontologically independent entity, in the sense that He does not depend for His existence upon anything else; (2) God is the ontological ground for everything else, in the sense that any entities distinct from God depend upon God for their existence; (3) God's existence is necessary, in the sense that if He exists at all, He exists necessarily.

What about the positive side? What do theists affirmatively mean by maintaining that God is in the universe?

It might be doubted whether they can coherently make the claim at all. That doubt could arise as follows. It might seem that the relation, x is in y, is satisfiable in only two kinds of situations. In the first, the entity which includes another entity is the spatio-temporal universe itself. An apple's being in the universe is an example of something's being in something else in this sense. In the second kind, the entity which includes another is itself a proper part of the universe. An apple's being in a box is a case of something's being in something else in this sense. Now, it seems that theists cannot consistently say that God is in the universe in either of these senses. For, necessarily, anything which is in something else in either sense is itself a spatial entity. But theists must deny that God is a spatial entity.

Of course, we agree that theists must deny that God is a spatial entity. But we reject the assumption that these two senses of "in" exhaust the possibilities. There is a sense of "in" in which one thing can be "in" another without being itself spatial. Suppose that a nonspatial entity exists with the power to causally interact with the universe in the following ways. It has the power to create the universe, the power to continuously maintain it in existence, the power to extinguish it at any time, and the power to causally interact with any part of it in a "direct" way, that is, without the need for causal intermediaries. We think that such an entity would be "in" the universe in *some* significant sense.

Is there such an entity? As orthodox Christians, we believe that there is. We could mention indefinitely many items: burning bushes, loaves of bread feeding thousands, the lame and blind healed, martyrs walking to their deaths singing the praises of God, relentless persecutors of Christianity spiritually transformed while traveling to Damascus, the dead raised and the mysterious persistence of the Church. We believe that these, along with many other events provide strong grounds for the belief in both the possibility and the fact of God's direct causal intervention in the world.

It is perhaps true that such evidentiary items fail to suffice for "demonstration" in the classical Aristotelian sense of furnishing the makings for deductively valid inferences from self-evident premises. There are at least two possible difficulties. First, strict demonstrations in this sense of God's existence may not be available. Second, even if they are, one might well doubt whether it is possible to demonstrate (again, in the strict sense) that this immaterial God is causally responsible for such events. For the individual Christian the question is: "Is the immaterial God whose existence may be demonstrable also working in my own life?"

There are at least two strong, albeit nondeductive, arguments supporting an affirmative response. The first invokes the idea of inference to the best explanation. It is difficult, though perhaps not impossible, to explain facts of this kind in any other way. The second takes the form of a practical argument. Expressed in the vocabulary of the individual believer, it can be (very schematically) put as follows: "My deepest desire is for spiritual integration and fulfillment. I have experienced in the past a significant degree of such integration and fulfillment. I believe that a necessary condition for those experiences is my own belief that the causal source of those experiences is God, the immaterial ontological ground of the universe. (That is, I believe that if I had not had this conviction, I would not have had the experiences.) The belief that the causal source of my experiences is God is epistemologically reasonable (although not strictly demonstrable). Hence, I ought to continue believing it." Although we cannot argue the matter here, we think that the use of practical arguments in metaphysics is not only philosophically legitimate, but at times necessary.

RICHARD SWINBURNE

No, I don't think we are all part of God. It seems to me characteristic of the sort of scientific pattern of an explanation which I was drawing attention to that we explain all the diverse and manifold things around us by a simpler beginning of them. Just as the scientist explains the whole range of chemical interactions by postulating that there are only a few kinds of chemical substances which interact in simple ways and thereby explains the manifold by something which is outside it as its cause, it seems to me that the metaphysician ought to proceed accordingly and not identify God with the world but try and look for something simpler outside the world, which leads us to explain the world, and that is characteristic of theism.

HUGO MEYNELL

I think theism is much more like pantheism than one might think. I've always liked Thomas Aquinas' formulation: God operates in every operation of nature and will. God is that which is active in everything. What then is wrong with pantheism? It is one thing for God to be the agent in practically every event, apart from human sins; it is another thing for God to be identical with all those events. Another formulation I like is Spinoza's distinction between *natura naturans* and *natura naturata*: God is *natura naturans*, the active principle working through nature.

ALVIN PLANTINGA

I don't believe in pantheism for a minute, because it seems to me an essential part of pantheism is the idea that God isn't a person, isn't a conscious, willing, intending being who has created the world, has plans, plans for me, for example, and to whom I can talk in the expectation of being heard. Pantheism is a totally different sort of view. I'm not even sure what it means to say that God can be identified with the world. Could a person be the same thing as the universe? I really don't see how. It doesn't make sense to me; from a rational standpoint, I find it very hard to understand. Somebody says, "everything there is, that is God." I don't know what is being claimed. It could be that what is being claimed is that God is the most impressive thing there is because he is the sum total of everything there is; or it could be that what is being claimed is something else, perhaps that God is the soul of the world, that the world is His body.

JOSEF SEIFERT

Having reached the conclusion that God exists, we also see that pantheism is an untenable position. For that which exists necessarily cannot be identical with all the beings in the world of which we understand that they could also not exist and that they exist contingently. That which is all-perfect and of which we can say that it is being itself, goodness itself, wisdom itself, justice itself and the infinite perfection of these pure attributes, can never be identical with the imperfect, finite, limited versions and forms of being in which we find these qualities in all beings in the world. Therefore the absolute transcendence of God, who is infinite in all of His perfections, over all of the world, and His radical distinction from the world, is evident and is an evident condition of the "divine immanence" in the sense of the indwelling and omnipresence of God in the world. For to be simultaneously present in all times, places, and creatures as the same identical God is possible solely for a being who is wholly transcendent to the world and different from it. Hence, the pantheistic idea that we are parts of God, or that God could be identified with the world, is untenable. As a matter of fact, we could agree with Schopenhauer who said that pantheism is only a polite form of atheism because to say that God is the world is to say the same thing as: there is no God.[2]

RALPH MCINERNY

To say that I, myself, am the cause of everything or some such version, or that I am part of the cosmic god is one of those fuzzy things but apparently it has an appeal. I'm sure there are a lot of sort of unreflective pantheists. Very often when people talk about death, they talk about returning, you know, to the ultimate capital of the world so that new coinage can be minted, or what have you. I just find that a very odd notion because what it tends to is materialism, it seems to me, or a real oddball kind of idealism.

In a sense is it incoherent?

Yes. It could be argued that it is. But most of the time I don't think it is held as anything like a thought-out position. It is sort of a sentiment that I am part of this whole and that is sometimes taken for pantheism. Maybe it is and maybe it isn't, but just to think of oneself as part of the cosmos, as part of the universe, is not pantheism. And yet sometimes pantheism sounds almost like that and then you figure it's not, it hasn't risen to the point of incoherence.

WILLIAM P. ALSTON

Would you say that in relation to the question of pantheism or some kind of panentheistic metaphysics, our experience of God generally tends to be of a being that is transcendent and all-perfect? Would you be able to reach that kind of a conclusion from experience?

Well, as you undoubtedly know, in the history of religion, experiences of God have been interpreted in various ways. Religious experiences have been interpreted theistically, pantheistically, in terms of some sort of nature mysticism, and all sorts of other ways. That again brings out the need for a diversity of sources or bases. If you are just going by personal religious experience, it obviously is open to a variety of interpretations and people do, no doubt, generally speaking, interpret it in terms of the religious belief system, the religious conceptual system, that they find themselves with. The experiences certainly reinforce this and, I think, quite properly. It is not that religious experience is so amorphous that you can interpret it in any way conceivable. If I have some experience that I am inclined to think of as an experience of the loving presence of God, it could not be interpreted as an experience of a spider crawling on the ceiling or an experience of somebody hitting me on the head. People do have those experiences too but they are very different. A religious experience is not a Rorschach blot. It is not totally amorphous even though it doesn't carry a precise interpretation on its face. But insofar as it does admit of different interpretations, then philosophical reasoning comes into play here as to which kind of general framework is most rational, most viable intellectually, and the kinds of arguments I was mentioning at the beginning all point in the theistic direction rather than some of these others.

NOTES

1. For a fuller account of this argument see Russell Pannier and T. D. Sullivan, "God and the World," in *Theos* (New York: Peter Lang).
2. Max Scheler, "Probleme der Religion" in *Vom Ewigen im Menschen*, 5 Aufl. (Bern und Munchen: Francke Verlag, 1968), S.101–354, distinguishes another form of pantheism which dissolves the being of the world into that of God.

DIVINE ACTION IN THE WORLD
AND HUMAN HISTORY

Great Question 14: *What is your view on the possibility of Divine action in the world and of the relation of Providence and history?*

RICHARD SWINBURNE

Well, if there is a God who has made us, loves us, cares for us, then clearly one would expect Him to interact occasionally with us. But one would also expect Him, because He values our having creative powers, our making a difference to things, and our influencing each other and helping each other, not to intervene in the world too often. God has entrusted us to each other. If parents have two children, an older child and a younger child, they may entrust the younger child to the care of the older child and they will not interfere in this arrangement too quickly because, if they do, the elder child will not have any serious responsibility and it is a good thing to have responsibility. But, on the other hand, they may interfere very occasionally if things get out of hand: if the elder child is too insensitive or cruel to the younger child. So I would expect, if there is a God, some intervention from time to time to deal with human needs, and I don't think that is incompatible with science in general ruling the way things behave in the world and human beings having a certain freedom with the way things behave in the world. As I said before, even if you think science, scientific laws, are all-dominant, the laws of quantum theory have plenty of gaps in them such that somebody could intervene without needing to suspend the laws of nature. But even if God does need, from time to time, to suspend the laws of nature, well, maybe He does. I don't see any problem in that. There might be evidence that He had done so, of course, and there are plenty of stories of miracles suggesting that, from time to time, that has indeed happened. How often God upsets the rule of nature I have no idea. But I've given arguments to suppose that He might do sometimes, and certainly I think He did, at any rate at least once, in the resurrection of Christ from the dead – though I think He does so a lot more often than that.

GERARD J. HUGHES

As a Christian, I of course believe that in Jesus of Nazareth God has "intervened" in our world in a particularly significant and quite unique way. I take it, though, that when someone asks whether God can intervene in the world, the questioner usually has in mind the kind of intervention which violates the laws according to which our universe naturally behaves.

We should be very cautious indeed in making claims about what God can and cannot do, or even about what God would and would not do. I know of no philosophical argument which shows that God could not intervene in the world, producing an effect which owes nothing to the causal powers of created beings. The more interesting and difficult issues are concerned with whether it would be possible for us to know that some event is due to the direct intervention of God, and why God should wish to intervene at all.

In the very nature of the case, if God does intervene, what happens will be from our point of view inexplicable. That is to say, in the nature of the case there will be no mechanism which we could invoke to account for such an event. In such a case, it has sometimes been argued that, rather than accept some miraculous intervention, the more prudent conclusion would be that the event must be due to perfectly ordinary natural causes which we simply have not as yet discovered. With hindsight, we can see that events once thought to be "miraculous" do indeed have straightforward scientific explanations, which we have subsequently been able to discover. There are indeed many such cases, and the call to prudence is perfectly sensible. Nevertheless, there could be occasions on which the most reasonable thing to say would be that there could be no natural cause of some event. If some event occurred which runs radically counter to some of the most fundamental laws of nature as we understand them, it might be more rational to accept that the event was caused by God than to suppose that we were so utterly mistaken about the most fundamental laws of physics. Of course, in so saying, it is always possible that we are mistaken. Not everything which we have the best of reasons for believing turns out to be true. In practice, it makes a good deal of difference which natural laws have allegedly been violated, since our knowledge of some of the laws of nature is a good deal more certain than our knowledge of others. Where our knowledge is uncertain, it will usually be more reasonable to suppose that there is some as yet unknown natural mechanism at work than to suppose that there had been a divine intervention. In every case, it will be a question of balancing the evidence.

Believers will often speak of some events as "providential," without wishing to claim that anything miraculous has occurred. If one believes that the world was created by a good God out of love for his creatures, one is thereby committed to believing that "all manner of things shall be well." But one is not committed to believing that we are always in a position to know what is best for us; it is possible that suffering could be just as providential as some fortunate escape from threatening tragedy. Equally, it is possible that some tragedies are just that, tragedies which serve no good purpose, but are the inevitable by-products of the workings of a world which is nevertheless good overall. To speak of divine providence, then, is an expression of confidence and trust in the goodness of the creator God, and is equally appropriate in adverse as well as in favorable circumstances.

ALVIN PLANTINGA

It is certainly possible for God to act in the world. In fact God acts in the world all the time by upholding it. If He weren't engaged in His upholding of the world, it would disappear like a candle flame in a hurricane. And of course God can act in history. How does He act in history; how does His part in what happens relate to our part in what happens? I don't know. God orchestrates history. He knows what is going to happen; He chooses a world which suits Him; out of all the possible worlds that He could have chosen, He chooses one that He approves of in the long run. And if you include in history what happens after the Second Coming, then, of course, in that part of it, what He does is much clearer, so to speak, than this present part of it. But as to just how providence and history are related now, in this dispensation, I don't know.

JOSEF SEIFERT

If it is evident from the preceding argument that the world does not exist by necessity and that many of the species and natures and laws which govern the world are not of an absolute inner necessity, then it is clear that all of these non-necessary (contingent) existences and natures must be, in the last analysis, a divine creature. But if God creates and sustains them by a free action, then He certainly can also enter the world by a free action, both through divine providence in human history, by bestowing grace or by accepting sacrifices or sacrificing His own Son on the Cross, by renewing His sacrifice, by pardoning sins, and also in the form of miracles.

To deny the possibility of divine action in the world, of providential, of miraculous or of sacramental divine interaction with the causal order of the world, presupposes either (a) atheism, or (b) the assumption of a totally closed causal order, or (c) a metaphysics according to which there are only necessary facts, no truly contingent ones. Even if we reject atheism, do we have to assume a causal order of the world that is closed and that does not stand open to possible divine interaction? Or is it intrinsically impossible to change nature because it obeys absolutely necessary laws of nature?

In response to (a) we conclude: In view of the arguments for the existence of God, the first reason can be dismissed. In response to (b) we might point out that the idea of a closed deterministic universe can be criticized from a scientific point of view, for example in light of Heisenberg's uncertainty relation which claims that microphysical laws are only statistical in nature. Yet a more philosophical response to the above objection is needed (because the difference between *strict and exceptionless* rules and merely *statistical rules* as such do not have to do with freedom or divine interaction). Determinism often rests on a definition of causality such as the one presented by Kant: "Every event follows upon another one according to a general law." From this definition of causality Kant concludes to a contradiction, an antinomy (and rightly so). For from this definition it follows that an absurd eternal change of causes must exist within which we find never an explanation of causality because – in such a scheme – each event requires a preceding one upon which it follows according to a law. Thus for causality to work at all an absolute beginning of causality is required which can only lie in freedom, i.e. in a free self-determination of a subject. Yet freedom contradicts the above given definition of causality. But in truth: the type of causality that corresponds to the Kantian requirement of "following upon another event according to a general law" does not apply to all causality but only to the one which moves within pure nature. In the higher sphere of persons, causality is primarily free causality, causality through freedom. And while this causality contains a general element of causality (forgotten by Kant), namely that *event A is brought about through the power of B*, it originates in the free agent and thus does not follow a general law of nature, or follows upon other events "according to a general rule." And yet, precisely this is the archetypical form of causality, as Augustine says. Only here is A truly the cause of B, and not only a link in a chain of causes that *transmits* causal force received from elsewhere. But if not all reality is dominated by laws of nature, there is no difficulty here.

If the principle of causality is correctly stated in the following way, the problem disappears entirely: "Every contingent being and every change requires a sufficient cause, i.e. a power and action through which they exist or occur." This true principle of causality "states more" than Kant's formulation of it, because it contains the all-decisive bond and characterization of efficient causality *through the power of which* X is or takes place. This is much more than the "following upon another thing according to a rule," for this applies also to the sequence of numbers, or to the relationship of day and night, which are not causal relationships.

On the other hand, the authentic formulation of the principle of causality "contains less" than Kant's formulation because it omits the phrase "according to a (general) rule" which applies only to a limited sphere of causality. For only when an event, for example the free fall of a body, is caused by another one, for example by dropping a heavy body in midair, the effect (the fall of the body) follows according to a general rule, namely the law of gravity. But it is no way of the essence of efficient causality to be of this kind, nor does the causality of impersonal nature which roughly corresponds to Kant's description dominate the whole of reality. As soon as we arrive at the level of understanding, motivation, and freedom, actions are caused spontaneously by free agents and do "not follow upon one another according to a general rule."

In response to (c) it is philosophically evident that not all events (existence) nor all natures are necessary. There are many forms of existence, but also natures such as the different species of fish and the distribution of their organs, their colors of skin, etc. which are not absolutely necessary. For this reason, when it comes to these contingent laws of nature and to these contingent facts, the free divine action in the world is entirely compatible with reason. Only when it comes to the eternal and unchanging truth, it makes no sense

to speak of a free divine action in the world. God would be transformed into an absurd being if one assumed, as Descartes did, that
he could make love of God evil and hatred of God good, or that He
could suspend the principle that nothing can both be and not be at
the same time. To be able to do such things would not increase
divine omnipotence or exalt it, but would not only transform God
into a meaningless, absurd and arbitrary tyrant, which is opposed to
the perfection of the divine nature, but would also postulate something that is intrinsically impossible.

Thus there is absolutely no philosophical, rational reason why
God should or could not interact in the world by free providential,
sacramental, or miraculous action. For not all events are subject to
the limited and relatively low form of causality "according to the
laws of nature." By far the most significant causes, which alone contain the ultimate origin of causality, are free ones. Since God is in the
supreme mode free, He can much more easily than humankind exert
His freedom and act in the world.

Moreover, when God acts freely in miracles, He does not alter
eternal and necessary laws which no power can change and which
are inseparable from God and from the very source of all change: the
divine being. On the contrary, God, being omnipotent, can change
all those things which are contingent and not absolute: such as the
characteristics of all species of animals or plants, or broken bones
which can be healed, blind eyes which can be opened, deaf ears
which can be made to hear, lame limbs which can be made able to
walk. Besides the condition of the contingency (nonnecessity) of that
which God produces or changes in miracles, divine omnipotence can
only act in accordance with God's own and infinitely good nature in
providence and in the bestowing of grace which can give rise to
countless changes in the world, such as those brought about by the
Franciscans and other orders in life and art, or such as those
involved in the work of Mother Teresa and the Sisters of Charity in
the whole world.

The mentioned two spheres which cannot be altered by omnipotence (acts against divine goodness or the change of absolutely necessary essential laws) are not restrictions of omnipotence but conditions of its greatness and beauty, and of its opposition to diabolical
arbitrariness of exertion of power.

Part IV:

WHAT CAN WE KNOW ABOUT GOD?

OMNISCIENCE, OMNIPOTENCE, ETERNITY, INFINITY

Great Question 15: *If God exists, what attributes can properly be described as divine attributes?*

GERARD J. HUGHES

If one is asked "What is God like?," the quickest and shortest answer is to list some of the things which have traditionally been said about God; He exists eternally, He is unchanging, knows all things, is all-powerful, personal, good; He created the world out of love for it.

But while I think those descriptions are indeed true of God, much caution is needed in understanding them. It is all too easy to suppose that the ordinary human words which we use of God are adequate to capture God's reality. As the early Greek philosopher Xenophanes once put it, "If horses had gods, they would depict the gods as horses." If we try to avoid such crudities and refuse to identify God with the universe, or with any particular kind of thing that we can grasp, we must recognize that it is impossible for our ordinary language to be applied in any straightforward way to God. I don't just mean that God is not an old man with a beard sitting on a throne. I mean that even if it is true to say that God is just, or loving, or personal, we have only the most slender grasp of what it means for God to be those things.

Still, our vocabulary gets its content from our own experiences of this-worldly things, and the very structure of our language makes us think of God as an individual, one being among others, one loving person among others. It just is not possible for us to think or speak of God in any other way, and I am certainly not advocating a radical revision of our theological or religious vocabularies. But we must recognize the extreme limitations of our understanding of a God who is not an individual, as we would normally apply that term, nor a member of any class such as the class of just beings or loving beings. It is no accident that much of the language of worship and prayer speaks of God in metaphors – as a boundless ocean, or a mighty fortress, or as a shepherd, or as light. Such talk removes much of the temptation to take it for more than it is. Metaphorical descriptions, whether in physics, or religion, or love-poetry, achieve truth by being suggestive, by pointing beyond what is said.

With those cautionary remarks, I shall try to say something of the attributes of God as I understand them.

I take God to be eternal and unchanging. To say that God is eternal is not to say that he exists at all times, everlastingly, but rather to say that his existence is not in time at all. He does not exist *at the same time* as the world, nor does he act *at some particular time*, nor yet at all times. Nothing in God is contemporaneous with anything in creation. Of course, in speaking about God we naturally and unavoidably used tensed vocabulary: God "revealed" himself through his prophets, "is" with us in our trials, "will" vindicate the righteous, and so on. Such talk reflects our own temporal viewpoint on these matters, but does not correspond to any succession of activities in God. Again, to say that God "was" angry but "then forgave" His people is to project on to God changes, not in God, but in the way we experience God's unchanging love. Once again, there is no need for us to abandon ways of speaking which are natural to us, provided that we remember that our ways of describing God are inaccurate and potentially misleading unless we are careful.

What about God's knowledge? I take God's knowledge to be a perfect act of self-awareness. We, in contrast, are aware of ourselves only in a piecemeal fashion: we have to go through a process of "fixing" our awareness by formulating statements about ourselves, and gradually coming to an understanding of who and what we are. We naturally enough tend to speak of God's knowledge as we speak of our own, in terms of the statements which God knows to be true. But, to be more accurate, we should remember that God does not need to express His knowledge by formulating statements (which takes time); rather His knowledge is a direct grasp of things and states of affairs; and His knowledge of things and states of affairs. For God, knowing just is His awareness of His own creative activity in sustaining those things in being.

God knows things as they are, irrespective of when they are. The world has only one actual history, one actual past, present and future, even though that history could, no doubt, have been different at any or every stage. It is that one actual history which is eternally accessible to

God's knowledge. That is not to say that God knows everything *simultaneously* (which would imply that God is in time); nor is it to deny that he knows that things succeed one another in time.

We often speak as though our past were fixed and our future open-ended. In a sense that is quite true, since we can no longer affect what is past, but we can affect what is still future. But there is also a sense in which it is misleading to talk in this way. For there are many past histories which we could have had but did not, and in just the same way many future histories which we could but will not have. Which of these possible histories we in fact have is, in part at least, dependent upon ourselves and our free choices. It is this one actual history which is timelessly known to God.

I believe that God knows the free choices we actually make because we make them. I thus disagree with the view that God's knowledge is in no way dependent on what we do. What about free choices which we *might have* made but never in fact make? I would say that God knows all of these as *possibilities*; but in my view it is a mistake to say that God knows what we *would have* (as distinct from *might have*) freely chosen had things been different; where freedom is concerned, I do not believe there are any truths of that kind to be known, by God or anyone else.

Plainly, God cannot do things which are impossible for an immaterial being, such as walking, speaking, or exerting physical force on things. Apart from such things, though, what can God do? It is often said that God can do anything which is in itself possible. This is no doubt true, but is not very illuminating since we have only a limited grasp of what is and is not possible. Many philosophers have tried to sort this out by saying that what is contradictory is impossible (like creating something which is at once circular and square), and that what is not contradictory is possible (like creating a human being 30 feet tall). I think this test for what is possible and impossible is very inadequate. What we take to be contradictory depends upon our own concepts and language, and that, in turn, depends upon the experiences of the world which we have had. But that tells us little about possibilities beyond our experience, or impossibilities which we can construct in our imagination, such as time-travel, or a talking horse. Descartes forcibly reminded us not to project onto God's infinite power the limitations of our own experience and imaginations. Apart from what God has done, it seems to me we have very little grasp of what God can or cannot do. Just as it is no limitation on God's knowledge to say that He cannot know where there is no truth to be known (as in "What would I have been doing now had I emigrated to Australia when I was twenty?" – a question to which there is no true answer, I would maintain), so it is no limitation on God's power to maintain that he cannot do what cannot be done. We know and understand some of the things which God has done; and that is too small a basis on which to make assertions about what is possible for God.

ALVIN PLANTINGA

I would give the traditional Christian and, more broadly, theistic list. God is a person, which means He holds beliefs (or at least does something very much like holding beliefs) and has knowledge. In fact, He is infinitely knowledgeable; He is omniscient. He is also all-powerful. He is an agent; that is, He has aims and ends and takes steps to accomplish these aims and ends, acts to accomplish them. He also has affections; that is, He hates some things, and loves others. He hates sin; He loves His children. He is perfectly good. Beyond that, He is loving, He is holy, He has created the world, He governs the world. These are some of the attributes that I would say God has.

It seems to me that there are really two ways of knowing God. I speak more or less as a Reformed Christian, or a Protestant, although Roman Catholics would say something very similar. There is first of all the *sensus divinitatis*, which is, according to John Calvin, a kind of way of apprehending God's existence that God has built into our nature, and which was ruined or at any rate damaged, wounded, in the Fall. Because of sin, our apprehension of God doesn't have the generality and the immediacy that it would otherwise have, but it is still there. Thus one may know that God is present upon seeing a mountain or a seascape, or when in danger, or when feeling guilty, and in other situations. In these situations, it is natural for human beings to form beliefs about God – such beliefs as that God created all this, God is almighty, God can help. But second, there is another source of knowledge about God: special revelation or scripture, or the testimony of the Holy Spirit. These sources renew the *sensus divinitatis*, and give us additional knowledge – knowledge of the central truths of the Christian faith. I would say those are the sources of the knowledge we have about God's attributes.

HUGO MEYNELL

The short answer is, in my view, whatever may properly be deduced from the thesis that God is that which conceives all possibilities, and wills those that actually obtain. One might say, well, we cannot apply terms in the same sense to God and to creatures, because that would be blasphemous. But if you take that principle too far, as David Hume in particular points out, you might as well join the atheists. If you say that God isn't good in anything like the sense in which the word "good" is used of creatures, or intelligent in any-thing like the sense in which we may be intelligent, then you might just as well say that God was bad as that God was good, or that God was stupid as God was intelligent. What's the way through this? The crucial thing here is a suggestion due to medieval philosophers, that God is in unrestricted act, that we are in very limited potency. We gradually develop in understanding from virtually nothing, and our wills are very restricted; but God is that whose understanding encompasses everything and whose will is almighty. God is either able to will this universe or another universe or no universe at all. Thus intelligence and will, it seems to me, have to be meant in the same sense as applied to God and creatures, as the medieval school-men used to say, univocally predicated of them; the difference is in their range and magnitude. Omnipotence, I think, follows from the fact that what sort of a world there is, and any contingent state of affairs, will be dependent on the divine action or, at the very least, the divine permission (this is where sin comes in). And omniscience, I would say, similarly follows from the fact that God conceives and wills everything. There are some ticklish problems, which have been variously resolved by theologians, around the question of in what sense and to what extent God knows the future, or what is future to us, if future events are not completely pre-determined by present cir-cumstances. But we can leave that question, I think, on one side, unless it actually comes up later on.

JOSEF SEIFERT

[I answered this question in my earlier answer to Great Question 10, on the existence of God] but could add that all those attributes which are "pure perfections" (the clear philosophi-cal discovery of which I take to be an equally epoch-making discov-ery of Anselm of Canterbury as the discovery of the ontological argument itself) must be attributed to God. Pure perfections are those of which we understand that they are not essentially limited, and therefore can and must be attributed to God. These so-called pure perfections differ from the mixed perfections which are only good under certain points of view and within certain limits. All species of plant and animal, and even human nature, are such essentially limited and mixed perfections. For while it is good, as Anselm of Canterbury said, to be gold rather than silver or a less-er metal, and much better to be human than to possess any nature lower than that of humans, it is not absolutely better to be gold rather than not to be gold; for to be a person or a spirit is beyond the material nature of gold and incompatible with it. And to be the infinite God is better than to be human. Similarly, all other species of animal and plant are intrinsically and necessarily limited and therefore the possession of these natures is not, absolutely speak-ing, better than their non-possession. For they are incompatible with higher perfections.

Quite different is the case with these pure perfections of which the mind can understand the most stunning thing: that it is not just bet-ter in certain respects but better absolutely speaking to possess them than not to possess them.

These perfections include:

1. the so-called transcendental properties of being which every-thing that is, and therefore also God, must possess: being itself, essence (*res*), to be something and distinct from nothing and from other beings (*aliquid*), to possess goodness (some value and positive importance in itself), some beauty (as the splendor of the good and of the true), intelligibility (*verum*), etc.;

2. many which not all beings possess but only some, such as life, per-sonhood, knowledge, wisdom, justice, freedom, power, etc. These perfections culminate in the characteristics of persons such as knowledge and wisdom, most of all in the moral perfections, such as justice and mercy. All these perfections can and must be attrib-uted to God and a god such as Zeus, who would not possess them, or not possess them infinitely, would not be God;

3. the pure perfections which we can and must attribute to God, including *those exclusively divine attributes*, which we can understand darkly in the intelligible mirror of the world: eter-nity as an all-presence of being in which nothing has to come

to be or passes away; absolute infinity of all perfections; omnipotence; omniscience; perfect necessity of real existence, etc. These attributes are exclusively divine attributes and no other being can possess them. Yet they are also pure perfections.

Of the pure perfections of the first and second group we can say that God not only must possess them but must be them and possess them in their infinite plenitude. For this reason, with regard to these pure perfections, the *via negativa* (the negative way of attribution by way of the negation of attributes) does not apply to God but rather to the world. God alone is good, God alone is just, etc. Of the world these pure perfections can be attributed only *secundum quid*, in certain aspects and in a purely analogous sense (as the Bible says: "Do not call me good, God alone is good"). The opposite is the case with respect to the mixed perfections. They can be literally only attributes of the world, and of God they must be negated (God is not a fish or a man), or they can only be attributed to Him analogously or super-eminently.

Having said all this as philosophers and having reached a true and profoundly significant rational knowledge of God as a supreme thinking and personal being, who has all the pure perfections in their infinity, we also possess, and I personally recognize as such, a second and quite different source of knowledge of God: divine revelation. Many attributes of the infinite perfection of God, such as the mystery of the Blessed Trinity and of the eternal community of persons who constitute God and possess the divine nature, are hidden from our pure human reason and intellect. With regard to these attributes, the truth about God, which we learn only through religious revelation, surpasses all that philosophy and pure human reason can know. Those most intimate and mysterious perfections of God can only be known by their being freely revealed to humankind by God Himself and taught to the Church and to us by the Holy Spirit.

The divine qualities hidden from purely philosophical knowledge also and particularly include the free actions of God in the world and towards us.

Before discussing supernatural relevation, let us first discuss the character of a "natural relevation" and of our natural human knowledge of God's free actions by the perception of the really existing world. That God chose to create the world and these meaningful species of beings in it, or this or that individual being, we can only grasp through our senses and intellectual perceptions based on sense-perception or on the inner awareness of our own existence in the cogito. Thereby we receive knowledge of the existing world, and, through it, of God's free creative will, by some natural revelation of God's free will which rests on the existential perception of the world and on our own inner experience of ourselves. The same type of perception and existential knowledge acquaints us with the order, finality, and beauty of the things that exist in nature and in the world, and which could also not exist but whose existence we learn through our concrete existential perception. And thereby we also receive some natural revelation of God's will and wisdom. This knowledge differs from an understanding of the most general and indispensable attributes of the world and of the necessary divine attributes. Rather, here the divine attributes of wisdom or goodness are concretely revealed to us through the specific creatures which God chose to create and, through knowing them, we learn about the free creative will of God.

This type of knowledge likewise underlies the "fifth way," the argument for the existence of God from the meaning and finality of the world, through which we understand God concretely as the origin of all the beauty and meaning embodied in the human body and human soul and in all other things which we witness in experience.

However, those even more hidden qualities of God, which involve also His free actions towards humankind, the infinity of his mercy and of His boundless love for us, especially, cannot be known through the observation of the existing world but only through the free act of God revealing Himself and his will to us, most of all through the divine revelation through Jesus Christ, who alone could reveal "that God loved the world so much that he sent his only Son to redeem us," as he says to Nicodemus and proves in its whole extension on the Cross. No philosophy can reach this mystery of a freely chosen action of God that reveals the infinity of His mercy and of His love but surpasses anything which could be known by mere human reasoning. Also the concrete ways in which the sinful humankind is called to be reunited to God, the ways which God chose of our redemption, of the communication of His grace, or of our resurrection from the dead, cannot be known purely philosophically. This follows from the nature of freely chosen acts and from the invisible effects of these acts. As no other human being can know my free acts if I do not reveal them through works, actions, or words, even less God's free acts stand in principle open to us without perceiving His Word and His works, or without our being informed about those divine actions which are not producing visible fruits but which require faith to be known and accepted, such as our redemption through the passion and death of Christ.

RALPH MCINERNY

Here again I am guided by two things and one would be the revelatory, as such, what God has told us about Himself, and second by the philosophical tradition, what people have, on reflection, thought it was fitting or appropriate to attribute to God. And the great tradition has been very cautious about claiming to have anything like comprehensive knowledge of what God is like. On the other hand, it is part of the cosmological argument base that you find perfections among creatures, probably limited and restricted in various ways, but that we can imagine in unrestricted form, like wisdom or knowledge or love and, we figure, if you can think away the restrictions and flaws of their finite appearance, then you would have a way of talking or thinking about God. But that is done with a great deal of caution. There is the famous three-stage approach of Dionysus the Areopagite – Pseudo-Dionysus – that you affirm things of God, you say that God is wise and then you say, but God isn't wise, meaning not like Socrates, who became wise and might lose it, but He is Wisdom – you get the eminent way. That is an effort to think beyond finitude and we can only have limited success in doing that, obviously.

There has been a lot of disagreement between those who've talked about the analogy between finite beings and God. Do you think that there are, at least, certain things held in common by those who held different theories of analogy?

Yes, well, you know analogy is what I am talking about, and I think that is what I cited from the three-stage process of Pseudo-Dionysus. It underlies analogy – you're trying to figure out how can a term like "wise" be common, analogously common, to creature and God. So it seems to me that analogy is going to show up – as a description of what you are doing – in any such cosmological proof or effort to talk about divine attributes and the like.

BRIAN LEFTOW

What is God's relation to space?

The Western religions hold that God is everywhere – that no matter where you are, God is present. The hard question, though, is what it means to say, in any place, that God is present here. My own view is that God is not literally in space at all. God's relation to history, including that of the universe itself, is like that of author to novel. This analogy is of course not perfect. (No analogy ever is.) For instance, I am free to do what God does not want or cause me to do. Sherlock Holmes is not free to do what Conan Doyle does not make or want him to do. Still, the analogy is suggestive. An author who writes a novel does not by so doing become part of the novel – Lewis Carroll was not at any place in Wonderland. If an author becomes part of the novel, this happens because the author writes himself or herself into it, as a character.[1] In that case, the author is in the novel and outside it as well. The author retains his or her nature, and also takes on a second nature or status, that of a fictional character. I believe that in the Incarnation, God did write Himself into our world. But apart from that, God is no more in our space than Lewis Carroll was in Wonderland.

Still, I do not think this keeps us from making literal sense of the claim that God is present here. When I say "the waiter is here," looking at my table, I do not mean that the waiter is sitting on the table. I mean that the waiter is nearby, close enough to hear me order my meal. I see "God is here" as making a like claim. It does not mean that God is in this space. It means that though He is not, He is literally near this space: though God is not located anywhere, He is just next to everywhere. He is not in any direction from here. But for any distance you care to name, God is closer than that to us.

Let me mention just two objections to this idea. One is that it does not seem to fit the author/novel analogy; Lewis Carroll was not literally near the Mad Hatter. But this is at least partly because there was no Wonderland and no Mad Hatter. Many Sherlock Holmes stories take place in London. Conan Doyle was literally in the London which was in the stories, because he made London a "character" in his story. So Conan Doyle could be near characters in *his* stories, even though he was not part of the story or near them in the story, because real things were parts of those stories. God can be near His characters even if He is not part of the story, because the characters are all real things. He relates to them outside the story, as Conan Doyle did. That is, He is near them although He is not in space.

This raises our other problem. How can something which is nowhere in space be *near* anything? To be in space is to lie at some distance in some direction from something else (or have parts which do). So whatever is in space stands in both sorts of relation (or has parts which do). If God is near everything but not in space, this means that for every point in space p, God is at some distance (namely zero) but in no direction from p. My claim, then, is just that God stands in just one of our two sorts of relation to every p. Thus He is not in space, since that requires standing in both sorts of relation to something. But He is near – that is a distance-relation. Can something be at a distance but in no direction from something? Each p is at a zero distance in no direction from itself.[2] There is a number for how far p is from p, namely zero. But there is no word for p's direction from p: there is nothing which is p's direction from p. So there are analogies to what I suggest about God. I could develop this a great deal further, but this would get more involved than is suitable to this format.

What is God's relation to time?

If universal history is a novel God writes, then God is outside the novel's time as well as the novel's space – that is, God is not in time at all. To be in time is just to exist or occur earlier or later than something. So if we say that God is not in time, what this means concretely is that no event in God's life is earlier or later than any event, in God's life or in time.

Thus God did not create the universe before now – say, at the first moment of time – even though that was when the universe started to exist. God is not sustaining the world in existence now, though now is when the universe exists. God will not sustain the universe tomorrow, though tomorrow is when it will exist due to His sustaining it. God simply creates the world, timelessly. There is no "when" He creates – that is, there is no part of time from which God causes the universe to exist. The times at which the universe exists are not times at which God causes it to exist. They are parts of what God causes. In the same way, there is no place from which God causes the universe to exist. All places are parts of what God causes.

This tells us at most a bit of what a timeless God's life is not. What is a timeless being's life like? I do not claim to know what it is like to be God. But I can say this. If God's life is outside time, everything that ever happens in God's life, happens all at once. Moses did not part the Red Sea at the same moment Paul preached to the Athenians. But God sees Moses part the sea neither before nor after He sees Paul preach. I think He sees the one in the very seeing which sees the other – and that the very seeing which sees the universe begin sees it end.

This being so, nothing is humdrum to God. What is humdrum has happened before, over and over. In God's life, nothing happens before anything. Further, everything happens only once. We see the morning newspaper come one day, then the next, then the next. For God, there is just a single seeing of all our lives' newspapers hitting all our lives' doorsteps. God knows all truth,[3] and grasps it in a single flash – as if the "got it" experience which can be the supreme moment in an inventor's life were multiplied to infinity. So to speak, He never has time to get used to it. What is eternal is eternally fresh.

LEO SWEENEY

Answering the question of whether God is perfect and infinite is not easy, as briefly looking at the answers philosophers and theologians have given it.

ARISTOTLE

Let us start with Aristotle (384–322 B.C.), who affirms God is perfect and subsistent being in a passage of extraordinary philosophical eloquence. After having indicated that locomotion is the perfection or actuation which is common not only to all existents on earth but also to all the heavenly spheres, he concludes that such ubiquitous locomotion must be caused by an existent which is itself without motion but which produces it as the goal-cause influencing all such movers. Then comes Aristotle's eloquent description of God, who is that final cause:

> On such a principle, then, depend all the heavens and the earth. And its life is such as the best which we enjoy – a life, namely, of contemplation and also of joy . . . If, then, God is always in that good state of actuation and perfection in which we sometimes are, this compels our wonder; and if God is in a better state this compels it yet more. And God is in a better state. And life also belongs

to God, for the actuality of contemplation is life, and God is that actuality; yes, God's subsistent actuality is life most good, and eternal. We say therefore that God is living, eternal, and most good, so that life and duration continuous and eternal belong to God, for this is God. (*Metaphysics*, Book XII, ch. 7, 1072b, 14–31)

But Aristotle is not finished: he next applies infinity to God. But before considering that application, let us turn to his notion of infinity, which means "that which cannot be gone through" and for Aristotle it primarily characterizes quantity, which fundamentally is infinite through division. For instance, let AO be a line divided at B, C, D, etc. so that $AB = \frac{1}{2}AO$, $BC = \frac{1}{2}BO$, $CD = \frac{1}{2}CO$, and so on:

```
├─────────────────────────┼──────────┼──────┼────┤

A                         B          C      D    O
```

The subtraction of AB, BC, etc. from AO can go on forever and some of AO will always be left. Through such division there emerges a series of parts, each of which is itself limited but has successors which follow it without limit; in a word, when division of a spatial magnitude is going on, a process which is in principle endless is progressively actualized.

Moreover, corresponding to that division is a process of addition. In fact, that which is infinite by way of addition is inversely the same as that by way of division. Having divided AO at B, C, D, etc., to AB without ever completing AO. Just as AO can be divided without limit, AB can be added to without limit.

In a way the infinite by addition is the same thing as the infinite by division. In a finite magnitude, the infinite by addition comes about in a way inverse to that of the other. For in proportion as we see division going on, in the same proportion we see addition being made to what is already marked off. For if we take a determinate part of a finite magnitude and add another part determined by the same ratio (not taking in the same amount of the original whole), and so on, we shall not traverse the given magnitude. (*Physics*, Book III, ch. 7)

What, then, does infinity mean when applied to quantity through addition and division? Or, more simply, how can the infinite be said to *be*? Aristotle's answer can be expressed in a syllogism. The word "is" means either what is in potency or what is in act; moreover, that which is infinite is so either by addition or division; but magnitude is not infinite in act, and yet it is infinite by division; therefore, a magnitude is infinite in potency and infinity is in potency as that which admits a progressive realization but is never completely realized at any one time.

Consequently, the infinite turns out to be not that which has nothing outside, but that which always has something outside it – i.e. in a quantity there is always some part beyond the point one has reached in dividing it or in building it up by addition. Hence, that is infinite according to quantity (*apeiron kata poson*) if it is such that we can always take a part outside what has already been taken.

Since, then, that which is infinite always has something absent or lacking from it (e.g. the parts of the line *AO* [see diagram above] which have not yet resulted from its bisection), it is not a "whole" or "complete" or perfect, and infinity itself is a privation, the subject of which is the sensible continuum (ibid.).

What, then, is the general picture of the infinity of quantity which Aristotle sketches? First of all, what actually is, is finite – for example, this line, *AO*, having such and such definite dimensions. Although actually finite, *AO* is infinite in so far as the process of going through it is without end: under certain conditions it is endlessly divisible. Yet it is only potentially infinite inasmuch as each part resulting from the division is actually finite (i.e. is *AB* or *BC*, etc.), and is infinite only because each can be again divided into smaller parts.

Thus that which is potentially infinite in the actually finite magnitude, *AO*, is its matter – that is, the composite, extended matter considered, however, as without the definite dimensions, limits and figure which it actually has and which make it actually finite.

Thus in *AO*, that which is potentially infinite is, precisely qua infinite, like matter without form; since completeness and integration come from form, the infinite as such is actually a part and only potentially a whole. Since form is the principle of perfection and of intelligibility, the infinite qua infinite is imperfect and unintelligible. That which is infinite, qua infinite, thus lacks completeness, perfection, and intelligibility, and infinity itself is the privation in *AO* of those three factors.[4]

For Aristotle, accordingly, infinity of extension, as well as of motion and time, implies imperfection, incompleteness, and unintelligibility.

His predicating infinity of God will turn out to be as simple and straightforward as his discussion of it was complex. He begins by repeating his proof of God's existence: "From what has been said [see initial paragraph of this chapter], it is evident that there exists an entity which is eternal and immovable and which is separate from [and thus unlike] the sensible existents on this earth and in the heavens." This entity is God, who as final cause moves all those sensibles and thus is the unmoved mover. But since this divine entity is the actuation of subsistent contemplation: "It cannot have magnitude or extension and, in fact, it is without parts and is indivisible. Why? Because it causes motion for an infinite time – a causation which requires its power to be somehow infinite, whereas no finite thing has such power." But infinity is predicable directly only of extension, motion, and time; since, then infinite power is required, infinity can be predicated of God's power only extrinsically – i.e. as subsistent actuation God is so perfect as to be capable of causing everlasting circular locomotion, to which alone infinity is properly and intrinsically predicated. (*Meta*, XII, ch. 7, 1073a4–13.)[5]

PLOTINUS

Aristotle builds all his positions on God, the physical universe and its existents in the heavens and on Earth, as well as the motion, time, and extension they entail – all these he builds upon a single foundation: to be of value and worth (and, therefore, to be real) is to be in a state of actuation, whether this last be locomotion (for all sensible existents whether on Earth or in the heavens) or contemplation (which properly belongs to human existents). Although coming four centuries after Aristotle, Plotinus (AD 205–270) uses the same technique in constructing his position: to be real (and thus to be of worth and value) is *to be one*. Once this is recognized, everything falls into place. God as supreme reality is the One. All other existents (Intellect and individual intellects, Soul and individual souls) are real to the extent they are one: each is the One on a lower level. Where does infinity fit into Plotinus' doctrine? One finds many texts on that topic and the best interpretation of those on God is that God is above both infinity and finiteness: He transcends both and is the One simply.

But before studying how God is infinite, let us first reflect on the texts disclosing what God is and how He produces the intelligible and physical universes. Consider Plotinus' description in *Enneads*,

V, 2 (11) 1, lines 22, of how this physical universe, of which He and we are parts, has come about.[6]

[a] The One [= God] is all things and yet is not a single one of them: it is the principle of all things [but is itself] not all things, all of which (so to speak) run back to it – or rather they are not there yet but they will be.

[b] How then do all things come from the One, which is simple and has in it no diverse variety nor any sort of doubleness? It is because there is nothing in It that all things come from It: in order that being may exist, the One is not being but That Which generates being . . which is (so to speak) its firstborn. Perfect because It seeks nothing, has nothing and needs nothing, the One (as it were) overflows and Its superabundance makes something other than Itself. What has thus come about turns back to the One and is filled and thus becomes Its contemplator and so is Intellect.

[c] The Intellect, because it thus resembles the One, produces in the same way – that is, by pouring forth a multiple power which is a product resembling its maker: just as That Which was before it did, Intellect poured forth alikeness of itself. This act originating from entity [for Intellect] is Soul, which comes about while Intellect remains at rest, for Intellect too came about while That Which is prior to it remains unchanged.

[d] But Soul does not remain unchanged when it produces: it is moved and thereby brings forth an image. It looks There whence it came and is filled and thereupon goes forth to another opposed movement and thus generates its own image [= the sentient and vegetal levels of the physical universe].

Plotinus' fourfold description discloses that reality is, despite first appearances, monistic.[7] Because superabundantly perfect the One overflows and this overflow produces something other than Itself (point b). Resembling the One, the Intellect also pours forth a multiple power like the Intellect's, its source (point c). If what is poured forth from the Intellect is power and the Intellect in producing is like the One, the One's overflow (i.e. what It pours forth) is power also.[8] This power actuates itself to be Intellect and intellects and, through Intellect, to be Soul and souls. The result is that all such existents are each the One-on-a-lower-level and each is real (= valuable) to the extent that it thus is the One. It is unreal to the extent it is other than the One – i.e. because of the actuations which each also entails and which precisely make it be Intellect (and intellects), Soul (and souls). Such actuation makes each be unreal because of the multiplicity which they introduce and in which they consist. The Intellect and its contents, the Soul and its contents do actually exist, as does the One, but their actual existence is not what makes them be of value and of worth. These consist rather in the degree to which they are one – either subsistently so or through participation.[9] As so understood, Plotinus' position on reality is a monism, wherein every existent consists of the same basic "stuff" – namely, oneness.

Now the question becomes: Where and how does Plotinus insert infinity into that monism? Let us return to the *Enneads*, where the reality of the One is portrayed as transcending both finiteness and infiniteness and, secondly, His power is said to be infinite but only through extrinsic denomination: God is capable of producing infinite effects.

Let *Enneads*, V, 5 (32), 6, 1 sqq., exemplify the first sort of text:

> The entity which is generated from the One is form . . . which is not the form of some one thing but of all, so that nothing is left outside it. The One therefore must be without form and, hence determined. But it is impossible to apprehend the One as a "this" for then it would not be a principle but only the "this" which one says of it. But if all things are in that which is generated from the One [that is, in the Intellect], which of the things in it are you going to say that the One is? Since It is none of them, it can only be said to be beyond them. Now since such existents are beings and being, the One is above and beyond being.

After warning that no one can know the One without first divesting himself of the intelligible and of every form, Plotinus then states that the One's most characteristic mark is not-to-have-any-characteristic, for what has no quiddity can have no properties. Therefore, the One is ineffable. "One" simply denies any multiplicity. In the beginning of someone's search for the First Principle, "one" indicates that which is most simple, but finally even "one" is to be dropped as an adequate term for that nature.

If Plotinus is thus presenting God as beyond entity, beyond "thisness," beyond determination and finiteness, even beyond unity, we must conclude that God is above infinity too. God exists,[10] and a human person encounters God only by losing his or her self and by becoming one with God through mystical union.[11]

Next, what of God's power: is it infinite? Yes, when carefully understood, as is clear from *Enneads*, VI, 7 (38), 1 sqq. Ascending from the material universe with its quasi-beauty to the genuinely beautiful existents of the intelligible universe, we must seek their source. That which has produced them is without form, not that it lacks one, but rather because all intelligible forms come from it. It is none of those beings and yet all of them – none, because they are posterior, yet it is all of them because all have come from it. Plotinus turns next to divine power:

> He who is thus capable of making all things, what greatness would He have? He is infinite [in power] and, if so, would have no physical magnitude. For such magnitude is found in the things which come after Him, and if He will produce their magnitude, then He should not Himself be extended. The greatness of any entity is not quantitative; only that which is after entity would have such magnitude. God would be great in this sense that nothing is more powerful than Him or even equally so. For what does He have in which beings who are in no way the same as Him could equal? (ibid.)

The greatness of the One, then, is not to be measured in terms of physical mass but of power, whose size is in turn computed *from without* – from what He effects. He is termed infinitely powerful and nothing is more powerful or even equally so because He is capable of making all things. This then is a description through extrinsic denomination: the power is named apeiron but only in view of its effects, which alone would be directly and properly so classified.[12]

CONDEMNATION OF 1241

From Plotinus (d. 270) to 1241 is a period of ten centuries, but this temporally long transition is justified in our study of divine infinity by two facts: no radically different theory of infinity or of God was introduced then[13] and, secondly, in 1241 there is evidence of such a radical difference.

In that year the following proposition was condemned by the chancellor of the University of Paris (Odo de Castro Radulfi) and the bishop of Paris (William of Auvergne):

> The divine essence itself will not be seen by either a man or an angel. This error we condemn and we excommunicate those who assert or defend it. We firmly believe and assert that God in His essence or substance will be seen by angels and all the saints, and it is seen now by all glorified souls.

Primus error, quod divina essence essentia in se nec ab homine nec angelo videbitur. Hunc errorem reprobamus et assertores et defensores auctoritate Wilhelmi episcopi excommunicamus. Firmiter autem credimus et asserimus, quod Deus in sua essentia vel substantia videbitur ab angelis et omnibus sanctis et videtur ab animabus glorificatis. (*Chartularium Universitatis Parisiennis*, I, 170.)[14]

What were the historical sources of that condemned proposition and who taught it at Paris? Its sources would be such statements in sacred scripture as John, 1, 18: "No one ever sees God" and John Chrysostom's commentary on that verse: "Not only the prophets but even angels and archangels have not seen that which is God" (*"Ipsum quod est Deus non solum prophetae sed nec angeli viderunt nec archangeli"*).[15] Under the influence of such sources and prior to 1241 some contemporaries (*"quidam"*)[16] of Thomas Aquinas and Bonaventure put forth this threefold doctrine on the divine essence or being. (a) God may be infinite in power but He is finite in essence. Why so? The properties of infiniteness or finiteness are linked with quantity, and since quantity can in no way be found in the divine essence, infinity cannot be found in the divine essence.[17] (b) Because the notion of perfection is identified with definiteness or determinateness, the divine essence is finite because it is perfect. (c) The divine essence is comprehended by the blessed in the beatific vision in heaven. Such comprehension is possible because the divine essence is absolutely simple, with the result that whenever it is grasped, it is grasped in its totality, so that nothing of it is left outside. If this simple essence is attained and thus comprehended by the finite intellect of the blessed, it too must be finite.[18]

Obviously, the condemnation by Chancellor Odo and Bishop William in 1241 concentrates upon the essence or substance of God: it will be seen by angels and saints, it is seen now by all glorified souls. It says nothing explicitly about whether or not the divine being is infinite. But reflecting on our seeing God's essence and our predicating infinity or finiteness of God are so intimately linked that teachers at Paris had to take a stand on infinity also.

One such teacher was Albert the Great, who in 1243 chose to predicate "finiteness" of God in the sense that He is the goal (*finis*) of all creatures. Thus understood, God, as well as His power and whatever else He is, is the most finite of all: *"finitione qua finis dicitur finitus, finitissimus omnium Deus et potentia sua et quidquid ipse est"* (*Commentarium in Librum Sententiarum*, I, d. 43, C, a.2, ad 1 [Borgnet ed., XXVI, 379]). Even when we affirm that God is infinite, it seemingly is in an extrinsic and relative fashion – i.e. it is with reference to creatures, "since neither time nor place nor created intellects can contain, limit, comprehend or define Him who surpasses all" (ibid., solution, pp. 38–9). In fact, if we wish to speak strictly, "God rather surpasses both finiteness and infinity in His excellence" (*Liber de Causis et Processu Universitatis*, II, tr. 3, c. 4 [Borgnet ed., X, 553]).

Another Dominican in approximately the same year but at Oxford asked, when also considering the beatific vision of God by the saints and angels, whether God is infinite – Richard Fishacre (d. 1248).[19] Yes, he replied, "God is both infinite and simple," provided one takes "infinite" not in terms of quantity, as Aristotle thought (ibid. 11, 287–88; on Aristotle, see my initial section above), but in terms of power. This latter is infinite not by infinitely increasing the power but by infinitely separating it from the impediments [to its action] coming from matter, and such infinity is entirely congruent with divine simplicity (*"non propter infinitam additionem virtuti sed propter infinitam elongationem ab impedimentis et a materia... infinitum virtualiter... congruit magis simplicitati"*).[20] But why is God's power infinitely separated from matter? Because God made matter from nothing, and since the power of a maker is as great as the distance between what is made and what it is made from and since the distance between matter and nothingness is infinite, God's power is infinite (ibid., 11. 10–12).[21]

God's power is infinite, Fishacre has established, but is His essence or being infinite? In 1254 Thomas Aquinas answers affirmatively and even bases the infinity of divine power upon that of essence. "Is the power of God infinite?" he asks *In I Sent*, d. 43, q. 1, a. 1 (Mandonnet ed., p. 1003). Yes, precisely because it is consequent upon God's essence or being, which is infinite:

> That which has absolute being and is in no way received in anything in fact, God is His being – that is absolutely infinite. Therefore, His essence is infinite, and His goodness and all other attributes predicated of Him are infinite, because none of them is limited to anything, as whatever is received in something is limited to the capacity of its recipient.

Illud quod habet esse absolutum et nullo modo receptum inaliquo – immo ipsemet est suum esse – illud est infinitum simpliciter; et ideo essentia ejus infinita est, et bonitasejus, et quidquid aliud de eo dicitur, quia nihil eorumlimitatur ad aliquid, sicut quod recipitur in aliquolimitatur ad capacitatem ejus.[22]

But what of divine power? Thomas answers in the immediately subsequent sentence: "From the fact that the divine essence is infinite, it follows that the divine power is infinite also." *"Et ex hoc quod essentia est infinita, sequitur quod potentia ejus infinita sit."*

Finally, does God's infinity of essence, as well as goodness, beauty, power and the like, prevent a saint or angel from seeing God Himself in the beatific vision (the issue which was, let us remind ourselves, at the heart of the 1241 condemnation)? No, Thomas answers, because God's subsistent essence is a subsistent intelligibility, which thus serves as the form by which the intellect of someone in heaven is entitatively actuated, an actuation which enables the saint or angel to efficiently cause its vision of God's essence (see *In IV Sent*, d. 49, q. 2, a. 2, solution and ad 6 [Parma ed., pp. 484–85]).[23]

KANT AND DERRIDA

The period between the death of Thomas Aquinas in 1274 and Immanuel Kant's *Critique of Pure Reason* (1st ed., 1781) and *Critique of Practical Reason* (1788) is five centuries. Why move directly and, one might say, precipitously from Aquinas to Kant? Because, according to James Collins, "All the highways in modern philsophy converge upon Immanuel Kant (1724–1804) and lead out again from him. The problem of God is no exception to his historical centrality."[24]

That Kant's own approach to God is itself problematic is clear from the fact that in the *Critique of Pure Reason* Kant allows us to think of but not to know God; in the second *Critique* we can affirm that God does exist but only because the human moral agent needs Him as a basis of his theory of morality. God is one of his three postulates of morality. Let me explain briefly.

According to the *Critique of Pure Reason* we *think* of God as "an *omnitudo realitatis*," we have a "concept of an *ens realissimum*," which "is the concept of an individual being. It is therefore a transcendental ideal which serves as basis for the complete determination that necessarily belongs to all that exists" (Norman Kemp Smith transl., pp. 490–91). On p. 492 Kant continues:

The possibility of that which includes in itself all reality . . . must be regarded as original. For all negations (which are the only predicates through which anything can be distinguished from the *ens realissimum*) are merely limitations of a greater, and ultimately of the highest, reality . . . [God as] the object of the ideal of reason, an object which is present to us only in and through reason, is therefore entitled the *primordial being* (*ens originarium*). As it has nothing above it, it is also entitled the *highest being* (*ens summum*); and as everything that is conditioned is subject to it, the *being of all beings* (*ens entium*). These terms are not, however, to be taken as signifying the objective relation of an actual object to other things, but of an *idea* to *concepts*. We are left entirely without knowledge as to the existence of a being of such outstanding pre-eminence (Smith, p. 492; italics in the original).

So far God has been described as *omnitudo realitatis*, as *ens realissimum*, as the primordial being, the highest being, the being of all beings. But for Kant we think of but do not know that such attractive (and, actually, traditional) descriptions fit God. But in the first *Critique* he on occasion anticipates the *Critique of Practical Reason* by mentioning how moral theology will affirm God's existence and thus will be complemented by the divine attributes which transcendental theology of the first *Critique* provides:

While for the merely speculative employment of reason the supreme being remains a mere ideal, it is yet an ideal *without a flaw*, a concept which completes and crowns the whole of human knowledge. Its objective reality cannot indeed be proved, but also cannot be disproved, by merely speculative reason. If, then, there should be a moral theology that can make good this deficiency, transcendental theology, which before was problematic only, will prove itself indispensable in determining the concept of this supreme being. Necessity, infinity, unity, existence outside the world (and not as world-soul), eternity as free from conditions of time, omnipresence as free from conditions of space, omnipotence, etc. are purely transcendental predicates, and for this reason the purified concepts of them, which every theology finds so indispensable, are only to be obtained from transcendental theology (Smith, p. 531).

The moral theology of which Kant speaks in that preceding quotation from the first *Critique* as hypothetical becomes actual in the *Critique of Practical Reason* when morality is seen to be based entirely upon duty (see Lewis, White, Beck transl., p. 83) as found within or even identified with a human being's will and personality:

> Duty! Thou sublime and mighty name that dost embrace nothing charming or insinuating but requirest submission and yet seekest not to move the will by threatening aught that would arouse natural aversion or terror, but only holdest forth a law which of itself finds entrance into the mind and yet gains reluctant reverence (though not always obedience) . . . What origin is there worthy of thee, and where is to be found the root of thy noble descent? It cannot be less than something which elevates man above himself as a part of the world of sense, something which connects him with an order of things which only the understanding can think and which has under it the entire world of sense, including the empirically determinable existence of man in time, and the whole system of all ends which is alone suitable to such unconditional practical laws as the moral. It is nothing else than personality, i.e. the freedom and independence from the mechanism of nature regarded as a capacity of a being which is subject to special laws (pure practical laws given by its own reason [and will]) so that the person as belonging to the world of sense is subject to his own personality so far as he belongs to the intelligible world (ibid., p. 89).[25]

After that rhapsodic description of duty Kant next sets forth the three factors needed to make that theory of morality work. The first of these is freedom of the will, which concerns a human action "which as belonging to the world of sense is always sensuously conditioned, i.e. mechanically necessary" but which can be free "as belonging to the causality of the acting being insofar as it belongs to the intelligible world" and thus has "a sensuously unconditioned causality as its foundation" (Beck, p. 108).

The second is the immortality of the human soul, the necessary object of whose will is the achievement according to the moral law of the highest good in the world, an achievement which "can be found only in an endless progress" of the will to its "complete fitness . . . to the moral law" and thus to holiness and happiness, which however "can be found only in an endless progress . . . This infinite progress is possible, however, only under the presupposition of an infinitely enduring existence and personality of the same rational being; this is called the immortality of the soul" and is the second "postulate of pure practical reason" (Beck, pp. 126–27).[26]

The happiness just mentioned as consisting in the endless process of an immortal soul to achieve the highest good requires that "everything goes according to [the soul's] wish and will," a requirement "which rests on the harmony of nature with [the man's] entire end and with the essential grounding of his will." But "his will cannot by its own strength bring nature, as it touches on his happiness, into complete harmony with his practical principles." Hence, "the existence is postulated of a cause of the whole of nature, itself distinct from nature, which contains the ground of the exact coincidence of happiness with morality" (Beck, p. 129). Therefore:

> The highest good is possible in the world only on the supposition of a supreme cause of nature which has a causality corresponding to the moral intention. Now a being which is capable of actions by the idea of laws is an intelligence (a rational being), and the causality of such a being according to this idea of laws is his will. Therefore, the supreme cause of nature, insofar as it must be presupposed for the highest good, is a being which is the cause (and consequently the author) of nature through understanding and will, i.e. God. As a consequence, the postulate of the possibility of a highest derived good (the best world) is at the same time the postulate of the reality of a highest original good, namely, the existence of God (ibid., pp. 129–30).[27]

With this third postulate Kant affirms the supremacy of the human person, which began in the *Critique of Pure Reason*, where the human person as knower through his a priori forms of space and time and the twelve categories constructs whatever is known as phenomena, and this supremacy has continued in the *Critique of Practical Reason*, where the human person as moral agent constructs God as what is needed to make the theory of morality work.

This affirmation of supremacy is equivalent to the subordination of God to the human person, which Kant admits in this triumphal claim:

> [Since] the pure moral law inexorably binds every man as a command . . . the righteous man may say: I will that there be a God, that my existence in this world be also an existence in a pure world of the understanding outside the system of natural connections, and finally that my duration be endless. I stand by this and will not give up this belief, for this is the only case where my interest inevitably determines my judgement because I will not yield anything of this interest (Beck, pp. 148–49).

That subordination of God will continue in subsequent modern philosophers to whatever factor they give primacy – e.g. the Absolute Spirit of Hegel, *Das Sein* of Heidegger, the *elan vitale* of Bergson, the creativity of Whitehead. That subordination continues even in such a postmodernist as Jacques Derrida (b. 1933), for whom the word "God" does not express any sort of subsistent being (even Kant's) but it stands for any sort of negations, whether these be grammatical or logical; or the privation of physical, moral or mental health; or the lifelong endlessly denying today what the human person affirmed/denied yesterday.[28]

In my eyes Thomas Aquinas' affirmation of God as subsistent, perfect, and infinite Being is much preferable not only to Derrida's but also to Kant's. Let the actual material existents in the concrete situations in the world of physical space and time, of which each of us is a part, determine the content of my metaphysical knowledge that actually to exist is to be real (= to be of value and perfection). The result? I am a single composite entity of this-individual-essence-and-existence, a composition which indicates there is an entity whose essence is existence (otherwise I would not exist) and who is my efficient, exemplary and final cause. This existent is God, subsistent and infinitely perfect being.

NOTES

1. I owe this thought to Paul Helm.
2. My claim, then, is that though God is not in space, He is as near each thing as it is to itself.
3. With a few exceptions, discussed in my *Time and Eternity* (Ithaca, New York: Cornell University Press, 1991).
4. See L. Sweeney, *Divine Infinity in Greek and Medieval Thought* [hereafter: *Divine Infinity*] (New York/Bern: Peter Lang Publishing Co., 1992), ch. 6, pp. 149–54.
5. In intrinsic predication one applies a predicate (here: infinity) to a subject (here: circular locomotion) because what the predicate signifies is itself found in the subject. Such intrinsic predication is contrasted with extrinsic predication or denomination in which what the predicate signifies is itself not in the subject, which however is related to something in which that signification is intrinsically verified. For an example and explanation, see ibid., p. xiv, n. 2.
6. In references to the *Enneads* the number in the parenthesis refers to the chronological order in which Plotinus wrote them.
7. Monism is the position of thought according to which all existents, however different they may seem, consist of one basic stuff, which in Plotinus' case is oneness.

8. See *Enneads*, III, 8 (30), 10, lines 1 and 25–26. Plotinus also calls the
    One's overflow "matter" as that which is shaped and differentiated (II,
    4 [12], 4, 6–7), as well as illuminated (ibid., lines 16–17), by the actua-
    tions which as dynamis it causes.

    Plotinus' conception of matter as the overflow from a higher to a
    lower level differs radically from Aristotle's since it is not essentially
    linked with physical extension and quantitative infinity at all. Matter as
    found on the higher levels of Intellect and Soul is indetermination and
    infinity with reference to forms because in and of itself it is their recip-
    ient – see L. Sweeney, *Divine Infinity*, pp. 177–84.

9. The "overflow" (see point b above) or "emanation" can also be viewed
    as amounting to a movement of what is increasingly less perfect from
    what is more perfect, of proceeding from the perfect to the imperfect.
    By this process lower existents become increasingly determined and,
    thereby, less real. For example VI, 9 (9), 11, 36 sqq.: "When [the human
    soul] goes down, it comes to evil and so to nonbeing." VI, 5 (23), 12,
    16: "[In ascending back to God] you have come to the All and not
    stayed in a part of it, and have not said even about yourself, 'I am so
    much.' By rejecting the 'so much' you have become all – yet you were
    all before. But because something else other than the All added itself to
    you, you became less by the addition, for the addition did not come
    from real being (you cannot add anything to that) but from that which
    is not. When you have become a particular person by the addition of
    nonbeing, you are not all till you reject the nonbeing. You will increase
    yourself then by rejecting the rest and by that rejection the All is with
    you." Determination so conceived helps preserve Plotinus' monism
    because what alone is real in any existent is the oneness it has from and
    with the one and not the apparent additions from individuation it has
    put on.

10. Although God is above entity and even above oneness, Plotinus explic-
    itly states that He does actually exist – see V, 5 (32), 13, 12–14: "If then
    one takes away everything and says nothing about him and does not say
    falsely about anything that it is with him, he allows him his 'existence'
    without attributing to him anything which is not there." Also see VI, 9
    (9), 3, 49–51; L. Sweeney, *Divine Infinity*, pp. 240–41.

11. For Plotinus' description of mystical union with God, see VI, 9, (9), 11,
    4–51. Plotinus, according to Porphyry (his student, companion, editor),
    achieved union with God several times during his lifetime – see
    Porphyry, "On the Life of Plotinus", trans. A. H. Armstrong (Harvard
    University Press, 1966), vol. 1, ch. 23, pp. 69–73: "[Plotinus] sleepless-
    ly kept his soul pure and ever strove towards the divine, which he loved
    with all his soul and did everything to be delivered and escape [from this
    physical world]. To this godlike man, who often raised himself in
    thought . . . to the first and transcendent God, that God appeared, who

has neither shape nor any intelligible form but is throned above intellect and all the intelligible . . . [Plotinus's] end and goal was to be united to, to approach the God who is over all things. Four times while I was with him he attained that goal in an unspeakable actuality and not in potency only . . . After his deliverance from the body he came to [heaven, where) affection rules and desire and joy and love kindled by God . . . [and where] life is filled full of festivity and joy and this life lasts for ever, made blessed by the gods."

12. See my *Divine Infinity*, pp. 195–209. On extrinsic denomination see n. 2 above.

13. Augustine's position on God is basically a Christianized Platonism: God is spiritual, immutable Being, Truth, and Eternity, in whom human persons participate through divine illumination – see L. Sweeney, *Christian Philosophy: Greek, Medieval, Contemporary Reflections* (hereafter: *Christian Philosophy*), ch. 3, paragraphs corresponding to footnotes 11a. On his position on infinity, see ibid., ch. 10, pp. 241–61, summarized in this sentence: Augustine "was not yet certain as to what divine infinity might mean in the light of his discovery, set forth in Confessions, Book VII, of God as completely incorporeal and thus as 'infinite in a way different' from how Augustine as a Manichean conceived Him to be an infinite body endlessly extended throughout space," (pp. 260–61).

14. See *Divine Infinity*, pp. 348–53.

15. "Homily 15" in *Nicene and Post-Nicene Fathers* (reprint; Peabody, Mass.: Hendrickson Publishers, Inc., 1994), vol. 14, p. 152.

16. On these "quidam" see *Divine Infinity*, ch. 16, pp. 337–60; ch. 19, pp. 416–25. Among those named are Stephen of Venizy and John Pagus; Alexander of Hales, Glossa in Quatuor Libros Sententiarum Petri Lombardi (1225); Guerric de San Quentin (at Paris 1233–1242).

17. A link made by Aristotle – see above paragraphs corresponding to nn. 1–2.

18. For documentation on the three doctrines see n. 13 above.

19. *Commentarium in Librum I Sententiarum*, Ermatinger ed., p. 216, 1. 2 sqq.: "*Hic de visione Dei quaeratur. Gratia cuius primo quaeritur an Deus sit infinitus.*"

20. Guerric de San Quentin took account of divine simplicity (vs. divine essence) in answering a *videtur quod non* (see *Divine Infinity*, esp. p. 419) and thus provides a background for Richard's sentence.

21. See ibid., ch. 18, especially pp. 391–404.

22. See ibid., ch. 19, pp. 432–37.

23. On the prominent place actuations "a" and "b" occupy in Aquinas' epistemology, see my *Christian Philosophy*, ch. 21. pp. 517–42.

24. James Collins, *God in Modern Philosophy* (Chicago: Henry Regnery, 1959), p. 162.

25. Kant's contrasting "the world of sense" with "the intelligible world" reveals the latent Platonism within his position, where Duty would correspond to what Plato calls a subsistent Form. The key, Kant explains, "to escaping from this labyrinth" and illusion of taking phenomena to be noumena is found when we discover " a view into a higher immutable order of things in which we already are, and in which to continue our existence in accordance with the supreme decree of reason we may now, after this discovery, be directed by definite precepts" found in the will and the moral law (Beck, pp. 111–12).

    Kant's explicit references to Greek philosophers are restricted to the Epicurean and Stoic schools – see Beck, pp. 115, 120, 131 and 145–46. See ibid., p. 146, where Kant contrasts Plato with Epicurus.

26. On existence after death see Beck, p. 128, note 1: "Naturally one who is conscious of having persisted, from legitimate moral motives, to the end of a long life in a progress to the better may very well have the comforting hope, though not the certainty, that he will be steadfast in these principles in an existence continuing beyond this life. Though he can never be justified in his own eyes either here or in the hoped-for increase of natural perfection together with an increase of his duties, nevertheless in this progress toward a goal infinitely remote (a progress which in God's sight is regarded as equivalent to possession) he can have prospect of a blessed future."

27. On attributes which can be applied to God, see Beck, p. 135, note 3: "Since we ascribe various attributes to God, whose quality we find suitable also to creatures (e.g., power, knowledge, presence, goodness, etc.), though in God they are present in a higher degree under such names as omnipotence, omniscience, omnipresence, and perfect goodness, etc., there are three which exclusively and without qualification of magnitude are ascribed to God, and they are all moral. He is the only holy, the only blessed, and the only wise being, because these concepts of themselves imply unlimitedness. By the arrangement of these He is thus the holy lawgiver (and creator), the beneficent ruler (and sustainer) and the just judge. These three attributes contain everything whereby God is the object of religion, and in conformity to them the metaphysical perfections of themselves arise in reason." Note that the concepts of "holy", "blessed," and "wise" imply unlimitedness (= infinity) and thus are exclusively ascribed to God.

    Would Kant, in the *Critique of Pure Reason*, by turning from the physical world of noumena, which are spatial and temporal, and by inserting space and time within the knower as a priori forms, have influenced current mathematical theories of infinity? These are only remotely (if at all) connected with physical extension (vs. Aristotle's conception of infinity, which directly issued from such extension). On Georg Cantor (1845–1918), who initiated the contemporary set-theory of infinite numbers, see the articles by A. W. Moore and Philip Clayton utilized in the initial pages of my chapter, "God: Subsistent and Infinite Being," *Theos*.

28. See L. Sweeney, "Three Approaches to Union with God – Plotinus, Aquinas and Derrida" in *Spiritual Life and Intellectual Work ed. D. Burke* (Philadelphia: LaSalle University, 1996), pp. 60–87.

INDEX

Romans, epistle to 140
Rorty, R. 33
Russell, Bertrand 143
Ryle, Gilbert 49, 82, 147–8

Sagan, Carl 169
sapiental sense 3–11, 14, 18, *see
also* common sense
Schopenhauer, A. 209–10
Schroedinger, E. 179
science: and intelligible universe
138–9, 166; limitations 117,
164–5, 170–8; and metaphysical questions 182–3; and miracles 169–70; neuroscience 86;
and religion 109–10, 112,
118–19, 137, 154–190; scientific laws 121, 154, 159, 169,
174, 175, 182; social sciences
32–3; and truth 26, 30, 31–2,
39, 157
scientism 112
scotosis 145
Searle, J.R. 58
self-knowledge 144–5
Sellars, Wilfred 112
'sensecontents' 48–9
sensus divinitatis 224
Simon, Herbert 161–2
sin 198, 200, *see also* evil; original sin
skepticism 1, 30, 31, 142
Skinner, B.F. 17–18, 46
Society for Psychical Research 47
Socrates 200
soul: and animals 50–1; existence
of 12, 15, 43–68, 236–7; as
form of the body 18, 49, 53; as
principle of unity 52, 55; separate from body 47, 49–50, 52,
53, 85, 86, *see also* life after

death; reincarnation; spirituality
Spinoza, B. 35, 208–9
spiritualism 56
spirituality 52, 54, 56, *see also*
soul
Stevenson, Ian 90, 91, 94
Strawson, Professor Peter 81
Strong Anthropic Principle (SAP)
181–2
superstring theory 175
Swinburne, Richard 15, 164

Teilhard de Chardin, P. 198
teleology 12, 148, 159
telepathy 89–90, 91
telescopes 171, 173
temporality 127, 160, *see also*
time
Teresa, St of Avila 156
theism 91, 111, 117–19, 136,
206, 208; 'dialectical theism'
125, *see also* religion
theological vocabulary 221–2
theology, as science 158–9
theoretical atheists 112
Thomas:
St (Aquinas) 36, 128, 130, 204
existence of God 124, 126–7,
185; God 208, 240–1, 245;
soul 49–50, 51, 52, 53, 55;
Thomism 11
thought 49, 52–3, 86, 134
time 176, 222, *see also* temporality
Trethowen, Illtyd 5
Trinity 227
trust in God 197, 214
truth 83, 124–5; correspondence
theory 36–7; perfection of
133–4; relativism 23–38, *see*